NEOCONSERVATIVE ECONOMICS IN THE SOUTHERN CONE OF LATIN AMERICA, 1973–1983

The Johns Hopkins Studies in Development
Vernon W. Ruttan and T. Paul Schultz,
Consulting Editors

Joseph Ramos

NEOCONSERVATIVE ECONOMICS IN THE SOUTHERN CONE OF LATIN AMERICA, 1973–1983

The Johns Hopkins University Press
Baltimore and London

© 1986 The Johns Hopkins University Press
All rights reserved
Printed in the United States of America

The Johns Hopkins University Press, 701 West 40th Street,
Baltimore, Maryland 21211
The Johns Hopkins Press Ltd., London

The paper used in this publication meets the minimum requirements of American
National Standard for Information Sciences—Permanence of Paper for Printed
Library Materials, ANSI Z39.48–1984.

Library of Congress Cataloging-in-Publication Data

Ramos, Joseph R.
    Neoconservative economics in the southern cone of Latin America, 1973–1983.

    (The Johns Hopkins studies in development)
    Bibliography: p.
    Includes index.
    1.   Southern Cone of South America—Economic policy.
2.   Economic stabilization—Southern Cone of South
America.   3.   Monetary policy—Southern Cone of South
America.   I.   Title.   II.   Series.
HC167.S67R36   1986   338.98   86-165
ISBN 0-8018-3040-0 (alk. paper)

*to Glorichu, Rocío, Barbara,
and la Comunidad José de Arimatea*

Contents

x   Contents

Tables
and Figures

TABLES

FIGURES

Preface

The emergence of economic policies based on neoconservative premises was one of the major developments of the 1970s in Latin America.[1] Up until then, and since the Great Depression, the prevailing paradigm in the region, especially in the Southern Cone, reflected skepticism concerning the possibility of achieving economic development based primarily on private initiative and the natural functioning of market forces. Thus the state came increasingly to intervene not only in macroeconomic management and the regulation of the economy but also in the promotion of industrial activities and even in production. All of this was accompanied by the increased imposition of direct controls on prices in diverse markets.

During the postwar period, the rest of Latin America achieved rates of growth unequaled in its history. Yet such was not the case with the countries of the Southern Cone, whose growth in this period was quite unsatisfactory. It is understandable, therefore, that the reaction against intervention and the movement for a paradigm based on the market emerged first in the Southern Cone. Neoconservative economic thinking influenced other countries as well, but in none of these did it take hold with the same force and "purity" as in Chile, Uruguay, and Argentina. An analysis of the experiences of the Southern Cone countries is, therefore, of obvious importance if one wishes to evaluate and understand the merits of the neoconservative approach for countries in the throes of development.

This book attempts precisely such an analysis, comparing the recent sta-

(handwritten margin note: Why they searched for new ideas but chic. Boys ready other.)

---

1. Throughout the text, *neoconservative* describes what in Spanish is called *neoliberal.* For English-speaking readers, *neoconservative* correctly connotes "right of center," "monetarist," and "economically conservative." It is associated with the Chicago school of economics and with the ideas of Friedrich Hayek. (It is not to be confused with the so-called neoconservative school of thought in the United States of which Irving Kristol, Daniel Bell, Michael Novak, James Q. Wilson, and Daniel Moynihan are the leading spokesmen, and for which the journal *Public Interest* is an important vehicle.)

bilization and economic liberalization experiences in Chile, Uruguay, and Argentina. The main purpose of the study is to extract lessons for the future. For this reason, the economic policies of the neoconservative experiences are analyzed from a wholly technical perspective, as if the economic rationale utilized by neoconservatives were the only motivation underlying their policies. It goes without saying that this was not in fact the case. Such policies reflected as well, and possibly even more importantly, particular value judgments and ideological positions. Nevertheless, I trust that such an omission is justified in this analysis, inasmuch as its principal interest lies not in writing economic history but in looking ahead. The study is addressed especially to policymakers who, without necessarily agreeing with the neoconservative ideology or with the authoritarian regimes that permitted it to take hold in the Southern Cone, nevertheless feel a certain attraction to the technical rationale behind the policies of stabilization and economic liberalization that were pursued and in the lessons these experiences provide. This exercise attempts to determine the contributions of these experiences as well as their defects and limitations.

The first part of this study (chapters 2 to 4) briefly describes in chronological order the experiences of each of the three countries. Chapter 5 evaluates these experiences comparatively, on the basis of the principal results—growth, distribution, inflation, and external equilibrium. The second part (chapters 6, 7, and 8) analyzes and evaluates the effectiveness of the policies themselves and, in particular, those dealing with price stabilization and adjustment, the opening up of trade, and financial liberalization.

Chapter 1 explains the origins of neoconservative thinking in the Southern Cone and describes its theoretical postulates, its basic diagnosis, and its fundamental policy views. The conclusions concerning each basic topic are found at the end of the corresponding chapter: the comparative analysis (chapter 5); price stabilization and adjustment (chapter 6); trade liberalization (chapter 7); and financial liberalization (chapter 8). More than a summary, chapter 9 presents conclusions concerning the relative merits of the market and state intervention in developing countries.

Any special merit in this study lies in its comparative approach. However many differences there may have been among the three countries in terms of their initial economic conditions, in the velocity and intensity with which the new policies were instituted, or in the sequence of those policies, the similarity in approach and in policies to stabilize and liberalize their economies is quite impressive. Therein lies the usefulness of a comparative approach. Many explanations of successes or failures that appear quite convincing when applied to one country are less so when applied to two or three. A comparative approach thus helps distinguish how much success or failure depended on the basic approach and economic policies of neoconservative thinking and how much depended on the specific situation facing each country or the way in which each policy was implemented.

Aside from the author's own weaknesses, this study suffers from various important limitations. First, it is not a base study; that is to say, it takes off from existing primary research often conducted with other purposes in mind. My effort has not been to improve on the individual studies but rather to concentrate on comparative work. For this reason, chapters 2, 3, and 4 are simply brief descriptions of what took place in each country. The reader interested in a better understanding of these individual experiences is advised to read the studies cited. Second, the study relies on aggregate macroeconomic information, for the firm-level analysis that would permit us to understand the microeconomic processes of stabilization, adjustment, and economic liberalization is only beginning to appear. Third and last, though a comparative approach is useful, it is nevertheless impossible to completely separate out those results attributable to the stabilization policy or the economic liberalization policies from those deriving from the initial conditions or the external environment—all the more so, if we take into account the relatively brief period being analyzed. The first two points affect the depth of the study. The last one conditions its conclusions. Nevertheless, I believe that the conclusions are fairly robust and should help us to distinguish the principal failures and successes of the three experiences and permit us to derive useful lessons for the future.

The stimulus for this study came from Enrique Iglesias when he was executive secretary for the United Nations Economic Commission for Latin America (ECLA). Mr. Iglesias felt that, given the influence of neoconservative thinking in the region, there was a need for a balanced evaluation of the Southern Cone experiences. Base studies were commissioned for each of the three experiences.[2] Eventually, the task of comparison and the drafting of the book was assigned to ECLA's economic development division, and to me in particular.

The period covered in this English version goes from the beginning of these experiences through the end of 1983.[3] By this time, the neoconservative approach had either gone by the boards (Argentina) or was clearly on the wane (Chile and Uruguay).

---

2. See Mezzera 1981, Sourrouille and Lucángeli 1983, Tironi 1981, and Wonsewer and Saráchaga 1980.

3. Thus this study includes one more year of data and analysis than the Spanish version, *Estabilización y Liberalización Económica en el Cono Sur* (Santiago: CEPAL, 1984), with considerable extensions in all chapters, especially in chapter 6 (which now includes adjustment programs) and chapter 8 (which includes much further probing into the reasons for low savings and the nature of the financial bubble). A version of chapter 6 was presented at the second session of the North-South Roundtable on Money and Finance held in Santiago in February 1984. This was later published in the proceedings; see Haq and Massad 1984. A version of chapter 8 was written during my stay at the Kellogg Institute for International Studies at the University of Notre Dame in January-February 1985 and presented at the United Nations University's Conference on Financial Liberalization in Tokyo (22–24 April 1985) under the title "The Rise and Fall of Capital Markets in the Southern Cone."

I am especially indebted to the authors of the six base studies, without which, obviously, no comparative analysis could have been done. Thanks are also due to Enrique de la Piedra, a colleague in the economic development division of ECLA, for drafting the first, and far more detailed, version of the chapter on Uruguay, which unfortunately had to be simplified to keep it in line with what I had written for Argentina and Chile. I very much appreciate the comments, critical and constructive, that were made in diverse stages of this work by colleagues at ECLA: Reinaldo Bajraj, Robert Devlin, Norberto González, Richard Lynn Ground, Martine Guerguil, Raul Gutierrez, Rodolfo Hoffman, Carlos Massad, Sergio Molina, Héctor Soza, Konrad Studnicki Gizbert, Larry Willmore, and Roberto Zahler. Equally fruitful for me has been the intense and continuing dialogue I have had on these topics in the course of the last years with Augusto Aninat, José Pablo Arellano, Edgardo Barandiarán, Vittorio Corbo, René Cortázar, Cristián Eyzaguirre, Ricardo Ffrench-Davis, Alejandro Foxley, Dominique Hachette, Carlos Hurtado, Lovell Jarvis, Rolf Lüders, and Patricio Meller. A special word of appreciation must be given to Andrés Bianchi, director of ECLA's economic development division: first, for his having confided this fascinating topic to me; and second, for his continued insistence on sticking to the facts, on avoiding the heights and delights of pure speculation, and on always returning to the empirical.

As is the tradition, I ought free them all, as well as ECLA, of any responsibility for defects that might still remain, and I herewith do so. But I do so reluctantly, for I suspect that what errors remain are largely due to the aforementioned. For by now my own thinking on this subject seems to me to be little more than the collective wisdom of this group.

And if it is not so as yet, I hope they will soon come to see it this way.

NEOCONSERVATIVE ECONOMICS IN THE SOUTHERN CONE OF LATIN AMERICA, 1973–1983

The Origins and Approach of Neoconservatism in the Southern Cone

ORIGINS

Three factors help to explain the emergence of neoconservative experiences in the Southern Cone: (1) frustration deriving from the poor economic evolution of these countries since the Second World War; (2) the emergence of neoconservative thinking in the industrial countries, which in addition to critically assessing social processes based on strong and active governments also offered both an alternative vision and concrete solutions based on apparently solid technical grounds; and (3) severe socio economic crises in all three Southern Cone countries, ending in the collapse of the then-prevailing political systems.

is it this act & day

Frustration concerning Economic Performance

At the end of the Second World War, Chile, Uruguay, and Argentina generated more than a third of the region's gross national product, even though they had only 17 percent of Latin America's population. Thus these three countries occupied the first three rankings in per capita income in the region. However, by the mid-seventies, the Southern Cone's participation in regional GNP had fallen to less than 24 percent. In the thirty years from 1945 to 1975, the rest of the region's GNP had grown at an average of 6.2 percent per year, while the Southern Cone's GNP had grown by only 3.5 percent per year. Argentina still had the highest per capita income of the region; however, Chile had fallen from third to seventh place, and Uruguay from second to fifth.

Because these three economies were endowed with a beneficent natural resource base (abundant and rich grazing lands in Argentina and Uruguay, rich mineral resources in Chile), a few traditional exports enjoyed a strong comparative advantage. Not only did the export earnings of these countries depend heavily on a very few products, but precisely because these products enjoyed such a strong, nature-given, comparative advantage, their earnings were more a form of rent than a return to productive innovation. Because of this, any general policy—such as devaluation—aimed at encouraging exports enormously increased the intramarginal rents of traditional exports. Thus export promotion policies had to be very selective or, failing this, nonexistent. Indeed, to have no export policies at all proved to be more attractive.

In different ways, the three countries chose to extract these rents from the traditional export sector by way of export taxes or a low exchange rate (thus discouraging all exports, nontraditional as well as traditional). They used these rents either to provide myriad services associated with a more developed welfare state or to pursue a tariff-induced, domestic-market-oriented industrialization policy. Not surprisingly, given their relatively small domestic markets (especially in Uruguay and Chile), such a policy of industrialization led to an excessively diversified industrial base, enjoying the advantages of neither specialization nor economies of scale. And so many industrial activities proved to be rent absorbing rather than rent generating (via innovation and efficiency).

In the same vein, the transfer of rents from traditional exports to government permitted these countries to provide their populations (at least their urban ones) with social services characteristic of more developed welfare economies. Thus social security programs (health, pension, dependent allowances, and so on) absorbed close to 10 percent of GNP in these three countries, double the median for the region, equal to Japan, and only surpassed by the more advanced industrial countries (see Mesa Lago 1985).

In view of their inability to use rents derived from natural resources to generate rents from innovation and productivity, it is not surprising that their overall economic performance in the postwar period proved to be mediocre. The only sector that showed some dynamism was manufacturing, whose

Table 1.1. Southern Cone and Rest of Latin America: Annual Growth, Comparative Indicators, 1945–1975 (*percentage*)

Indicator	Southern Cone			Rest of Latin America
	Chile	Uruguay	Argentina	
Gross national product	3.6[a]	2.1[b]	3.7[a]	6.2[c]
Gross national product per capita	1.5[a]	0.7[b]	2.0[c]	3.2[c]
Manufacturing product	4.4[a]	3.3[b]	4.6[c]	7.8[c]
Agricultural product per capita	0.2[a]	−0.2[b]	−0.1[c]	0.9[c]
Volume of exports per capita	−0.2[b]	−2.3[b]	−1.2[b]	1.3[b]
Consumer prices	30.0[d]	29.0[d]	24.0[d]	8.0[d]

Source: CEPAL, on the basis of official data; International Monetary Fund, *International Financial Statistics.*

[a] 1945–73.
[b] 1950–75.
[c] 1945–75.
[d] 1950–70.

growth had been favored by the policy of tariff-induced, import substitution (table 1.1). Nevertheless, even its growth was sluggish, limited as it was to relatively small domestic markets and sheltered as it was from efficiency-inducing foreign competition. Thus manufacturing in the three countries grew between 3.3 and 4.6 percent per year as compared to 7.8 percent per year in the rest of Latin America. And the cost of this particular development strategy naturally fell upon the "taxed" sectors—agriculture and exports. The volume of exports per capita *fell* in the three countries of the Southern Cone between 1950 and the beginnings of the neoconservative experience, whereas it grew at a rate of 1.3 percent per year in the rest of the region. Similarly, agricultural output per capita fell (Argentina and Uruguay) or grew only slightly (Chile), whereas it grew at a rate of 0.9 percent per year in the rest of the region. However, the Southern Cone countries, along with Bolivia and Brazil, had the highest rates of inflation in Latin America, averaging 25 to 30 percent per year, with a very high variability from one year to the next.

In view of such mediocre economic performances (especially given the seeming potential of these countries) and the burden of their social legislation, it is not surprising that frustration was widespread, as awakened expectations were dashed.

The Emergence of Neoconservative Thinking

As frustration increased in the Southern Cone and their economic strategies were increasingly challenged, doubts began to be raised in industrial countries, also, with respect to the Keynesian paradigm, which had prevailed since the Great Depression. Keynesian macroeconomics had come to replace the traditional monetary approach, which argues that changes in aggregate demand give rise to changes in prices without significant effects on output (in short, a theory of inflation and deflation but not of severe recession). The Keynesian approach, on the other hand, argues that, in the short run, changes in aggregate demand affect output above all, whereas prices tend to remain constant. Thus, it was up to governments to maintain strong aggregate demand by means of counter-cyclical fiscal policies, even if this requires, as it did, deficits for some time. The key objective of the Keynesian approach was to maintain full employment, rather than stable prices.—

The emergence of stagflation in industrial countries in the late 1960s proved to be a serious challenge to the Keynesian approach. Since inflation was expected to emerge only when full capacity and employment were achieved, the coexistence of inflation along with recession was hard to explain. As creeping inflation became generalized, these doubts grew. Moreover, at a theoretical level, how was one to explain how a monetary and fiscal expansion systematically increased output, as Keynesians argued, if in the long run, as both Keynesians and monetarists argued, prices rose with money? Might it not be that economic agents were increasingly tending to anticipate deficit spending? If so, fiscal intervention would become increasingly ineffective; that is to say, in order to maintain full employment, progressively higher rates of inflation would be required. Precisely for this reason, some began to argue against the use of discretional countercyclical policy, inasmuch as it would be increasingly ineffective; rather, they argued for the pursuit and maintenance of objective policy rules for the principal macroeconomic variables (for example, a predetermined and fixed rate of money growth for large countries and a fixed exchange rate for small ones).

At the same time, the school of public choice and decision making made an even more penetrating and global criticism of the then-prevailing Keynesian paradigm. It argued that government intervention knew no limits, for by its very nature government is far more sensitive to the direct pressure of organized interest groups than it is to the diffuse interest of the common good. Thus it concluded that it was necessary to counteract this inbuilt tendency to overexpansion by clearly limiting not only the sphere of the government but government intervention within its sphere.

Thus the school of public choice and the new macroeconomics based on neoconservative thinking, by stressing the need to buttress market mechanisms, to minimize state intervention, and to return initiative to the private sector, directly challenged the assumptions underlying the development strategy the Southern Cone had followed since the Great Depression.[1]

The Immediate Crisis

These neoconservative views came to be taken seriously in the Southern Cone countries not only because of frustration with economic performance but, more importantly, because of the severity of the immediate crisis, both sociopolitical and economic.

In the years immediately preceding the collapse of the preneoconservative political and economic system in each of these countries, output per capita fell (Chile and Uruguay) or barely grew (Argentina); the deficit in current account rose to unprecedented levels (between 20 and 36 percent of exports of goods and services); and inflation grew to triple-digit rates, approaching hyperinflation in Argentina and Chile. The resulting short-run economic disequilibria were thus of such a magnitude that they made the public more receptive to drastic measures.

---

1. An excellent summary of neoconservative economic thought can be found in Lepage 1979. The key figures in macroeconomics, especially as pertain to our subject, are Friedman and Lucas—the former in reformulating the quantity theory of money, the latter in developing the theory of rational expectations. As for the open economy and "global monetarism," the work of Mundell is central, especially its eventual expression of the monetary approach to the balance of payments. Finally, the work of Buchanan and Tullock is central to issues of public choice and to limits to the expansive tendencies of the state.

Moreover, social and political forces in the Southern Cone became extremely polarized toward the end of the sixties and the beginning of the seventies, as the development strategy heretofore in vogue was increasingly challenged by both the right and the left. This, together with the acute distributive impact of recent economic disequilibria and the long-run mediocre growth, led to social upheavals bordering on civil war. Indeed, political conflict had become virtually intolerable in Chile, and Argentina and Uruguay were rampant with guerrilla activity and counterinsurrectional repression. The crisis was thus not only economic but political and social, culminating in the overthrow of the constitutional process through military coups.[2]

The need to put an end to spiraling conflict and disorder and to reestablish basic macroeconomic equilibria could be expected to provide the coups with far broader public support than that of the economic elites, whose interests were being directly endangered. Yet the neoconservative program appealed to only a limited clientele. Indeed, it is far from obvious that even the interests of the traditional economic elites, or of the military itself, are best served by a neoconservative strategy of liberalization and stabilization. Hence—however much it lies beyond the scope of this book—the reason for the adoption of the neoconservative approach needs to be briefly discussed.[3]

Given the disequilibria and the frustration with past development strategy, it is likely that any new policy would have reestablished fiscal discipline, enlarged the role of the market and the price system, and looked outward for markets. However, such a pendular swing admits of a far more varied mix of instruments and intensities than those that were used. For example, military governments in Brazil after 1964, although likewise ideologically attached to private property and to providing a leading role for the military, gave an active role to the state and chose their policy instruments eclectically and pragmatically, both for short-term stabilization and long-run development, thus producing what came to be known as the Brazilian miracle (see Foxley 1983).

Why then was such a pure and extreme strain of neoconservatism adopted in the Southern Cone? My answer, in a nutshell, is that the reasons were more political than economic. Because of the polarization, social conflict, and disarray that characterized the periods immediately preceding the coups, order and

---

2. The recent literature on the breakdown of democracies is ample. Indeed, in the case of Latin America, it even gave rise to a theory all its own, that of bureaucratic authoritarianism. While I share Hirschman's misgivings (Hirschman 1979) as to its excessive economic determinism and so consider the theory of bureaucratic authoritarianism as fundamentally off base, it is nevertheless rich in insights, and it provides much needed background for a fuller understanding of the experiences of the three countries dealt with here. Basic readings are Collier 1979, Linz and Stepan 1978, and Valenzuela 1978.

3. The question I here address is not to be confused with another: whether a neoconservative strategy could have been adopted and implemented without authoritarian governments. The answer to the latter, I think, is clearly no. Certainly the changes could not have encompassed so many fundamental spheres, so quickly, and so drastically.

discipline had to be restored, and insurrection could not be countenanced. For such a limited task, the military could no doubt have counted on widespread, if not majority, support. But rather than seek such an explicit popular mandate (via plebiscite, for example), the military chose to act on the basis of an implicit or presumed mandate, which permitted it far more leeway. The military thus sacrificed legitimacy for the sake of "efficiency"—to avoid the constraining hand a popular mandate would have entailed. Unchecked, extraconstitutional, political repression was thus the characteristic trait of the three regimes.

But such a high political cost could more easily be justified were there to be the promise of a radical restructuring of the society rather than simply of a putting of the house in order. Neoconservatism in its purest strain offered these regimes the prospect of just such a political and economic structural transformation of society. Moreover, its criticism (through its public-choice theorists) was not only of past economic policy but of pluralist democracy as currently practiced.[4] Thus despite the military's instinctive proclivity for planning and intervention—and the fact that the traditional economic elites were never enthusiastic about neoconservative policy—the military came to adopt, for political reasons, the neoconservative program of economic liberalization.

Neoconservatives for their part were not above effecting their program via imposition. First, they stood little chance of having their full program adopted by a democratic government. Second, given the prevailing social conflict and economic disarray, a military coup might seem to them the lesser of two evils, and certainly such a regime would need economic advice. Thus the seeming contradiction of pursuing freedom via repressive means could be rationalized by seeing repression as transitory and freedom as an eventual result of economic liberalization. For neoconservatives argued, as Friedman did early on (1962), that a prerequisite for political freedom was economic freedom. Finally, neoconservatives used the sharp distinction between normative and positive economics (drawn by at least one important variant of the Chicago tradition) to justify their role as technocrats and spare them responsibility for the political sphere.[5] That such a distinction is valid for analytical purposes but untenable

---

4. This in no way suggests that public-choice theorists were responsible for, or abetted, or were favorably disposed toward these military regimes. Public-choice theories were simply used by these regimes to discredit previous democratic structures and to further legitimize their "emergency" measures of repression.

5. Although the distinction between normative and positive economics certainly formed part of an important tradition at Chicago (see Friedman's celebrated 1953 essay or Harberger's 1982b restatement), and though Southern Cone policymakers were in fact disproportionately drawn from the University of Chicago, it would be unfair to hold this Chicago tradition responsible for, or supportive of, political repression in the Southern Cone. Theory is one thing; the values that orient a theory's implementation is another. In fact, the values and ideological proclivities of most Southern Cone policymakers were shaped well before studying at Chicago or being inspired by its thought. The Chicago tradition simply served the ideologies and values these policymakers had long entertained and that they could now justify

for policymakers—who must both analyze (positivism) and propose (fix priorities according to norms)—was lost on the neoconservatives. Moreover, the justification for repression grew increasingly less plausible as repression became more permanent. Thus some combination of political casuistry or naivete, the temptation of power, the fanaticism of the "true believer," and simple, self-serving interest led many Southern Cone neoconservatives to act as if all that really mattered was the economic structure and to treat the political sphere as a mere superstructure. It is thus a tragic paradox that this school of thought should so stress economic autonomy and liberalization as key structural bulwarks against tyranny that, in privileging the means—economic liberalization—it sacrificed the end—freedom itself, both freedom from coercion and freedom of participation. Rather late, Friedman introduced a major modification to his former aphorism, now stating (1982) that without political freedom economic freedom would not long endure. But by this time the damage had been done, and the Southern Cone neoconservative experiences were on the verge of collapse.

Friedman changed his mind

In short, military repression and economic liberalization was a marriage of convenience between military regimes in need of a program for radically restructuring society to justify their harsh political repression and technocrats who had just such a program, a program that claimed scientific excellence and was critical of the structures of pluralist democracy as then known.

This coincidence of interests between the military's political goals and the neoconservatives' economic ones held true at more practical levels. The military's political need not only to dissolve congresses and political parties but to serverely restrict labor unions coincided with the neoconservatives' tendency to view with suspicion and distaste (as incipient monopolies) all such intermediate organizations. Thus there was an extraordinary congruence for dismantling the institutions of a pluralist society in pursuit of what each party considered to be the essence of a new democracy.

APPROACH

Diagnosis

According to Southern Cone neoconservatism, the poor economic performance of these countries in the postwar period was due to the exaggerated and increasingly discretional intervention of the state, which replaced the market as

---

technically and through a more broad-based ideological tradition (that of freedom from coercion). As for economic liberalization, that is another issue. Here the influence of Chicago (or more properly, "greater Chicago," which includes parts of Stanford and Columbia) was far more supportive, and the lessons of these three experiences say much about the soundness and limitations of this approach.

the principal mechanism of resource allocation. Limited in this way, private initiative naturally tended to zero-sum activities (attempting to secure higher prices, or preferential credits, or higher tariffs, and so on), thus neglecting its natural mission, which is the creation of new wealth; and even when it did create new wealth, private investors did not necessarily invest it in activities with the highest social rate of return.

According to the neoconservative diagnosis, state intervention begun in the thirties, though perhaps justified to minimize the devastation of the Great Depression, nevertheless failed once it was transformed into a development strategy. For, in the long run, the principal bottleneck for developing countries is not so much a lack of demand as it is insufficient productive capacity.

For example, strong protective tariffs may have been justified to protect industrial production during the Depression, when exports were quite inelastic to price; but once the Depression was over and demand was back to normal, it would have been far more sensible to promote new exports via higher exchange rates and lower tariffs rather than invest in new import substitutes or in old lines of heavily protected production. To maintain protective tariffs in these new circumstances meant promoting an excessively diversified industrial sector, with insufficient specialization and without the economies of scale possible in a larger domestic market.

To protect the domestic market when the international market collapsed, as it did in the thirties, was reasonable. Quite the opposite was the policy to protect the domestic market when the international economy boomed, as it did in the postwar period. In the same vein, to "prime the pump" when there existed heavily underutilized capacity, as in the thirties, was one thing. Quite another was to continue deficit spending when there was no longer any under-utilized capacity. The former policy minimizes recession, the latter is simply inflationary. For, after all, deficit spending is simply a form of expenditure, not savings; and savings are what, in fact, are necessary to expand the productive capacity of a developing country.

To grow inward implied slowing exports, for which reason the Southern Cone suffered a chronic shortage of foreign exchange. Governments tended to meet this shortage through increased controls over imports and capital move-ments. Inasmuch as inflation was by now endemic and fiscal expenditures were increasingly inflexible, it was often necessary to rely on the administrative fixing of prices, especially of basic foodstuffs. In this way, inflation was re-pressed in the short run but at the expense of a slow growth in output. There-fore, the role of prices became increasingly distributive and not allocative. Distributive conflicts worsened, centering no longer in the market, where they might have been resolved impersonally, but in the government bureaucracy. This fact alone would explain the increasing politicization of these societies.

To the extent to which prices were no longer used to encourage production, selective credits and subsidies came increasingly to the fore. In short, slowly but surely, market mechanisms came to be replaced by discretional decisions taken by the government bureaucracy. Inasmuch as these really were not fully planned economies, such an approach implied a loss of the advantages of both a market economy and of a centrally planned one. At least, so read the neoconservatives' indictment.

It is not the purpose of this introduction to analyze the validity of the neoconservative diagnosis, a diagnosis which in many respects was shared by others of different technical and political views.[6] The diagnosis was, at least on the surface, consistent with many of the central phenomena observed during the postwar period in the Southern Cone: (1) the overall slow rate of growth; (2) the persistence of inflation and the worsening of distributive conflicts; (3) the stagnation of agriculture and exports and the excessive diversification and consequent low productivity of the industrial sector; (4) the frequent balance-of-payments crises. Moreover, the neoconservative approach had the further attraction of being a global interpretation, which explained all of these phenomena on the basis of a single factor—namely, the tendency to replace the market by direct government intervention. Finally, it was an interpretation that fit in quite nicely with the well-known thesis that the sociopolitical development of the Southern Cone (especially of Chile and Uruguay) had far exceeded the economic base on which it rested, resulting in unnecessary conflicts, tensions, and disequilibria, and poor economic performance.[7]

Strategy

The strategy of Southern Cone neoconservatism was aimed at strengthening the private sector and restoring the role of the market. The free play of prices as determined by supply and demand would be the principal mechanism both to allocate resources and to reorient the economy from its distributive function toward its productive one. The natural counterpart of this change in orientation was a reduction in the role of government in the economy. This involved not only reducing its importance as a producer and entrepreneur but in minimizing the use of its discretional authority. From now on, the dynamic agent of the economy would be the private sector, and the state would limit itself to creating the conditions whereby market signals and incentives (prices) would be free of distortion and interference.

Such a strategy implied, among others, the following: (1) freeing prices so they would reflect opportunity costs and not simply distributive purposes; (2) reducing tariffs and establishing an exchange rate that, together with the open-

---

6. Possibly what give these criticisms and proposals a very specific neoconservative touch are, one, the virtually limitless faith they exhibit in the dynamism of the private sector and the efficiency of the market and, two, their correspondingly negative, almost diabolical, view of the state.

7. See Pinto 1973, who, however, reached political conclusions quite different from those of the neoconservatives.

ing of trade, would permit economies of scale and the use of comparative advantage; (3) promoting a domestic capital market by freeing interest rates and eliminating quantitative and qualitative controls over the allocation of credit; (4) promoting the free entry and exit of capital to fully utilize external savings and to help domestic and international interest rates to converge; (5) preventing all forms of collusion that might alter the free play of supply and demand, which implied minimizing or compensating for the actions of intermediate groups (especially those not subject to foreign competition, like labor unions and professional groups); (6) reducing the participation of the public sector in GNP; and (7) above all (since it was considered a necessary condition for market efficiency), achieving and maintaining price stability by eliminating fiscal deficits and strictly controlling monetary growth.

Assumptions

In the following chapters the assumptions behind the neoconservative model are analyzed.[8] At this stage, I simply wish to draw attention to two central assumptions: (1) the intrinsic dynamism of the private sector as an agent for development and (2) the unquestionable efficiency of the market when free of state controls and monopolistic interference.

Neoconservatism, certainly Southern Cone neoconservatism, paid little attention to the possible defects or limitations of the market or of the private sector. For example, it tended to minimize the difficulties entailed in preventing the collusion of private agents and in establishing an effective competitive environment. This problem is especially acute during periods of transition, when disequilibria transitorily accentuate monopolistic situations, giving rise to sizable quasi rents, which prolong the disequilibria.

Likewise, neoconservatism overlooked the possibility that (1) there is not one market but many markets or segmented markets, and these are not perfectly integrated but adjust at different speeds or initially diverge from, rather than converge toward equilibrium; and (2) sometimes no market exists at all, as is the case of futures markets (in practice, the case for virtually all products), or only incipient markets exist (for example, medium- and long-run capital markets). Nor does neoconservatism adequately take into account the fact that the achievement of individual plans depends very much on what others do. Should our expectations be erroneous, not only would our own plans be dashed but those of others, for our effective behavior differs from what was expected. The automatic harmonization of the plans of multiple private agents by the market is

---

8. There are of course even more important assumptions of a philosophical and political nature in neoconservatism. Given the nature of this study, I shall not go into these. The reader who is interested should see Hayek 1960, probably the most influential philosophical work among neoconservatives in the Southern Cone; for local reformulations see Cáceres 1982 and Lavín 1980; for different and critical views see Ramos 1982 and ILADES 1983.

thus oftentimes a slow and even divergent process (vicious circle) rather than a rapid and convergent one (virtuous circle).

Each of these defects—none of which are due to government intervention—requires for its correction that someone at the level of the widest national community (thus the state) anticipate, compensate, and harmonize such behavior. No other agent would have the incentives or sufficient capacity to assume alone the cost of correcting such possible defects, for these costs naturally fall on the society as a whole.

It is not necessarily the case that such defects in the market or in private agents are incompatible with the theoretical principles on which neoconservatism is based. Nevertheless, neoconservative policymakers in the Southern Cone acted as if these defects were remote possibilities of second-order importance—an attitude responsible for many of the costs of the neoconservative experiences. Suffice it to say at this stage that the neoconservative diagnosis would have difficulty explaining why, before the Great Depression, these countries (certainly Chile and Uruguay) had not achieved a stage of development similar to Europe's and the United States'. For between their independence and the thirties, these countries' economic activities had been almost exclusively in private hands, and government control of the economy had been quite slight.

Chile, 1973–1983

Policies and Principal Results

Two overriding concerns marked the economic policy of the Chilean junta upon taking power at the end of 1973: (1) the unavoidable need to restore basic macroeconomic equilibria, and (2) the intention to instill dynamism in an economy whose performance in recent decades was considered quite unsatisfactory. (See table 2.1 for economic indicators during these years and through the neoconservative era.) The first objective had clear priority during the first years. Nevertheless, the development aspirations of the junta not only affected the structural policy changes it implemented but also the speed and manner with which the price-stabilization policy was pursued from the very beginning.[1]

[handwritten margin note: Couldn't have anyone have seen that the policies of the Chic Boys were needed?]

THE INITIAL CONDITIONS

Unable to finance its revolutionary program via taxes—for this required parliamentary approval and the parliament was in opposition hands—the Allende government (Unidad Popular, or UP) nonetheless persisted in its plans, financing them via massive deficit spending. Inasmuch as such fast-growing deficits risked runaway inflation, the UP chose to control most prices, including exchange and interest rates. Although it managed to repress inflation in this way,

---

1. Perhaps because it was in many respects the purest form of neoconservative economic policy, the Chilean case is the one most studied in the literature. Among the most important evaluations of Chile's neoconservative experience, in addition to those already noted in the introduction, are Balassa 1984; Corbo, Edwards, Lüders, and Koenig 1984; Edwards 1985; Ffrench-Davis, Fontaine, García, and Wisecarver 1983; Foxley 1983; Harberger 1982a; and Zahler 1983. How firms adjusted to the various reforms is very well treated in Galvez and Tybout 1985. This chapter gives but a thumbnail and descriptive sketch of the events. The issues are treated more analytically in chapters 5 through 9. Readers interested in the historical antecedents of the neoconservative experience in Chile are referred to ICHEH 1978 and Mamalakis 1976.

it did so at the expense of acute shortages, queuing, and black markets. Even so, in August 1973, official inflation proceeded at the unprecedented rate of 300 percent per year. It is therefore understandable that the central objective of economic policy after the military coup was to restore basic macroeconomic equilibrium: control inflation, eliminate shortages, and improve the balance of payments.

Subsequent economic policy was forced to face these disequilibria, and it was natural that this policy would strengthen the very weakened role of the market, given the extreme distortions in relative prices resulting from previous government intervention. Therefore, what is most characteristic of neoconservative economic policymaking in Chile is not so much its decision to restore basic equilibrium nor the greater role it gave to the market but rather how it decided to do so (with what instruments, at what speed, at what cost) and with what orientation.

natural decision-policies or Chic Boys

The resulting approach was an exclusively monetarist stabilization policy within a neoconservative development strategy. The slow growth of output since the early forties (1.5 percent per capita per year versus over 3 percent for the rest of Latin America excluding the Southern Cone) was attributed by the neoconservatives to ill-conceived market intervention by the government, especially through protective tariffs, subsidized credits, and price controls, as well as to the rising ratio of public expenditures to GNP. Thus they saw as imperative the need to restore the market as the principal determinant of economic decisions and to make the private sector the privileged agent of development.

ECONOMIC POLICY AND ITS RESULTS

At times the goals of price stabilization and development required similar policies. Reduction of fiscal expenditures, for example, tended simultaneously to correct fiscal deficits and to reduce the weight of the state in the economy. On other occasions, however, such goals were in conflict, at least in the short run. For example, the freeing of prices corrected many distortions (a long-term development objective), but unleashed inflationary expectations (which wrought havoc on its stabilization policy). Generally speaking, major priority was given to restoring price stability rather than to promoting development; yet, there was little concern, or even awareness, concerning possible conflicts in time between these objectives: both goals tended to be pursued simultaneously. It is, therefore, not always clear to what we should attribute the successes and failures of the economic policy that was followed: to the monetarist stabilization policy or to the neoconservative development strategy.

Economic policy in Chile can be fruitfully divided into three fairly separate phases: (1) September 1973 to June 1976, in which inflation as well as output declined; (2) June 1976 to the middle of 1981, in which inflation con-

Table 2.1. Chile: Basic Macroeconomic Indicators, Postwar Period and 1971–1983

Indicator	1950–1970	1971	1972	1973	1974	1975	1976	1977	1978	1979	1980	1981	1982	1983
Real sector														
Per capita GNP growth rate	1.9	7.1	−2.9	−7.1	−0.7	−14.4	1.8	8.0	6.4	6.5	6.0	3.9	−15.7	−2.4
Gross-investment/GNP coefficient	16.8	20.8	15.2	14.3	25.8	14.0	13.6	14.4	16.5	19.6	23.9	23.9	9.6	11.2
Savings/GNP coefficient[a]	14.6	17.8	10.4	9.5	25.3	8.5	15.4	10.7	11.6	13.7	17.9	11.3	1.0	6.5
Unemployment rate		5.7	3.7	4.6	9.2	16.8	19.4	18.6	17.9	17.7	17.4	15.6	28.2	24.5
Real wage index		119.3	108.2	80.0[a]	64.8	62.1	63.0	71.1	75.7	82.0	89.4	97.5	97.1	86.8
Monetary and financial sector														
Inflation rate[b]	30.3	26.7	108.3	441.0	497.8	379.2	232.8	113.8	50.0	33.4	35.1	19.7	9.9	27.3
M1 growth rate[c]	37.7	102.0	100.0	259.1	314.6	239.2	216.0	156.7	81.2	60.0	62.6	−6.0	9.4	26.6
M2 growth rate[d]		100.0	147.1	472.6	338.0	255.7	166.4	130.1	90.5	67.6	57.3	55.8	31.3	−0.8
Public-sector-surplus/GNP		−10.7	−13.0	−24.7	−10.5	−2.6	−2.3	−1.8	−0.8	1.7	3.1	1.7	−2.3	−3.8
Real interest rate[e]						−46.8	39.4	55.3	33.4	2.3	14.7	58.1	16.8	14.0

	C1	C2	C3	C4	C5	C6	C7	C8	C9	C10	C11	C12	C13	C14
Growth rate of exports														
Value	7.7	−9.4	−13.0	48.7	59.1	−21.0	31.3	7.9	13.0	57.1	29.2	−16.1	−7.3	−0.9
Volume	3.0	9.0	−12.2	10.1	18.0	9.2	18.7	7.4	7.9	24.3	15.3	−7.7	10.8	1.6
Indexes														
Real effective exchange rate^f	91.9	96.4	107.2	93.5	100.2	87.1	84.4	97.7	87.4	75.1	67.4	78.9	83.5	
Terms of trade, goods and services	80.6	75.5	84.7	88.3	55.4	59.3	54.1	48.6	54.7	51.6	44.6	39.8	40.7	
Current-account-surplus/exports	−17.8	−48.1	−19.7	−12.9	−27.1	5.4	−21.8	−37.8	−26.1	−33.9	−88.4	−48.6	−26.6	
External debt (billions of dollars)	2.8	3.0	3.6	4.4	4.7	4.5	5.2	6.7	8.5	11.1	15.5	17.2	17.5	
External-debt/exports	2.5	3.1	2.5	1.9	2.6	1.9	2.0	2.3	1.8	1.9	2.8	3.7	3.8	

Source: CEPAL, on the basis of official data; growth rate of *M*1, International Monetary Fund, *International Financial Statistics*, August 1985, and *Statistical Yearbook*, 1982.

Note: 1970 = 100, Year 1983; preliminary figures.

^a January–August.

^b Variation in the consumer price index.

^c *M*1 = bills and coins in circulation plus demand deposits.

^d *M*2 = *M*1 plus time and savings deposits.

^e Nominal interest rate deflated by the wholesale-price index.

^f Exchange-rate variation deflated by the difference between the internal and external wholesale-price index.

tinued to subside but in which output more than recovered—although at the expense of heavy foreign indebtedness; and (3) mid-1981 through 1983, in which the weight of indebtedness, both domestic and foreign, brought on a severe financial crisis and recession, even worse than that of 1975, resulting in the demise of the model.

Phase I, September 1973 to June 1976

The most immediate problem that faced the military junta was how to restore basic equilibria without bringing on hyperinflation. The decisions taken in the last quarter of 1973, and the sequence in which they were taken, decisively determined the resulting hyperstagflation.

Since inflation and the acute shortages were considered to be basically monetary phenomena—that is to say, at the prevailing level of prices there was "too much money chasing too few goods"—the following decisions were taken: (1) To free virtually all prices, in this way ending shortages, black markets, and repressed inflation. (2) To devalue the exchange rate by approximately twenty times its shadow value of late 1969 (in short, by an amount equal to the increase in the supply of money since the last period of "normalcy"), with the purpose of closing the deficit in the balance of payments. (3) To control wages by demobilizing labor unions, a bastion of UP support, and by changing the readjustments of wages from looking "backward" (adjusting in accordance with 1973 inflation) to looking "forward" (adjusting in accordance with the programmed inflation for 1974). The feeling, no doubt, was that if wage readjustments incorporated the total increase in prices of 1973, prices would cease to be flexible downward, so that a restrictive monetary policy would be virtually impossible to execute. (4) To follow a restrictive monetary policy to reduce the fiscal deficit.

Economists of almost all schools of thought would agree that policies of this sort were necessary in the long run. But what characterized neoconservatism in this phase was its clear conviction that a policy that is correct in the long run is also correct in the short run, or—what amounts to the same thing—that the short run was so short that it was pointless to concern oneself with the optimum sequence and speed during this phase. Hence, the economic team rejected the most radical stabilization policy of all to correct repressed inflationary pressure but without unleashing wild inflationary expectations: freeing prices but accompanying this with a semiconfiscatory monetary reform. (This was the approach followed in post–Nazi Germany.) Nor did the team consider a more gradual price liberalization, which would have reduced shortages and queuing while avoiding the risk of price overshooting and its concomitantly high inflationary expectations.

On being freed in October 1973, prices, which up until then had been well below equilibrium, jumped well above equilibrium. They "settled" at a level thirty times above that of December 1969, the last period of "normalcy" (pre-

Allende days), overshooting by some 50 percent the cost pressure (as measured by the increase in the exchange rate and in wages in that same time period) and by 25 percent the demand pressure (as measured by monetary growth in the same period). In a matter of days, the economy moved from one in which money was abundant and goods were scarce (queuing and shortages) to one in which goods were abundant and money was scarce.[2] At the same time, as a result of wage controls and the freeing of prices, real wages fell some 20 percent below what they had been in the first eight months of 1973, and so some 35 percent below what they had been in their last period of normalcy, in 1969 (see Cortázar 1983a); and all of this with a per capita output similar to that of 1973 and 1969.

Shortages were thus eliminated but at the expense of an excessive increase in prices and a resulting collapse in real wages. As a result, internal demand plummeted and a recession ensued. This especially affected the industrial sector, whose final sales and output declined. Overall unemployment shot up as well, from 3 to 7 percent in a matter of one quarter, and it would reach 10 percent, a heretofore unprecedented level, by the end of 1974.[3]

Fiscal expenditures were lowered 25 percent in real terms in 1974, thanks largely to the decline in current expenditures, mainly wages. Fiscal income increased 15 percent in real terms. Hence, the fiscal deficit was reduced from 25 percent to 11 percent of GNP, enabling monetary growth to decelerate sharply, from 410 to 250 percent, and inflation to decline from 600 to 370 percent.[4]

Thanks to the sharp increase in the exchange rate,[5] to the fall in real

2. A detailed treatment of this period can be found in Ramos 1975.

3. Final sales to consumers fell immediately in October. Nevertheless, industrial production reached its historic maximum that month, because the demand of firms, at least the transitory demand, was quite strong in order to build up stocks depleted during the UP regime. Once this demand for inventories was satisfied, however, industrial output and sales began to decline. In December, output was in fact 10 percent below its average for October-November, and this fall was to continue in a systematic fashion for the next couple of years. This behavior of the industrial sector is a clear indication of significant idle capacity at the end of 1973. Moreover, it shows that the recession, at least in the industrial sector, began at the end of 1973, for reasons of inadequate demand and as a result of the stabilization policy, and not in 1975, in response to the so-called shock treatment to address balance-of-payments problems. If this decline in output was not so noticeable in 1974, it is because at the beginning of 1973 (the base period for such comparisons), production was falling because of restrictions on the supply side (shortages, strikes, and work stoppages).

4. Monetary growth and inflation are measured from December to December in the text (as opposed to midyear to midyear as in table 2.1) in order to better capture the points of inflection. The inflation rate is the variation in the consumer-price index as corrected in Cortázar and Marshall 1980 and not the official index, which was grossly manipulated by government authorities to understate inflation in 1973 as well as in 1976–78.

5. The real effective exchange rate (calculated on the basis of the corrected consumer-price index or on the basis of wages in relation to the exchange rate) rose more than 50 percent

wages, and to the recovery of the price of Chile's principal export, copper (which more than compensated the increase of the price of petroleum), Chile's competitiveness improved enormously, and its deficit in current account was substantially reduced. However, at the end of 1974, once the price of copper began to decline sharply from its previous peak and as it became increasingly difficult for the government to secure foreign credits, another sharp devaluation was decreed, which led to an important acceleration in the rate of inflation in the first quarter of 1975.

In order not to lose all that had been gained in slowing inflation, in mid-1975 the government chose to intensify its restrictive policy, reducing fiscal expenditures by another 28 percent in real terms, this time centering the reduction on public investment.[6] In this way, the fiscal deficit was lowered once again, to less than 3 percent. This draconian and procyclical reduction in domestic expenditures, which aimed at coping with the deterioration in the terms of trade, brought on the sharpest reduction in Chilean GNP (13 percent) since the Great Depression. To this must be added the further decline in gross national income (5.5 percent), which resulted from the worsening in the terms of trade. Unemployment shot up from 13 percent in the first quarter of 1975 (already above its previous historic maximum) to 19 percent one year later, and this notwithstanding the fact that real wages had fallen almost 40 percent below normal levels (1970). Even then, inflation continued at 250 percent per year.

While the government was understandably oriented toward the short run—restoring basic macroeconomic equilibrium—it nevertheless also set in motion in this phase the bulk of its long-term development policies: (1) most activities in the public sector were returned to the private sector; (2) trade was opened up; and (3) the domestic capital market was created.

First, the bulk of industrial firms that the UP regime had "intervened" in (over 200, among them the most important firms in the country) and those farms that had been taken over in extralegal fashion by peasants or government agencies were returned to their owners. Between 30 and 40 percent of all expropriated land, or 15 to 20 percent of the country's total agricultural arable land, was returned (see World Bank, 1979 and Jarvis, 1985). The government

---

between the first eight months of 1973 and all of 1974. The real effective exchange rate shown in table 2.1 does not show this rise, since it refers to all of 1973 and since it was calculated by deflating by the wholesale-price index. In the Chilean case, the basket of goods in the wholesale-price index is quite small and the weight of petroleum and its derivatives is exaggerated, so that it poorly represents the evolution of internal costs in this period.

6. This was the so-called shock treatment, which, rather than bring on the recession, as some unwary observers believe, worsened the recession that had already begun by lowering demand even more. For by May 1975, before the announcement of the shock program, industrial output was 40 percent below that of October of 1973 and 20 percent below that of December 1969. In addition, unemployment reached 13 percent in March and 16 percent in June (before the impact of the shock program could be felt), compared to the historic average of 6 percent and the historic maximum (which lasted for only one quarter) of 10.5 percent.

also auctioned off the bulk of firms and banks (another 200) either bought or legally expropriated in the previous regime. Nevertheless, inasmuch as it chose to auction these firms during a severe recession, the prices and the conditions of sales were quite disadvantageous for the government and for the country. One estimate is that their selling prices were 30 percent less than their real value (Foxley 1983). In any case, twelve of the fifteen largest nonfinancial firms in the country continued to be owned and run by the government, including the largest copper mines, which had been Chileanized under Frei and nationalized under Allende.[7]

As a result of the military coup, stock-market values doubled in real terms between August and December of 1973; indeed they sextupled in terms of constant dollars. If one takes into account the immense capital gains that the coup thus brought about—gains that were not taxed—it is clear that the government missed a splendid and unique opportunity to redistribute wealth in a nonconflictive way. For example, 51 percent of the ownership of each firm could have been returned to its owners, and the remaining 49 percent could have been retained as a capital gains tax to be distributed to workers or unions. Indeed, even with 51 percent, entrepreneurs would still have made important gains compared to the situation previous to the junta.

Second, in order to stimulate competition, tariffs were reduced from 94 percent on average in December 1973 to an average of 33 percent by mid-1976, the maximum tariff not exceeding 60 percent. Nevertheless, since the real effective exchange rate rose sharply between 1973 and 1976, the lowering of tariffs did not imply a significant loss of competitiveness for domestic output during this first phase.

Third, with the purpose of eliminating assigned and subsidized credit, a domestic capital market was created, thus furthering the market's role in the determination and allocation of savings and investments. Interest rates were freed; the creation of private financial intermediaries was permitted, both to raise and lend resources; and quantitative controls on the use of credit were eliminated, as were some of the limitations on the entry of foreign banks.

As a result of these measures, real interest rates rapidly changed from negative to sharply positive—3 percent real per month for the borrower, with a 15 percent per year differential for the financial intermediary, on a typical loan of thirty days. These two characteristics proved to be of a long-term nature, and thus the hopes for improvement in savings and investment failed to materialize. Indeed, both of these characteristics would contribute to building up the financial bubble, which finally burst in 1981–82.

For both political and economic reasons, during this first phase it was difficult for Chile to secure foreign credits. Moreover, the central bank, fearful of the potentially inflationary effects that a massive affluence of foreign capital

7. At the end of 1977, 78 percent of the assets of the hundred largest firms in the country belonged to the state. See *Economía y Sociedad* 1978.

might imply, imposed limitations on such entry. For these reasons, the volume of foreign lending was rather modest, and foreign indebtedness maintained itself around four and a half billion dollars (which, of course, meant that in real terms it actually fell).

Phase II, June 1976 to mid-1981

This was the golden phase of the Chilean economy under the military junta; the economy recovered and expanded at a rate between 6.5 percent and 8 percent per year.[8] Yet, notwithstanding the severe reduction in real wages as well as the important reduction in the fiscal deficit, inflation was still advancing at 250 percent per year as this phase began. As a result, the price-stabilization strategy was modified. Emphasis from now on was placed not on monetary and wage restrictions (it was difficult after all to explain such a high inflation in the midst of such a sharp recession solely in terms of excess demand) but on controlling expectations and pressuring domestic prices downward via foreign competition.

The key instrument in this new strategy was the exchange rate. In June 1976, the exchange rate was suddenly revalued, putting an end to three years of continued devaluation. A further revaluation took place in March 1977. From then on, monthly devaluations were programmed and preannounced but at a rate substantially lower than past inflation. The object of these measures was to alter inflationary expectations in hopes of lowering inflation. It was further hoped that reduced tariffs would put a ceiling on increases in domestic prices.

Thanks to these new policies, inflation dropped from 90 to 40 percent between the first and second semesters of 1976. Moreover, this implied an increase in real wages, for by this time wage readjustments were again indexed by law to past inflation. Surprising to those who believed in a microeconomic explanation of unemployment (to wit, government economists), unemployment began to fall while real wages rose. In fact, this was the result of the increased *aggregate* demand, resulting from the higher wage bill. This demand more than compensated the incentive to hire fewer workers, which higher wages implied (the microeconomic view then in fashion). By 1978 the annual inflation rate was 50 percent, production was increasing, and the fiscal deficit was close to zero. In mid-1979 the exchange rate was fixed for an indefinite period at thirty-nine pesos to the dollar, a rate that would hold for the following three years.

Unfortunately, since domestic inflation, though lower and falling, continued to substantially exceed international inflation, the level of domestic

---

8. Official figures show a growth rate of 8 percent. Yet a recent and most important paper (Meller, Livacich, and Arrau 1984) suggests serious errors in the methodology of the official national accounts—among others, the supposition of constancy in the relation between value-added and gross value of production, despite trade liberalization—which would lead to overestimating growth by 20 percent.

prices moved well above that of international prices plus tariffs and transport costs. The consequences of such a loss in competitiveness were not immediately made manifest, for three reasons: (1) The real devaluation of the exchange rate during 1975 and 1976 was so strong that it continued to be advantageous to export for a good time beyond, notwithstanding the subsequent revaluation. (2) Thanks to greater international liquidity and the progressively liberalized domestic capital market, capital inflows kept increasing, attracted by the large differential between internal and external interest rates. These capital movements thus financed ever-increasing deficits in current account and in the trade balance. (3) The strong inflow of foreign credits and the increase in real wages strengthened aggregate demand, so that the vast majority of productive sectors in the economy were able to recover—and in several cases to surpass—their level of output and sales of 1974. This was so despite the fact that imports were steadily gaining a wider share of the internal market.

During this second phase, the government completed its trade and tariff reform and its opening up of the capital account. The affluence of foreign credit was so massive that the level of net foreign debt almost doubled in just two years (1979–81). Nevertheless domestic interest rates, while declining somewhat, remained well above international ones.

Finally, two key structural reforms were implemented: the labor plan and the new social security system. The first reestablished collective bargaining but limited it to the level of the firm. The government expected that the atomization of the labor movement together with the pressure of foreign competition would keep wage demands in line, holding them close to productivity increases. At the same time, the plan guaranteed workers a minimum floor in such negotiations equal to the conditions in their previous contract and readjusted according to the rate of inflation. Strikes were once again legalized but with two important limitations: (1) the employer would have a right to lockout and to hire a new labor force; and (2) if at the end of sixty days no agreement had been reached, workers would either have to accept their last contract or quit.[9]

The old system of social security had entered into a financial crisis, partly because of the ease with which benefits had been increased in the past when the ratio of contributing participants to those retired was large. Financing such

---

9. Though the restrictions on strikes were quite in line with the neoconservatives' desire to correct what for them was one of the economy's most serious rigidities, the floor on wages, with a built-in cost-of-living escalator appears to have been based on other considerations: (1) to make the whole plan more appealing to workers; and (2) to remove the most frequent source of conflict in collective bargaining, hoping thereby to limit negotiations to increases in labor productivity. Moreover, though the wage floor left no room for real wage declines, it was thought that this would not normally be a serious constraint, for, should it be necessary, the firm could keep all of the productivity increase for itself, thus permitting actual declines in unit labor costs. The predicted productivity increases of 3 to 4 percent per year would provide a sufficient margin to adjust to most cyclical fluctuations. To be sure, the wage floor could be a serious constraint in case of a serious recession—especially from a neoconservative perspective.

ample benefits, once this ratio declined as the system matured, became increasingly difficult. The new system, established in 1980, extended the age of retirement and reduced some of the benefits. These two measures alone resolved the financial crisis. Nevertheless, this opportunity was seized to change the previous system, based on sharing, to one based on "individual capitalization." From now on, and above a certain minimum pension guaranteed by the state, each worker would receive at the end of his or her working life a pension directly proportional to his or her personal contribution. Similarly, in accordance with the general philosophy underlying neoconservative thinking, private firms were put in charge of administering the social security system. To some, this would guarantee their efficiency; to others, this risked putting large amounts of capital in the hands of a few economic conglomerates, at least to the extent to which capital markets, especially long-term capital markets, were only slightly transparent and not at all competitive.

With the establishment of the new system, the social security contribution, which heretofore was based on the wage bill (a form of tax on labor), was replaced. During the transition, this cost was absorbed directly by the state: it continued to pay the benefits of retired workers in the old system and of those who were close to retirement, while no longer receiving contributions from those transferring to the new system. This cost has been estimated of the order of 2.5 to 4 percent of GNP (see Arellano 1981).

Phase III, mid-1981 through 1983

The third phase began in mid-1981, when the Chilean economy went into a nosedive. The continued buildup of disequilibria in the foregoing period, especially the increased disparity between domestic and international prices and the persistently high real rates of interest, led to a very sharp fall in output as well as in the value and volume of exports (the latter fell 8 percent in 1981 versus an average rise of 12 percent per year in the previous five years). The deficit in current account at the end of 1981 reached the unprecedented level of 90 percent of the value of exports. The massive entry of foreign capital thus became a critical factor in the operation of the model.

The deterioration of virtually all indicators of economic activity—the worsening of the lag in the exchange rates and the sharp increase in interest rates—all led to a sudden increase in nonperforming loans. For it was not possible for firms to continue paying real interest rates averaging 25 to 30 percent per year for six years when output was growing at about 7 percent per year.[10] By the end of 1981, bad loans constituted one quarter of banks' capital

---

10. Behind all this, to be sure, was a speculative fever, as can be seen by the behavior of the stock-market index. Between December 1973 and December 1980, the index of the value of stocks rose 8.5 times in real terms; indeed, it even rose 33 percent during the 1975 depression. And all of this rise was in addition to the doubling of stock value that followed the military coup. Obviously, such a situation could not continue indefinitely. The bubble, its causes, and consequences, are dealt with at length in chapter 8.

and reserves, jeopardizing the stability of the entire financial system. The intervention by the government in eight financial institutions in November 1981 avoided the imminent collapse of the system, but this proved to be the signal for foreign banks to drastically cut back their loans.

Because of the crisis, the government was obliged to take drastic steps. The year 1982 began with a series of sharply restrictive economic policies aimed at deflating the economy and avoiding devaluation; these policies proved ineffective and unnecessarily costly. A massive devaluation was finally forced upon the government; there followed a period of generalized uncertainty and a massive run to the dollar. Output fell 14 percent in 1982, a greater fall than in the recession of 1975; and unemployment (counting those employed in the emergency work program) reached the unprecedented level of 30 percent.

The massive devaluations of 1982 tended to correct the disequilibrium in external accounts. But the deterioration of firms' debt-to-equity ratios and the consequent erosion of the financial soundness of the banking system persisted. Hence, in early 1983 the government closed three financial institutions and intervened in five others, including Chile's two leading private banks, each of which was at the core of one of the country's two largest conglomerates. The measure avoided a financial run, which would certainly have taken place upon the inevitable bankruptcy of any one of Chile's major firms (most of which were overly leveraged, with dangerously high debt-to-equity ratios). Moreover, the intervention permitted a reordering of banks' and firms' finances, began the process of deciding who was to absorb Chile's excess debt (variously estimated between 2.5 and 4 billion dollars), and avoided the total cutoff of capital inflows.[11] Yet it achieved this at the cost of largely exempting foreign creditors from absorbing their share of the costs of Chile's bad debts, for the measure served as a pretext and justification for foreign creditor banks to insist upon the government's guaranteeing the private financial sector's heretofore unguaranteed foreign debt.

Given the greater domestic financial stability and the important devaluations of 1982, the substitution of imports by domestic production began to take hold in 1983. Nevertheless, the value of exports continued to be limited by the international recession. This, plus the continued decline in the entry of foreign capital, severely constrained the improvement that might have been expected because of the real depreciation. Consequently, output fell by another 1 percent, and the economy "stabilized" at a level of per capita income even below that of Allende's low of 1973.

---

11. See in this regard Arellano 1984 and Lüders' important article (Lüders 1985), in which he justifies the intervention (which he himself effected as the then minister of finance and economics).

Uruguay, 1974–1983

Policies and Principal Results

3

Short-run crises in the balance of payments and high inflation were the immediate problems that induced the adoption of the neoconservative approach to policy in Uruguay in 1974. (See table 3.1 for Uruguay's economic indicators before and during the neoconservative era.) Nevertheless, more than the immediate problems themselves it was their chronic reappearance that brought about this change in approach, for these problems were attributed by neoconservative thinking to the development strategy pursued by Uruguay since the thirties. Consequently, efforts focused on revitalizing the private sector by means of a far greater use of market mechanisms and on raising the productivity of the public sector.

In the final analysis, the neoconservative approach followed in Uruguay turned out to be far more pragmatic and, in this sense, less pure than that followed in Chile. On the other hand, Uruguayan policies were very intimately related and conditioned by the economic policies of its neighbors, Argentina and Brazil.[1]

THE INITIAL CONDITIONS

Between the end of the Second World War and 1973, per capita income in Uruguay grew by a mere 0.7 percent per year, the slowest growth rate in Latin America except for Haiti. Moreover, together with Argentina and Chile, Uruguay had one of the highest rates of inflation in the continent. Despite its small size, it had a very low export coefficient (less than 10 percent of GNP), exports

---

1. The reader interested in a fuller view of the antecedents of neoconservatism in Uruguay is referred to Instituto de Economía 1969 and World Bank 1982. As for the neoconservative period, in addition to the base studies on Uruguay earlier cited, see Macadar 1982 and, very especially, Esser, Almer, Greischel, Kürzinger, and Weber 1983 and De Melo, Pascale, and Tybout 1985.

growing quite slowly even in the boom period of the sixties (2.1 percent per year nominal versus 9.4 percent per year for the rest of the world).

Given its democratic tradition and relatively high per capita income, Uruguay had, at a fairly early stage, adopted social legislation characteristic of an advanced welfare state. For its financing, it relied heavily on the taxing of "rents" in the traditional export sector (wool and beef). This worked well enough in times of export price booms, but in times of falling export prices, the squeeze was on—the distributive issue became paramount, and inflation soared. Moreover, in the long run, this squeeze of the export sector took its toll, discouraging export expansion. The quantum of Uruguay's exports in the postwar period stagnated and so the growth of per capita income was minimal.

According to neoconservative thought, the very same policies that had helped Uruguay pull out of the Great Depression limited its long-run development. The feeble growth of its output and exports were seen as resulting from exaggerated state intervention, which focused much too heavily on distributive issues at the expense of productive activity and relied excessively on administrative controls rather than on market mechanisms. Neoconservatives especially criticized the tendency to face balance-of-payments crises with an extensive use of quantitative restrictions on imports, a policy that normally ended in massive devaluations once the situation became intolerable (as was the case after the Korean War). Similarly, the tendency to meet inflationary pressure through a generalized system of price controls was sharply criticized.

Quantitative restrictions over imports sometimes permitted Uruguay to ride out the immediate external crises but, argued neoconservatives, at the cost of the stagnation of nontraditional exports. Moreover, when these controls proved insufficient, devaluation—with its considerable inflationary impact— was made necessary. Something similar occurred when the prices of traditional exports rose, for, since these were agricultural products consumed domestically, inflation rose unless a special tax was also levied on external sales. The need to break this close and recurrent link between external disequilibria and domestic inflation played a dominant role in neoconservative thinking. It was considered indispensable to look outward if the foreign exchange bottleneck and the unending cycle of external crisis and inflation was to be overcome.[2]

The size of the state was seen as being excessive on all counts. Its participation in output and employment exceeded 20 percent. Market mechanisms, on the other hand, were increasingly diminished: ever since 1968, the vast majority of goods and services, except for real estate and products normally auctioned, had their prices set via administrative decree. It was the use of such discretional instruments that explained to neoconservatives the slow and unstable development of the Uruguayan economy.

---

2. In Uruguay, as in Chile and to a lesser extent in Argentina, the need for an outward-looking orientation to development was not peculiar to the neoconservatives. To a greater or lesser extent, this view was shared by most alternative schools of thought.

Table 3.1. Uruguay: Basic Macroeconomic Indicators, Postwar Period and 1971–1983

Indicator	1950–1970	1971	1972	1973	1974	1975	1976	1977	1978	1979	1980	1981	1982	1983
Real sector														
Per capita GNP growth rate	0.7	−0.2	−1.6	0.3	3.1	5.6	3.5	0.7	4.6	5.5	5.1	1.2	−10.3	−5.3
Gross-investment/GNP growth coefficient	12.6	11.9	10.2	9.6	9.7	11.6	13.5	15.7	17.0	19.8	21.4	17.8	14.5	11.1
Savings/GNP coefficient	12.4	9.6	11.6	10.1	7.1	8.5	12.3	13.3	15.3	16.2	15.8	14.4	13.5	11.3
Unemployment rate		7.6	7.7	8.9	8.1		12.7	11.8	10.1	8.3	7.4	6.6	11.9	15.5
Real wage index	105.2	87.2	85.7	85.0	77.5	75.6	69.9	66.9	64.8	65.1	69.9	69.7	55.3	
Monetary and financial sector														
Inflation rate[a]	29.4	24.0	76.4	97.0	77.2	81.4	50.7	58.2	44.5	66.8	63.5	34.1	19.0	51.5
M1 growth rate[b]	29.5	32.3	49.2	63.5	80.0	50.1	67.9	45.3	53.0	99.5	34.9	8.3	19.8	11.1
M2 growth rate[c]		51.5	60.4	70.9	70.6	91.6	97.1	78.0	89.3	84.7	72.5	63.9	90.0	−8.6
Public-sector-surplus/GNP		−5.8	−2.5	−1.2	−3.8	−4.3	−2.1	−1.3	−0.9	0.0	−0.3	−1.5	−9.1	−3.9
Real interest rate[d]								14.4	9.0	−6.5	29.5	39.6	13.7	11.9

Growth rate of exports

Value	−0.4	−12.9	38.8	16.9	22.0	10.2	26.4	16.1	12.9	30.8	27.8	11.4	−9.6	−10.1
Volume		−16.7	18.0	−14.4	17.3	24.3	24.1	5.7	4.3	0.6	6.3	7.1	−1.2	4.3

Indexes

Real effective exchange rate[e]	92.0	113.7	97.3	93.8	108.0	115.0	114.1	111.2	94.0	90.5	86.7	100.3	123.8
Terms of trade, goods and services	102.2	109.9	139.8	106.4	80.4	78.6	84.7	89.1	96.6	94.5	89.1	87.5	78.5
Current-account-surplus/exports	−28.7	13.5	4.4	−27.3	−35.9	−11.8	−21.2	−14.5	−30.4	−46.9	−27.5	−15.3	−4.0
External debt (billions of dollars)	0.6	0.8	0.7	1.0	1.0	1.1	1.3	1.2	1.7	2.1	3.1	4.3	4.5
External-debt/exports	2.4	2.2	1.8	1.9	1.9	1.6	1.6	1.4	1.4	1.4	1.8	2.8	3.2

Source: CEPAL, on the basis of official data; growth rate of *M1*, International Monetary Fund, *International Financial Statistics*, August 1985, and *Statistical Yearbook*, 1982.

Note: 1970 = 100. Year 1983; preliminary figures.

[a]Variation in the consumer price index.

[b]*M1* = bills and coins in circulation plus demand deposits.

[c]*M2* = *M1* plus savings and time deposits.

[d]Nominal interest rate deflated by the wholesale-price index.

[e]Exchange-rate variation deflated by the difference between the internal and external wholesale-price index.

This typical cycle of external disequilibria and inflation repeated itself once again in the period 1967–73: a balance-of-payments crisis in 1967; a massive devaluation at the end of 1967; a freezing of the exchange rate in 1968, yet followed by creeping inflation notwithstanding price controls; a new massive devaluation at the end of 1971, followed by a strong resurgence of inflation—76 percent in 1972 and almost 100 percent in 1973, once prices were freed and the effects of the devaluation made themselves felt. Finally, the rise in the price of petroleum toward the end of 1973 and the need to finance huge deficits in current account in 1974 provided the decisive impetus for development strategy based on outward-looking growth.

ECONOMIC POLICY AND ITS RESULTS

The approval of the National Development Plan for 1973–77 (in the second semester of 1973, following the collapse of Uruguay's institutional system) marked the beginning of the implementation of the neoconservative strategy in Uruguay. Three stages can be usefully distinguished in this process: (1) July 1974 to October 1978, in which emphasis was placed on a policy of indiscriminate export promotion, while output recovered and grew and nontraditional exports expanded.[3] (2) October 1978 through 1980, in which a policy of preannounced and programmed devaluation was pursued, revealing the dominance of the monetary approach to the balance of payments. The key goal was price stabilization. A lag in the exchange rate emerged, though production continued to grow, thanks to the massive entrance of foreign capital. (3) 1981 through 1983, in which the crisis in Argentina, the growing lag in the exchange rate, and the deficit in the trade balance increasingly braked the entry of foreign capital on which Uruguay was by then heavily dependent. A financial crisis occurred, both domestic and external, and an unprecedented recession ensued.

Phase I, July 1974 to October 1978

The explosive increase in petroleum prices at the end of 1973 signaled the urgency for Uruguay to overcome its by now chronic foreign exchange bottleneck. It has been estimated that the loss in output attributable to this external shock was the equivalent of 7 percent of GNP, one of the largest losses in the entire region (see Balassa 1980). Thus, unlike Chile, and notwithstanding

---

3. This phase began when Alejandro Vegh Villegas became minister of finance. To some extent, July 1974 is a rather arbitrary date, inasmuch as it could be argued that the new economic policy began in 1973, when the policy of export promotion was implemented. Nevertheless, the neoconservative approach did not become operational in most of its dimensions until July of the following year.

Uruguay's severe inflation, the first priority of economic policy during this first phase was not price stabilization but the reestablishment of equilibrium in its external accounts. To do this, the government effected a massive devaluation, which left the exchange rate in 1975–76 some 20 percent higher in real terms than in 1974; and this rate was maintained subsequently via a crawling peg. In the four years of this phase, the multiplicity of exchange rates that had existed up until then were virtually eliminated.

Moreover, and quite importantly, the government used a wide set of instruments in support of the external sector, especially in favor of exports with high domestic value-added: preferential and subsidized credits, the anticipated provision of foreign exchange, tax exemptions, and so on. At the beginning, such instruments were justified as transitorily compensating the negative effects of tariffs and other policies, which heretofore had implicitly taxed exports. But by the second phase, such instruments began to be used as simple subsidies to promote nontraditional exports. Indeed, so generous was this support that, as of mid-1977, 60 percent of credit for the industrial sector was for such exports; moreover, and quite significantly, these credits were provided at a nominal interest rate of 20 percent, less than half the rate of inflation.

In contrast to Chile, a policy of gradual rather than abrupt price stabilization was adopted, prices being freed bit by bit throughout this period, so that even at the end of 1978 as much as 40 percent of the basket of goods included in the cost-of-living index was still under price controls.[4] Collective bargaining was suspended and real wages were purposely compressed, so that between 1974 and 1978 wages fell over 20 percent with respect to the already depressed levels at the end of 1973.[5] This wage policy had three principal objectives: (1) to reduce domestic spending, in this way freeing domestic resources so as to increase exports; (2) to lower costs in order to improve Uruguay's competitiveness; and (3) to raise profit margins to induce increased investment. The stabilization policy as a whole aimed at controlling the fiscal deficit (3.8 percent of GNP in 1974), in this way constraining monetary growth.

During this phase, no significant attempts were made at reducing the size of the state in the economy. Though import quotas were eliminated, the highly protective tariff system was left basically intact. Nevertheless, important decisions were taken with respect to the financial system. Domestic interest rates were freed; capital movements, both inflows and outflows, were widely liberalized; and deposits in foreign currency were authorized.

---

4. At the beginning of phase I, 94 percent of the basket of goods in the consumer-price index was under price controls. See Notaro and Wonsewer 1980.

5. The wage series available for this period probably overestimates the fall in real wages up to 1975, inclusively, for it refers to the movement in legal minimum wages and not to wages actually paid. The central bank of Uruguay began a new series of wages actually paid in industry as of 1976. This latter series is the one used in table 3.1 from 1976 onward. In any case, the decline is quite sharp.

The results of this phase undoubtedly showed a break with past economic performance. Per capita output first recovered and then grew at a rate close to 4 percent per year, quadrupling the rate of previous decades. At the same time, the share of investment in GNP grew from 10 to 17 percent between 1974 and 1978. Exports, both in value and in quantum, grew at a strong rate, especially nontraditional exports, in clear contrast to the stagnation of previous decades; and though inflation continued high, by 1978 it had fallen slowly and gradually to 45 percent per year, from close to a 100 percent in 1973.

The fiscal deficit did not decline until 1976, reaching 0.9 percent of GNP only at the end of the first phase. This reduction was due principally to increased taxes and a decline in current expenditures, especially wages. Public investment was not reduced; quite the contrary, it grew at a real rate of 45 percent per year during this phase, almost quadrupling its participation in GNP. This, together with the favorable evolution of exports, explains the bulk of the growth in demand and output observed during this period. In short, the recessive impact of the wage policy on domestic demand was compensated in large part by the dynamic expansion of public investment. Consequently, rather than following a contractive stabilization policy, Uruguay gradually shifted its demand, chaneling it from domestic consumption to either investment or exports.

The one clear cost of the otherwise successful policy during this first phase was in the distribution of income. The already depressed wages of 1973 suffered a further reduction of some 20 percent in real terms, without compensating improvements in employment, while output and national income were growing 4 and 3 percent per year, respectively. Last, and to the good, despite financial liberalization and the good performance of exports, foreign debt rose only moderately, at an average of under 10 percent per year in nominal terms during the four years, all of which implied a significant reduction in the debt-to-export ratio.

Phase II, October 1978 through 1980

Phase II is identified with a major modification in exchange-rate policy. By October 1978, the first priority of short-run economic policy was the reduction of inflation. This implied going from a policy of export promotion at almost any cost to a policy that privileged price stabilization. The path chosen was that of preannounced and programmed devaluations in an ever-decreasing rhythm. It was hoped that in this way the rise in domestic prices could be kept equal to the rate of devaluation plus international inflation. Once the monetary approach to the balance of payments became the dominant approach to policy, monetary growth was transformed into a passive variable. At the same time, since the initial external disequilibrium seemed to be resolved, the system of very costly incentives for export promotion began to be dismantled. It was hoped that in this way the fiscal deficit could be closed, helping to further reduce the rate of inflation.

The policy of gradual price liberation was continued, so that by the end of this phase the number of goods whose prices were controlled fell to less than 30 percent of those in the basket making up the consumer-price index. Moreover, the sale of beef, traditionally controlled in Uruguay, was freed. Controls were also removed from the pricing and wholesaling of cereals and oil-producing seeds. These products, especially beef, were and are quite critical in Uruguay, for these are not only exportables but also basic foodstuffs for domestic consumption. Hence, when the price of these goods rises in international markets, it hurts the consuming population of the country. This explains, no doubt, the traditional attempts by the government to separate internal price movements and domestic consumption from the ups and downs of international markets.

Finally, at the end of 1978 a tariff reduction and reform program was announced. It was to be put into effect by January 1980 and completed in five years. The final goal was a nominal tariff of 35 percent on all imports, to be reached in six successive reductions.

Despite the fact that the fiscal budget was brought into equilibrium during this period, inflation continued to advance faster than the rates of devaluation and international inflation. Consequently, an important lag in the exchange rate began to show up (20 percent between 1978 and 1980). The growth in the quantum of exports slowed from 15 percent per year between 1974 and 1978 to less than 4 percent per year in 1979–80, and the export of nontraditional goods actually fell in absolute terms. Nevertheless, there was a very strong inflow of capital into Uruguay toward the end of the 1970s as a result of (1) financial liberalization and the free movement of capital; (2) the preannounced exchange rate, which amounted to a virtual guarantee of foreign exchange, as long as this policy was maintained; and (3) high interest rates plus Argentina's larger lag in its exchange rate. Indeed, in 1979 and 1980, foreign debt rose 75 percent, increasing more in these two years than in the preceding four years.

Thanks to this heavy indebtedness, Uruguay was able to finance the new hike in the price of petroleum and to increase the volume of imports by almost 50 percent. Moreover, output continued to grow (6 percent per year), but no longer on the basis of export but rather because of increased domestic demand. Particularly dynamic was the growth of the construction sector (both in Punta del Este and in Montevideo) and of private consumption. Private consumption was fueled by the large inflows of Argentinian tourists, attracted by the low cost of Uruguayan products. (Because Argentina's exchange rate lagged behind Uruguay's, Uruguayan prices relative to Argentina's fell 50 percent between 1977 and 1980.) In short, the sensation of sustained growth was created, despite the fact that the basis for such growth was becoming increasingly less solid, for neither the growing foreign debt nor the overvaluation of the Argentinian peso could be sustained indefinitely.

Phase III, 1981 through 1983

The key objective of economic policy in this phase continued to be price stabilization. The privileged instruments were preannounced and programmed devaluations and reduced tariffs. The latter, begun in 1980, in fact never came close to being put fully into effect.

Thanks to the increasingly lagged exchange rate, inflation finally came down sharply in 1981, and in 1982 it actually fell below 20 percent. Yet by this time the economy was in crisis, both pillars of its growth having yielded. First, Argentinian demand for Uruguayan products was drastically curtailed by Argentina's massive devaluation of the peso in 1981, which by the third quarter of 1982 tripled in real terms the relative cost of Uruguayan products for Argentinians. This loss might have been compensated in 1981 by the significant increase in real wages resulting from the sudden decline in inflation, but because of the lag in the exchange rate, a good part of this increased demand was chaneled toward the importation of consumer goods, whose volume increased by a third in 1981.

Second, the inflow of foreign capital was sharply cut because of uncertainty about the exchange policy, despite the authorities' efforts to offer greater security to the banking system through such means as exchange guarantees and limits on the size of loans to firms. In 1981, this decline in the entry of foreign capital to the private sector was compensated by a substantial increase in official indebtedness, but by the end of 1982 this was no longer practicable either. Uruguay's loss of competitiveness with respect to both Argentina and Brazil, together with the international recession, brought on a decline of 1 percent in the volume of exports in 1982. Moreover, the poor situation of financial intermediaries, whose nonperforming loans skyrocketed due to firms' inability to pay high interest rates (which reached 40 percent per year real in 1981), increasingly weakened and jeopardized the financial system. This forced the central bank to buy up part of the banking system's portfolio of nonperforming assets to facilitate the renegotiation of the private sector's debt. Moreover, the deficit in current account, though sharply lowered, still equaled 15 percent of the value of exports. Given the outflow of foreign capital, there was a huge reduction in international reserves. Output fell 9 percent, and the unemployment rate shot up to 12 percent.

In the face of such an acute crisis, it was no longer possible to maintain exchange policy; toward the end of 1982, the central bank allowed the peso to float freely. After a somewhat chaotic first month, the exchange rate "stabilized" at a rate some 50 to 60 percent above the previous rate. With this, the real effective exchange rate recovered its previous levels. In 1983, in an effort to adjust to external disequilibria and to minimize the inflationary impact of the devaluation, a contractive policy was set in motion. While this managed to hold inflation "down" to some 50 percent, it did so at the cost of a further contraction in output: by the end of 1983, GNP per capita was 16 percent below 1981.

Nevertheless, it was still some 10 percent above what it had been ten years before, when the experience began. While exports had grown sharply in the neoconservative period, thus proving that it was possible to overcome the external bottleneck, foreign debt had quadrupled. As a result, the ratio of debt to exports was of the order of three to one. So closed this third phase of Uruguay's neoconservative experience.

4

Argentina, 1976–1983

Policies and Principal Results

In the beginning of 1976, in the midst of a severe economic, social, and political crisis, the armed forces once again took power in Argentina. The political objectives were to reestablish order to put down the guerrillas; the economic ones, to correct the basic macroeconomic disequilibria and to re-orient the inward-oriented development strategy, which had been followed ever since the Great Depression.[1] (see table 4.1 for economic indicators during these years and through the neoconservative era.)

Though Argentina's growth in the postwar period had not been all that bad (3.7 percent per year), it was quite disappointing not only in comparison to its former dynamic performance (5 percent per year between 1870 and 1930) but also to that of the rest of Latin America in the postwar period (6.2 percent per year, outside the Southern Cone). Whereas in 1930, Argentina possessed a standard of living on a par with that of many developed countries of Western Europe, because of its lackluster economic performance since then, Argentina was now classified with the developing countries of the Third World. Indeed, during the late 1970s its per capita income was surpassed in Latin America by Venezuela, as its overwhelming manufacturing predominance in the region had given way in the late fifties and early sixties to Brazil and Mexico.

The neoconservative model was adopted not only because of the relatively poor performance of the traditional strategy and because of the urgency to correct basic macroeconomic disequilibria, but also because its neighbors, Chile and Uruguay, were both following neoconservative strategies with apparent success. Nevertheless, inasmuch as Argentina is a larger economy with a

---

1. Among the important works on the historical antecedents of the neoconservative experience in Argentina are Díaz-Alejandro 1970, Di Tella and Zymelman 1970, Ferrer 1977, and Mallon and Sourrouille 1975. For evaluations of the neoconservative experience, see, in addition to the base studies cited in the Preface, Canitrot 1982, Dagnino Pastore 1984, and the discussion that followed his paper, and Ferrer 1979. How firms adjusted to the reforms is treated in detail in Petrei and Tybout 1985.

much more developed technology, its industry was seen as more complex and efficient. Neoconservatives here were less critical of industrialization per se; the accent was placed not so much on reducing the weight of industry in GNP as on raising its productivity and improving international competitiveness.[2]

THE INITIAL CONDITIONS

The economic situation at the beginning of 1976 was intolerable. In the previous year, inflation had approached 350 percent[3] and was worsening, threatening to reach four-digit rates within the next year. At the same time, the fiscal deficit exceeded 10 percent of GNP.

Since Argentina was self-sufficient in petroleum, it was not affected by the energy crisis. Indeed, its terms of trade actually evolved in a fairly favorable fashion, at least through 1974. Nevertheless, in 1975 it found itself in the midst of a serious external crisis: the quantum of its exports had fallen 11 percent; and its terms of trade, though not unfavorable judged by its historic trends, had fallen 25 percent. The deficit in current account reached an unprecedented 37 percent of the value of its exports of goods and services, international reserves fell by a billion dollars, and output fell one percent.

The new military government claimed that the economic crisis was not simply the consequence of mistaken policies of recent years. It claimed that the crisis had its origins in the Great Depression, when the previous strategy of outward-oriented growth, based on the export of agricultural products, was replaced by a strategy of inward-oriented growth. This strategy centered on import-substituting industrialization aimed at the domestic market and was based on high tariffs, tax exemptions, and subsidized credits—all at the expense of traditional exports. The latter were taxed and a low exchange rate was maintained. It was not strange then, according to the neoconservative view, that the quantum of exports per capita did not increase at all during the preceding three decades.

The new economic authorities argued that past strategy had led to a very inefficient form of industrialization and so to a slow rate of overall growth. And this was so despite Argentina's large potential, both in human and natural resources, and the fact that the country regularly saved and invested a fairly high proportion of GNP, unlike Chile and Uruguay. Neoconservatives argued that the growth of the last thirty years had been quite unstable and, paradox-

---

2. For a good analysis of this point, see Ferrer 1981.

3. This percentage is the rate of inflation between January and December 1975, and not the variation in the average level of 1975 prices with respect to 1974 prices, which is what table 4.1 shows. The January to December rate more accurately reflects the acceleration, and that is why it is used in the text.

Table 4.1. Argentina: Basic Macroeconomic Indicators, Postwar Period and 1971–1983

Indicator	1950–1970	1971	1972	1973	1974	1975	1976	1977	1978	1979	1980	1981	1982	1983
Real sector														
Per capita GNP growth rate	1.9	2.0	0.1	1.8	4.4	-2.5	-2.1	4.7	-5.0	5.4	-0.5	-7.4	-6.8	1.2
Gross-investment/GNP coefficient	17.3	22.5	22.2	20.5	19.6	20.2	21.2	23.9	21.4	22.0	23.8	20.5	17.4	14.3
Savings/GNP coefficient	16.8	21.3	21.6	22.2	19.8	18.3	22.1	25.3	23.6	21.5	19.5	16.8	15.4	12.8
Unemployment rate		6.0	6.6	5.3	3.4	2.6	4.5	2.8	2.8	2.0	2.3	4.5	4.8	4.0
Real wage index		103.4	98.3	104.4	117.9	111.1	74.7	73.6	72.3	83.0	92.8	83.0	74.1	90.8
Monetary and Financial sector														
Inflation rate[a]	23.8	34.9	58.9	61.2	23.3	182.5	443.2	176.1	175.5	159.5	100.8	104.5	164.8	343.8
M1 growth rate[b]	24.3	6.9	35.2	86.3	93.0	90.5	399.4	176.2	142.8	131.4	115.8	53.9	195.7	361.7
M2 growth rate[c]		38.5	47.2	98.1	69.5	136.5	359.6	239.2	164.9	187.6	91.6	118.5	131.5	422.3
Public-sector-surplus/GNP		-3.1	-3.3	-4.7	-5.3	-10.3	-7.2	-2.8	-3.2	-2.7	-3.6	-8.1	-7.2	-11.0
Real interest rate[d]								26.7	11.9	2.6	25.9	-1.5	-13.5	

Growth rate of exports														
Value	2.1	-0.2	9.5	60.9	23.1	-23.2	31.8	42.9	13.6	22.6	7.8	9.7	-16.9	4.0
Volume	2.6	-12.1	-1.2	13.5	-3.3	-10.7	31.9	40.5	6.0	-2.8	-10.3	14.5	0.7	9.8
Indexes														
Real effective exchange rate[e]		94.9	107.3	102.7	87.8	134.2	88.5	114.0	102.9	77.2	69.2	87.0	112.9	104.1
Terms of trade, goods and services		108.1	117.3	141.8	128.7	97.1	93.1	88.9	89.9	97.6	110.3	100.2	89.1	86.8
Current-account-surplus/exports		-18.4	-9.7	18.9	2.6	-36.8	14.3	17.1	24.5	-5.8	-48.3	-43.4	-27.5	-27.4
External debt (billions of dollars)		4.5	5.8	6.2	8.0	7.9	8.3	9.7	12.5	19.0	27.2	35.7	43.6	45.5
External-debt/exports		2.1	2.5	1.7	1.7	2.3	1.8	1.5	1.7	2.1	2.8	3.3	4.8	4.9

Source: CEPAL, on the basis of official data; growth rate of $M1$, International Monetary Fund, *International Financial Statistics*, August 1985, and *Statistical Yearbook*, 1982.

Note: 1970 = 100. Year 1983; preliminary figures.

[a]Variation in the consumer price index.

[b]$M1$ = bills and coins in circulation plus demand deposits.

[c]$M2$ = $M1$ plus savings and time deposits.

[d]Nominal interest rate deflated by the wholesale price index.

[e]Exchange rate variation deflated by the difference between the internal and exteral wholesale price index.

ically, too dependent on the ups and downs in the prices of traditional exports.[4] It was thus considered necessary to orient growth outward, basing it on new exports, which implied raising the productivity of the industrial sector by taking advantage of economies of scale and forcing it to meet the rigors of foreign competition.

ECONOMIC POLICY AND ITS RESULTS

The neoconservative model that began in Argentina in 1976 had potential advantages over similar situations in Chile and Uruguay: (1) Argentina could take advantage of the experiences of these countries during the two or three years they had been applying the model. This probably explains why the Argentinian government opted for a more gradual stabilization policy and why it was reluctant to reduce public investment. (2) By 1976, the international economy was no longer depressed. This meant not only that the demand for exports would be increasing but that the availability of capital for the periphery was now substantial, a fact that Argentina's public sector would make great use of by 1977. (3) Only one minister was in charge of implementing Argentina's model for most of the period. Martínez de Hoz was in charge of the economic team for five years, thereby providing a stability and consistency seldom seen before in economic policymaking in Argentina. Unfortunately, when, as is endemic in dictatorships, there is little feedback, consistency ceases to be a virtue, for it lends itself to dogmatism and to the continued postponement of necessary corrections. Moreover, while easy access to external capital provides more freedom to economic policy, it also permits the pursuit of easier courses, many of which in the long run proved to be far too precarious (as for example, the temptation to lower inflation by resorting to the massive use of foreign indebtedness).

Three stages can be clearly distinguished in Argentina's application of this model. In phase I (April 1976 to May 1978) there was a notable improvement in the balance-of-payments situation, but inflation slowed down only partially. This phase was characterized by wage controls and by a high real effective exchange rate. Phase II (May 1978 to early 1981), was characterized by the

---

4. Much of this criticism and diagnosis, though certainly not all the policy prescriptions, was shared by schools of thought not of a neoconservative bent. It would be well in this regard to quote Díaz-Alejandro's concluding remarks in his seminal work 1970: "The economic history of Argentina since 1930, but especially since 1943, should be required reading for planners of countries beginning their industrialization. It is a dramatic example of the dangers arising in the development process when a balance between the production of exportables, importables, and home goods is neglected. In an economy with a severe exchange bottleneck, not even a gross savings rate of 20 percent will bring rapid growth. . . . The most ironic lesson of postwar Argentina experience is that if there had been less discrimination against exports, manufacturing expansion would have been greater" (p. 138).

ready availability of foreign capital and the extensive use of such capital to reduce inflation. The exchange rate was used principally to control inflation, and tariffs were lowered. What progress there was in this phase was at the expense of an increasingly artificial exchange rate. In phase III (early 1981 through 1983, heavy internal and external indebtedness led to a financial crisis, both domestic (bankruptcies) and external (a sharp fall in reserves). This crisis forced the country to make a series of massive devaluations and ultimately led to sharp falls in output in both 1981 and 1982. Output stabilized in 1983 but at the cost of an extraordinarily high and rapidly accelerating inflation.

Phase I, April 1976 to May 1978

The immediate objectives of the new economic policy were to improve the balance-of-payments situation and to slow inflation. In the medium run, the objective was to raise the relative price of agricultural products so as to stimulate their production and export.

Labor unions were neutralized not only for obvious political reasons but also in the hope that wage controls would help bring down inflation and make exports more competitive. At the same time, an attempt was made to maintain the real effective exchange rate at the level to which it had been raised at the end of the preceding government, and to do this via a form of crawling peg—that is to say, by devaluing at a rate similar to that of domestic inflation. Inasmuch as wages (the principal component of value-added in costs) deteriorated sharply, the competitive position of the country improved notably, cheapening (relatively speaking) both exports and domestic substitutes for imports. At the same time, the fiscal deficit was gradually reduced by lowering current expenditures (wages).

In contrast, public investment rose (from 9 percent to almost 13 percent of GNP), in order to maintain output and employment. Prices were generally freed (*sinceramiento*) in the hope of improving the prices of public services and of agricultural foodstuffs (repressed in preceding times) relative to industrial products (heretofore most favored). Taxes on traditional agricultural exports, which had ranged between 10 to 50 percent of their value, were lowered by half. Incentives for nontraditional exports and tariffs on manufactures were also reduced (average nominal tariffs, once 90 percent, were now 50 percent). The purpose of this last policy was to improve the relative price of exportables (mainly agricultural products) in relation to import substitutes (mainly industrial goods).

These policies initially brought about two quite favorable results. First, a large surplus was generated in 1976 in both trade balance and current account. Second the quarterly rate of inflation was reduced from 75 percent at the beginning of the year to 25 percent at the end of the year, and the fiscal deficit was lowered by one third.

Less favorable were the effects of these policies on production, which fell

1 percent in 1976, and especially on real wages, which fell by a third from their 1975 level and by 25 percent from the pre-Perón period of 1970 to 1972. At the same time, the much-desired improvement in the relative prices of agricultural goods was only partially successful, rising only 11 percent in 1976. In short, industrial prices adjusted in accordance with the variation of the exchange rate, which was large, rather than in accordance with wage costs. This implied (1) a growth in profit margins, despite the fact that sales did not rise, and (2) the existence of redundant margins of tariff protection, for the lowering of tariffs did not significantly increase the pressure of imports on domestic prices or on the growth of profit margins.

This downward price rigidity for industrial goods kept the rate of inflation at 7 percent per month from the beginning of 1976 onward, thus affecting the efficient allocation and full employment of resources. Since industrialists were raising profit margins to compensate (and overcompensate) the fall in sales (see Frenkel 1979), the government decided to change its anti-inflationary policy. As of March 1977 and for the following four months, it controlled prices for the products of 700 leading industrial firms. In addition, as of June, bank interest rates were freed to stop the subsidy of debtors via negative interest rates. A more restrictive monetary policy was thus made possible and put into effect.

In 1977, the fiscal deficit was lowered by two-thirds, but real interest rates skyrocketed, and inflation, rather than slowing down, continued to advance at rates of 25 percent per quarter.[5] In the last month of 1977, sales and output began to fall once again, thus aborting the recovery that had been taking place.

Phase II, May 1978 to Early 1981

Unwilling to accept the cost of a severe and prolonged recession, the government in May 1978 instituted a new price-stabilization policy—which it would perfect toward the end of the year—in order to lower the 25-percent-per-quarter inflation rate. It decided to control the exchange rate and prices of public services rather than monetary growth, for it was then believed that the tight monetary policy, by making domestic interest rates (28 percent per year real in 1977) attractive to foreign capital, was actually inducing its entry and rendering the control of the money supply impossible. In short, the monetary approach to the balance of payments now came into its own, much as it had in Chile and was about to in Uruguay.

The idea was to adjust the rates of public services and of the exchange rate not in accordance with past inflation, which would tend to reproduce indefinitely the trends of the past, but rather to adjust them in accordance with the

---

5. The hypothesis that increases in real interest rates initially pressure prices upward (via the increased weight of financial costs) rather than downward (via the forced sales of inventories and increased sales, at least while they do not face foreign competition), was first formulated by Cavallo 1977.

expected or programmed or desired rate of inflation. There was no theoretical reason why slowing inflation would require a recession and unemployment; it sufficed that economic agents recognize that the prices of nontradables need eventually evolve in accordance with the prices of tradables. Because of this, a policy of devaluing at ever-decreasing rates would mean not that the relative prices of nontradables would grow but rather that inflation would be much lower. Hence there would be no recession or increase in unemployment (subject, of course, to agents acting in accordance with rational expectations).[6]

This change of approach in the stabilization policy had an additional advantage—namely, it was consistent with the policy of commercial and financial liberalization, which was part of the development strategy. It was expected that opening up trade would increase the pressure on domestic prices, especially on downwardly rigid industrial ones, and would increase the efficient allocation of resources, at least in the long run. For this reason, at the end of 1978 a program of additional tariff reductions was announced. It envisaged the gradual reduction of tariffs from an average of 50 percent to 35 percent in 1981 and 20 percent by 1984.

In complementary fashion, financial liberalization was further pursued. Capital entry was facilitated by eliminating the need for previous deposits and by shortening from two years to one year the minimum period such capital had to remain in the country. This restriction was expected to be eliminated fully in 1980. It was hoped this would assure a more fluid flow of capital between the domestic and international markets, so that the domestic interest rate would approximate the international one plus the announced rate of devaluation. (To be sure, this assumed that economic agents believed in the announced devaluation.) Thus, while the active and restrictive monetary policy of phase I implied a control on capital accounts so as to limit monetary growth, the new policy required a further integration between the domestic and international capital markets, both for short-run stabilization and for growth and long-run liberalization.

The inflow of foreign capital was in fact quite strong. Private foreign debt more than doubled in one single year, 1979, while the total foreign debt of Argentina tripled in the period 1978–81. Nominal interest rates (to borrowers)

---

6. According to the rational-expectations approach, economic agents adjust their prices in accordance to expected inflation, for it is only in this way that they can keep prices in equilibrium. This view has several difficulties; among others, it assumes that, because in the long run the price of nontradables tends to maintain itself relative to that of tradables, economic agents instantly and always move to that long-run price. But a producer of nontradables could well choose a slow adjustment toward equilibrium, giving the producer a monopolistic, though transitory, gain. It would also be rational for a group of producers of nontradables to adjust prices in accordance with each other's prices rather than moving prices rapidly to their long-run equilibrium values, thus maintaining the monopolistic gain for themselves as a group—a form of spontaneous collusion. The expectation of such behavior would suffice to make the decline in inflation of nontradables much less than that of tradables.

well above domestic inflation and a devaluation rate well below that of inflation implied that there was a very strong incentive for foreign investors to bring dollars into the country, and in fact the effective interest rate paid in dollars was well above LIBOR (the London Interbank Offer Rate). For similar reasons, it was very advantageous for Argentinians to borrow in foreign currency, for so long as the domestic inflation was superior to the rate of devaluation, such interest rates in real terms (and in domestic currency) would be either very low or negative. Therefore, so long as there was confidence in the preannounced and programmed exchange policy and so long as it was believed that inflation would be substantially above the rate of devaluation, the inflow of foreign capital would be quite strong.

The persistence of domestic inflation well above the rhythm of devaluation plus international inflation during this second phase resulted in a sharp fall in the real effective exchange rate (a lag in the exchange rate). Hence the current account shifted from a surplus in 1978 equivalent to 25 percent of the value of exports to deficits of over 40 percent in 1980 and 1981. These deficits implied a heavy volume of imports at the expense of domestic industry, leading to a 4 percent fall in industrial output in 1980 and an even greater one in 1981. At the same time, since it was quite clear that such deficits could not be sustained in the medium run, an important exchange risk began to emerge. Because of this increased risk, domestic interest rates rose to 4 percent real per month by the beginning of 1981. Increased financial costs and the loss of external and domestic markets to foreign competition affected the solvency of innumerable firms, eventually jeopardizing the financial system itself.

This phase concluded with a belated deceleration in the rate of inflation (to 100 percent in 1980) for the first time since the beginning of the neoconservative experience. Nevertheless, the lag in the exchange rate and the high interest rates were slowing the level of activity. Output, which thanks to the massive entry of foreign capital had grown significantly in 1979, grew by only 1.1 percent in 1980 and was clearly falling in absolute terms at the end of phase II (early 1981). Argentinian competitiveness (expressed as the relation between wage costs and the exchange rate) fell to one third of what it had been between May 1978 and early 1981. In other words, the cost in pesos of Argentinian output tripled relative to imports in the three years of this phase. And, all along, the financial crisis was absorbing ever more resources.

Phase III, Early 1981 through 1983

From the beginning of 1981, the economy was facing quite serious disequilibria. Domestic prices were well above international prices thanks to the lag in the exchange rate. The domestic interest rate was 4 percent real per month. Such a rate was "payable" only if firms, kept increasing their debt and postponing the payment of amortization and interest.[7] Their demand for credit was thus a way of postponing the capital losses (or even bankruptcy) they would have had to endure were they to try to amortize their loans. Hence the domestic debt jeopardized the solvency of the entire financial system. Moreover, the level of foreign indebtedness had doubled in a mere two years, so that the relation of foreign debt to exports (a measure of the country's capacity to pay) had grown by almost two-thirds in this period. Notwithstanding strong capital inflows in 1981, which increased Argentina's debt by another 30 percent, the government's exchange policy lost so much domestic credibility that capital flight proved massive, resulting in a net outflow of financial resources.

In view of such circumstances—massive losses in reserves, the persistent and growing belief that the exchange policy could no longer be maintained, and grave and worsening disequilibria—the government was finally forced to devalue. Unfortunately, not only did it devalue too late but it devalued by too little, first, by 10 percent, then by 30 percent, and so on. Moreover, multiple exchange rates were created for specific commercial and financial transactions. So great was the uncertainty stemming from these changes in the rules of the game that the pressure on the exchange rate continued rather than diminished, notwithstanding the heavy devaluations. The dollar was seen as the only secure investment; indeed, more than eight billion dollars in short-run capital left the country in 1981. With this fall in the net inflow of capital, the government was forced to let the exchange rate float. By the end of 1981, the exchange rate reached five times the value it had at the beginning of the year. However, since inflation had been much less, the real effective exchange rate recovered substantially what it had lost in the preceding phase.

The real devaluation and the fall in economic activity reduced the deficit in current account. Nevertheless, the financial problems, internal and external, dragged on during 1981, worsening the decline in output. In 1982, to deal with the problem of internal debt, the government fixed interest rates on past debt (negative in real terms), so that by the end of 1982 the level of domestic debt in real terms had been reduced by a third, at the expense of both the government and bank depositors (see FIDE 1982). At the same time, negotiations began with the international banking system regarding servicing the foreign debt.

By 1983, the level of economic activity stabilized and picked up slightly. Nevertheless, by the end of the eight years of the neoconservative experience in Argentina, per capita income had fallen 10 percent; inflation (at almost 350 percent) was little changed; and the level of foreign debt had grown five times—by the end of 1983, the relation of debt to exports more than doubled that of 1975. So came to a close the neoconservative experience in Argentina.

---

7. See Petrei and Tybout's 1985 illuminating paper on firms' microeconomic adjustments to the crisis in this period.

5

A Comparison of the Neoconservative Experiences

Earlier chapters examine the extraordinary similarity in the initial conditions, diagnoses, strategies, and economic policies of the three neoconservative experiences in the Southern Cone. All three grew out of conflictive and polarized sociopolitical situations and from economic circumstances characterized by high and growing inflation and by severe disequilibria in external accounts. When these situations reached crisis proportions, they served to justify the military coups that ensued.

Even more important to the neoconservatives were the long-run trends. They argued that the crises were simply the final but inevitable result of the development strategy followed since the Great Depression. More specifically, they attributed the slow growth and high inflation of the thirty years after the Second World War to extreme state intervention. Policies that might have been justified to combat demand-deficient cyclical recessions were doomed to failure when enacted as long-run development strategies. Neoconservatism condemned especially the inordinate emphasis placed on import-substituting industrialization based on tariff protection, since such tariffs do not take into account opportunity costs and thus encourage inefficiency. Although many of these criticisms were shared by other schools of thought, at that particular time, the most outspoken and persistent critics were the neoconservatives.

Southern Cone neoconservatism thus proposed not only stabilization policies to restore basic macroeconomic equilibrium but a development strategy based on the following: (1) an outward-oriented growth policy; (2) the maximum use of market mechanisms to allocate resources, rather than administrative controls; and (3) replacement of the state by the private sector as the principal dynamic agent for growth, the state retiring to a subsidiary role (see Boeninger 1983). Such a strategy encompassed not only a price-stabilization program but an opening of trade and finances to the outside world as well; at the same time, it aimed to reduce the size and role of the government. The principal policy instruments consisted of freeing prices, setting a realistic exchange rate (though not a free one), reducing the fiscal deficit, lowering tariffs, freeing interest rates, and relaxing the restrictions on the entry and exit of capital.

While there were important differences among the three countries in the sequence and speed with which these policies were put into effect, the package of measures was quite similar. Moreover, inasmuch as the goals were not simply short run, the three experiences not only happened to have been carried out under strongly authoritarian regimes but would have been unimaginable without such regimes, given the radical nature of the changes desired and the time expected for these to bear fruit.

This chapter compares the results of the three experiences with respect to growth, price stabilization, external equilibrium, and the redistribution of income and wealth, examining the explanatory factors for similarities and differences. Subsequent chapters analyze in detail the policy instruments used.

ECONOMIC GROWTH

In studying the impact of neoconservative policy on economic growth in these countries, one must take into account several mitigating factors: (1) the magnitude of initial disequilibria; (2) the unfavorable international situation in which these experiences took place (coinciding with two international recessions and huge increases in the price of petroleum and its derivatives, neither of which was fully compensated by the increased liquidity of international capital markets); and (3) the relatively brief period being analyzed. Thus this section on economic growth examines the economic evolution of these countries' neoconservative experiences both overall and by phase, distinguishing between short-run tendencies and those that have made long-run modifications in the structure and productive capacity of these economies.

The Overall Period

Growth during the neoconservative experience was quite different for the three countries (table 5.1). Only Uruguay experienced any growth at all. Its per capita output was some 10 percent higher at the end than at the beginning of the period; Chile's was marginally lower; Argentina's was 10 percent lower. This evolution is in marked contrast to historic trends, for it was Argentina, the country that had heretofore experienced the greatest dynamism of the three, whose output fell the most. Inversely, only Uruguay showed signs of reversing its secular stagnation; whereas Latin American growth fell during this period to less than a third of what it had been in the postwar period, Uruguay doubled its previous rate and actually equaled the regional average (though to be sure, at a not very spectacular rate of 1 percent growth in per capita output).

It is not surprising that the share of agriculture and mining in GNP generally increased in the neoconservative period, for these are activities in which these countries might be expected to have comparative advantage. Nevertheless, and surprisingly, the share of nontradables in GNP rose, for the growth of these was far superior to that of tradables (table 5.2). This latter result is largely due to the behavior of manufactures, whose share both in GNP as well as in tradables fell substantially (especially in Argentina and Chile, where manufacturing production fell in absolute terms at −2 and −1 percent per year over the entire period—with important variations depending on the phase).

The expansion of productive capacity, without which sustained growth is impossible, also showed important variations from country to country (table 5.3). Though Uruguay, with 15.8 percent of GNP as investment, had the lowest coefficient of the three countries, it registered the greatest increase.[1] By contrast, the coefficients of Argentina and Chile are quite similar to those of the preceding ten years (slightly above in Argentina, somewhat below in Chile). This suggests that Uruguay's growth was in fact based on an acceleration in the expansion of productive capacity. The deterioration in Argentinian and Chilean

Table 5.1. Southern Cone and Rest of Latin America: Annual Growth of Per Capita Gross National Product, Historic and Neoconservative Periods (*percentage*)

Period	Chile	Uruguay	Argentina	Rest of Latin America
Historic	1950–73: 1.5	1950–74: 0.6	1950–75: 1.7	1950–74: 3.4
Neoconservative[a]	1974–83: −0.4	1975–83: 1.0	1976–83: −1.3	1975–83: 1.0
Phase I[a]	1974–76: −4.6	1975–78: 3.6	1976–78: −0.9	1975–78: 2.9
Phase II[a]	1977–81: 6.2	1979–80: 5.3	1979–80: 2.4	1979–80: 3.8
Phase III[a]	1982–83: −9.0	1981–83: −4.8	1981–83: −4.3	1981–83: −2.7

Source: CEPAL, on the basis of official data.

Note: Year 1983, preliminary figures.

[a]There are differences between the text and the table in the years included in each period and phase. The text refers to the exact amount when each period and phase can be considered to have begun or ended. The table lists the yearly averages that were, in fact, included in the calculation of the average of each period and phase, which do not necessarily coincide with the exact interval, because the data are available only for annual periods. However, much of the difference is only apparent, for the table lists the rate of growth for each period and phase, including both the beginning and end years. Thus, for example, the data for the average growth rate for 1974–76 is the average of the *three* years 1973–74, 1974–75, and 1975–76, and not of the two-year span from January 1974 to January 1976.

---

1. Because of methodological differences in the manner in which investment, especially the construction component of investment, was calculated, not too much importance should be attached to differences among countries. These coefficients are useful mainly for historic comparisons within a country.

Table 5.2. Southern Cone: Annual Growth of Gross National Product by Sector, Historic and Neoconservative Periods (percentages)

Sector and Product	Chile Historic Period 1950–73	Chile Neoconservative Period 1974–83[a]	Uruguay Historic Period 1950–74	Uruguay Neoconservative Period 1975–83[a]	Argentina Historic Period 1950–75	Argentina Neoconservative Period 1976–83[a]
Gross National Product	3.6	1.5	1.6	1.7	3.3	0.1
Tradables	3.3	1.1	1.9	0.2	3.9	−0.2
Agriculture	1.0	4.6[b]	0.7	1.5	2.3	1.8
Mining	2.3	4.7			8.2	3.0
Manufacture	4.6	−1.4	2.6[b]	−0.9[c]	4.6	−1.6
Nontradables	3.9	2.1	1.5	2.6	3.0	0.4
Construction	2.0	1.0	0.2	4.5	3.1	−0.7
Basic services	5.2	2.7	1.2	2.1	3.5	1.7
Commerce and finance	4.4	3.2	0.9	0.2	3.0	−1.0
Government services	4.0	0.1			1.9	0.5
Other services	3.1	0.1	4.8	2.2	3.8	1.8

Source: CEPAL, on the basis of official data.

Note: Year 1983, preliminary figures.

[a]There are differences between the text and the table in the years included in the neoconservative periods. The text refers to the exact moment when each period can be considered to have begun or ended. The table lists the yearly averages that were, in fact, included in the calculation of the average of each period, which do not necessarily coincide with the exact interval, because the data are available only for annual periods. However, much of the difference is only apparent, for the table lists the rate of growth for each period, including both the beginning and end years. Thus, for example, the data for the average growth rate for 1976–83 is the average of the *eight* yearly variations between 1976 and 1983, beginning with 1975–76 and ending with 1982–83, and not of the seven-year span from January 1976 to January 1983.

[b]Half of the growth in this period is accounted for by the recovery in 1974 of agricultural output lost between 1970 and 1973. If one excludes the recovery component of 1974 growth, the average growth rate over the period is 2.3 percent per year.

[c]Includes mining.

per capita output, on the other hand, was due to cyclical crises or errors in economic policy more than to declines in the rhythm of investment.

As important as the behavior of investment was that of national savings, for in the last analysis it is the capacity to mobilize one's own resources that determines how solidly based one's growth is (table 5.4). Once again, it was Uruguay that showed an improved rate of domestic savings, raising the share of savings in GNP by 3 percentage points. On the contrary, Chilean national savings fell substantially, from 17 percent of GNP in the preceding ten years to 12 percent in the neoconservative period.[2] While it is understandable that savings declined during the recession of 1975, in no other year thereafter, not even in 1980 in the midst of the boom, did national savings in Chile exceed the average levels of the ten years preceding the neoconservative period—despite unusually high interest rates and an even more regressive distribution of income. Thus, in the neoconservative period, investment in Chile was based on an ever-increasing share of foreign savings and a diminishing share of national savings. This situation obviously could not persist indefinitely.

Argentina continued to save a high proportion of GNP (19 percent), slightly below its rate of savings in the previous ten years. Nevertheless, not

Table 5.3.   Southern Cone: Share of Investment in Gross National Product, Preneoconservative and Neoconservative Periods (*percentage*)

Period	Chile	Uruguay	Argentina
Preneoconservative	1964–73: 19.7	1965–74: 10.2	1966–75: 20.0
Neoconservative[a]	1974–83: 17.3	1975–83: 15.8	1976–83: 20.6
Phase I[a]	1974–76: 17.8	1975–78: 14.5	1976–78: 22.2
Phase II[a]	1977–81: 19.7	1979–80: 20.6	1979–80: 22.9
Phase III[a]	1982–83: 10.4	1981–83: 14.5	1981–83: 17.4

Source: CEPAL, on the basis of official data.

Note: Year 1983, preliminary figures.

[a]There are differences between the text and the table in the years included in each period and phase. The text refers to the exact moment when each period and phase can be considered to have begun or ended. The table lists the yearly averages that were, in fact, included in the calculation of the average of each period and phase, which do not necessarily coincide with the exact interval, because the data are available only for annual periods. However, much of the difference is only apparent, for the table lists the average for each period and phase, including both the beginning and end years. Thus, for example, the data for 1974–76 is the average of the *three* years 1974, 1975, and 1976, and not of the two-year span from January 1974 to January 1976.

---

2. This calculation underestimates the domestic savings effort, for, because of higher interest rates, interest payments to the rest of the world grew sharply. Moreover, there were important losses in the terms of trade in this period. In any case, this does not alter the conclusion that domestic savings were insufficient to sustain significant and stable growth.

only did Argentina not grow, but indeed it did so negatively, per capita output declining at the rate of 1.3 percent per year (table 5.1). This suggests that the productivity of this investment was negatively affected both by cyclical factors and by its poor allocation.

The Period by Phase

Previous chapters distinguished three fairly similar phases in each of the three neoconservative experiences. The first phase, based on a monetarist view of a closed economy, emphasized price stability through monetary and wage controls and used the exchange rate to achieve external equilibrium. In the second phase, based on the monetary approach to the balance of payments, monetary growth became a passive variable; the exchange rate was used to stabilize prices, and it was believed that external equilibrium would be automatically achieved through the impact on the capital account and the trade balance of interest-rate variations. In the third phase, the accumulation of disequilibria from the preceding phases (due to overindebtedness, the lagged exchange rate, and high interest rates) led to a financial crisis and acute recession, and major devaluations were required to bring about the needed adjustments in external accounts.

Given the size of the initial disequilibrium, it could be expected that during the first phase the countries of the Southern Cone would not grow very strongly, which is not to say that it was inevitable that they suffer a recession, for there is

Table 5.4. Southern Cone: Share of National Savings in Gross National Product, Preneoconservative and Neoconservative Periods (*percentage*)

Period	Chile	Uruguay	Argentina
Preneoconservative	1964–73: 17.0	1965–74: 10.4	1966–75: 19.9
Neoconservative[a]	1974–83: 12.2	1975–83: 13.2	1976–83: 18.9
Phase I[a]	1974–76: 16.4	1975–78: 12.4	1976–78: 23.7
Phase II[a]	1977–81: 12.0	1979–80: 16.0	1979–80: 20.5
Phase III[a]	1982–83: 3.8	1981–83: 13.1	1981–83: 15.0

Source: CEPAL, on the basis of official data.

Note: Year 1983, preliminary figures.

[a]There are differences between the text and the table in the years included in each period and phase. The text refers to the exact moment when each period and phase can be considered to have begun or ended. The table lists the yearly averages that were, in fact, included in the calculation of the average of each period and phase, which do not necessarily coincide with the exact interval, because the data are available only for annual periods. However, much of the difference is only apparent, for the table lists the average for each period and phase, including both the beginning and end years. Thus, for example, the data for 1974–76 is the average of the *three* years 1974, 1975, and 1976, and not of the two-year span from January 1974 to January 1976.

no theoretical reason why a slowing down of inflation necessarily requires a recession. Nevertheless, it is true that most stabilization programs bring on recessions for reasons we examine in detail in chapter 6. Indeed, only Uruguay, the country with the lowest initial inflation and that thus ranked price stabilization behind external equilibrium, showed positive growth in this phase.

Nor is it surprising that the fastest rates of growth of output in all three countries should have been exhibited during phase II. For one thing, the underutilized capacity brought on by the recession or stagnation of phase I in Argentina and Chile permitted an accelerated recovery without the need of important increments in investment. For another, the massive inflows of capital during phase II raised domestic demand enough to more than compensate the loss in competitiveness brought about by the lag in the exchange rate caused by the inflows.

The collapse of output during phase III was more difficult to anticipate. In the three years 1981 through 1983, per capita output fell over 13 percent in each of the three countries. To be sure, this result was due in part to the deterioration in their terms of trade and the high rates of interest in international markets.[3] Nevertheless, this does not explain why their performance was so much worse than that of other nonpetroleum-exporting countries of Latin America, whose output per capita fell much less.

Two immediate domestic factors common to the three experiences seem to explain the collapse in the last phase. First, the depression in the last phase was accompanied, and to some extent preceded, by a series of widespread domestic financial crises, which forced the governments to intervene in the banking system and supply it massively with resources. The mechanism typically chosen was the purchase by the central bank of nonperforming loans and risky loans, which exceeded the capital and reserves of many, if not most, private banks. The deterioration in the quality of these loans was the result of the high interest rates (2 to 3 percent real per month) charged to firms during most of the neoconservative experience. Firms probably could not long service such loans at these interest rates even in a growing economy (6 to 8 percent per year), never mind in a declining one.

Once the decline began, the financial bubble burst. Although the banks knew the firms would be unable to pay, they were forced to renew credit simply to avoid having these loans appear as nonperforming assets. Governments were finally forced to absorb a good part of these losses, intervening in banks and buying nonperforming assets or renewing loans at interest rates well below the market. Nevertheless, while the uncertainty remained as to who would absorb the losses—and as long as banks were renegotiating loans—firms tended to

---

3. The Argentinian situation was further aggravated by a noneconomic factor—the conflict in the southern Atlantic.

keep their operations to a minimum and to use their cash flows not for investments or deposits in the financial system or repayment of debts but for the purchase of foreign exchange. Capital flight thus added to the pressure on the exchange rate in phase III and explains the huge reduction in reserves, the sharp increases in the exchange rates, and the collapse of aggregate demand.

The second factor in the collapse in phase III was the use of the exchange rate during phase II to stabilize prices rather than to achieve external equilibrium. For reasons to be examined in detail in the next chapter, the domestic inflation rate failed to fall rapidly in accordance with the international inflation rate plus the rate of devaluation. Domestic prices thus diverged increasingly from international prices, leading to a lag in the exchange rate and implying a loss of competitiveness for all tradables. Imports became cheaper and exports more costly, generating balance-of-trade deficits. To be sure, such an exchange policy was made possible only by the heavy capital inflows available in this phase. However, rather than perceiving the intrinsically transitory character of these inflows, policymakers persisted in their exchange policy as if these inflows would continue indefinitely.[4] When these inflows slowed in 1981, aggregate demand collapsed.

Hopes that the lag in the exchange rate would be automatically corrected by a rapid slowing of inflation rather than by a fall in output led to a postponement of a devaluation. While it is true that the growth of domestic prices slowed somewhat toward the end of phase II, the real depreciation achieved by deflation was minimal (1 to 2 percent) compared to the lag in the exchange rate (30 to 50 percent). Thus the contraction in aggregate demand fell mostly on output and not on prices.

The cost of putting off the devaluation for so long was a severe recession. By the time maxidevaluations were finally decreed (by Argentina in 1981, by Chile and Uruguay in 1982), the inflows of foreign capital had so slowed that the devaluations were necessarily large in order to correct the trade disequilibrium and to discourage the flight of capital in the brief time available. The loss of competitiveness (brought about by the lag in the exchange rate, which especially affected tradables) and the severe recession hit especially the industrial sector, which explains why, despite the outward-oriented policy, the share of tradables in GNP diminished so sharply and why manufacturing, specifically, was the activity most negatively affected.

---

4. Suddenly increased capital inflows thus acted as a windfall price rise for traditional exports. Such a price rise, if not neutralized, would discourage nontraditional exports and increase imports. To be sure, this ailment differed in critical ways from the Dutch disease, of which it was a Creole variant. For one thing, the Latin American inflows were clearly of a once-and-for-all nature, a stock adjustment to greater world liquidity and savings. More decisively, these inflows were not the product of windfall profits but were in fact debt. They had to be paid. And the day of reckoning, unfortunately, proved to be not far off.

PRICE STABILIZATION

Despite the similarity in antiinflationary policies among the three countries,[5] important differences in results emerged (table 5.5). Undoubtedly, Chile met with the most success in this regard: it lowered inflation from something of the order of 600 percent at the end of 1973 (January through December) to 0 percent during the first semester of 1982. Uruguay brought inflation down to 11 percent toward the end of 1982, but it began with a much lower rate. Moreover, with the devaluation at the end of 1982, inflation quickly picked up, reaching 50 percent per year in 1983. The least progress was made in Argentina. For one thing, it never lowered inflation below 100 percent and, once the maxidevaluation of 1981 was forced upon it, inflation moved to 340 percent in 1983, close to what it had been at the beginning of its neoconservative experience.

The greatest success in reducing the fiscal deficit was also achieved by Chile (table 5.6): it had a deficit of 25 percent of GNP in 1973, whereas in 1979, 1980, and 1981 it had a surplus; and even in 1983 its deficit was a relatively low 4 percent. Uruguay also virtually achieved a fiscal surplus in 1979–80, but the implicit effort involved was much less, since its initial deficit was only 4 percent of GNP. To be sure, the relation between inflation and fiscal deficits is not one to one, for many additional factors influence this, such as the proportion of income maintained in money balances and the monetary expansion implicit in a deficit. Indeed, similar fiscal deficits (between 2 and 3 percent of GNP) have coincided with quite different inflation rates: close to 380 percent in Chile (1975), 160 percent in Argentina (1979), and 76 percent in Uruguay (1972). The same phenomenon can be observed within a country: in 1982, Uruguay had its highest deficit of the decade (9 percent of GNP), and yet it had one of the lowest inflations of recent years (19 percent). In any case, it is important to note that the only country that failed to achieve a balanced budget, Argentina, failed to bring inflation down below three digits. In other words, however flexible in the short run the relation between these two variables may be, one cannot reach low inflation (international rates) and maintain it without reducing the fiscal deficit to relatively modest proportions of GNP.

Somewhat surprisingly, notwithstanding the importance to neoconservatives of reductions in the fiscal deficit, except in Chile, public expenditures in GNP for the period did not go down. This may be attributed to the greater pragmatism of Argentinian and Uruguayan policymakers, or to their lesser control over policy, or to the fact that the initial ratio of public-sector expenditures to GNP was far greater in Chile. In any case, in Argentina the weight of public expenditures declined only in relation to the two years preceding the neoconservative experience, and then only up to the final crisis, when it shot up. In Uruguay, except for a modest decline in phase II, there was no significant change at all.

---

5. See chapter 6 for a detailed analysis of stabilization policy.

Table 5.5. Southern Cone: Inflation Indicators during Neoconservative Phases (*percentage*)

Neoconservative Phase[a]	Chile				Uruguay				Argentina			
	Dates	Public-Sector Surplus/ GNP	Growth Rates		Dates	Public-Sector Surplus/ GNP	Growth Rates		Dates	Public-Sector Surplus/ GNP	Growth Rates	
			Consumer Prices	Money[b]			Consumer Prices	Money[b]			Consumer Prices	Money[b]
I												
Beginning	1973	−24.7	441.9	259.1	1974	−3.8	77.2	80.0	1976	−7.2	443.2	399.4
End	1976	−2.3	232.8	216.0	1978	−0.9	44.5	53.0	1978	−3.2	175.5	142.8
II												
Beginning	1976	−2.3	232.8	216.0	1978	−0.9	44.5	53.0	1978	−3.2	175.5	142.8
End	1981	3.1	19.7	62.6	1980	−0.3	63.5	34.9	1980	−3.6	100.8	115.8
III												
Beginning	1981	3.1	19.7	62.6	1980	−0.3	63.5	34.9	1980	−3.6	100.8	115.8
End	1983	−3.8	27.3	26.6	1983	−3.9	51.5	11.1	1983	−11.0	343.8	361.7

Source: CEPAL, on the basis of official data; money growth rate, International Monetary Fund, *International Financial Statistics.*

Note: Year 1983, preliminary figures.

[a]There are differences between the text and the table in the years included in each phase. The text refers to the exact moment when each phase can be considered to have begun or ended. The table lists the years that were, in fact, included, which do not necessarily coincide with the exact phase interval, because the data are available only for annual periods. However, much of the difference is only apparent, for the table lists the rate of growth for each phase, including the beginning and end years.

[b]Money growth rate is *M1* (bills and coins in circulation plus demand deposits).

Stabilization policies were based on the two monetary approaches already described: (1) in phase I, controlling the money supply by reducing the fiscal deficit, and (2) in phase II, controlling the exchange rate by either a programmed and preannounced devaluation or a fixed exchange rate.

In phase I, important advances were achieved with respect to stabilization. Inflation was reduced by half or more in Chile and Argentina, and by almost half in Uruguay. These achievements were not merely transitory, for they were accompanied by significant reductions in fiscal deficits—from 25 percent of GNP to a little over 2 percent in Chile; from 4 to 1 percent in Uruguay; and from 7 to 3 percent in Argentina.

And during phase II and up until the maxidevaluations, Chile reduced inflation remarkably, from 230 percent to 0 percent per year; Uruguay brought it

Table 5.6. Southern Cone: Share of Public-Sector Expenditures and Surplus in Gross National Product, 1971–1983 (*percentage*)

	Chile		Uruguay		Argentina	
Year	Expenditures	Surplus	Expenditures	Surplus	Expenditures	Surplus
1971	31.1	−10.7	20.1	−5.8	16.9	−3.1
1972	31.2	−13.0	24.6	−2.5	16.2	−3.3
1973	44.9	−24.7	22.6	−1.2	16.4	−4.2
			(25.4)	(−1.2)		
1974	32.4	−10.5	23.8	−3.8	19.4	−5.3
	(33.1)	(−10.5)	(25.9)	(−3.7)		
1975	27.4	−2.6	23.5	−4.3	19.4	−10.3
	(28.2)	(−2.6)	(24.5)	(−4.0)		
1976	25.8	−2.3	24.2	−2.0	17.7	−7.2
	(26.9)	(−2.3)	(25.6)	(−1.8)		
1977	24.9	−1.8	23.5	−1.3	15.7	−2.8
	(25.7)	(−1.8)	(26.2)	(−1.1)		
1978	23.8	−0.8	22.9	−0.9	17.9	−3.2
	(24.6)	(−0.8)			(30.2)	(−5.2)
1979	22.8	1.7	20.2	0.0	19.1	−2.7
	(23.5)	(1.7)			(30.4)	(−4.5)
1980	23.1	3.1	21.8	−0.3	22.4	−3.6
	(26.7)	(0.6)			(32.8)	(−5.7)
1981	24.9	1.7	24.9	−1.5	20.3	−8.1
1982	28.5	−2.3	29.6	−9.1	22.5	−7.0
1983	28.4	−3.8	24.9	−3.9		−11.0

Source: International Monetary Fund, *International Financial Statistics;* and Banco Central de Chile, 1983.

Note: Coefficients in parenthesis include provincial and municipal public expenditures. Year 1983, preliminary figures.

down by more than half. When maxidevaluations were made necessary in Uruguay and Chile during phase III, inflation was below or similar to the international rate. Argentina also lowered its inflation by close to one half in phase II—and kept it low as long as it was able to maintain the lag in the exchange rate. But once it was forced to devalue, inflation more than doubled.

THE BALANCE OF PAYMENTS AND FOREIGN DEBT

At the beginning of their neoconservative experiences, the three countries faced two problems in their external accounts: (1) unsustainable deficits in current account (20 to 35 percent of the value of exports at the onset of the neoconservative period), and (2) a low proportion of GNP dedicated to exports, which together with a slow growth in exports restricted foreign exchange, and limited economic growth (table 5.7).

It is without a doubt in this area that the neoconservative experiences had their greatest success (at least up to phase III).[6] Thanks to the real devaluation effected at the beginning of these experiences (or just before) and the maintenance of a high and realistic exchange rate for the balance of phase I, it was possible to make an appreciable dent in the deficits in trade and current account. In part, this reflected a cyclical recovery in traditional exports. But there was also a substantial net expansion, so that the overall volume of exports grew quite rapidly, reaching average growth rates of 15 percent in Chile and Uruguay and 26 percent in Argentina during this first phase (the growth was even greater for nontraditional exports).

However, in phase II, because of the lag in the exchange rate, the rate of growth of the volume of exports slowed sharply: it actually fell 7 percent per year in Argentina and decelerated to 9 percent per year in Chile and to 4 percent per year in Uruguay.

In any case, throughout the neoconservative period, the volume of exports grew in each of the three countries at least three times faster than historic rates and, of course, much faster than GNP. Hence exports became one of the most dynamic activities in the economy, and their weight in GNP grew substantially: from 13 to 33 percent in Chile, from 9 to 15 percent in Uruguay, and from 6 to 10 percent in Argentina.[7]

To be sure, this growth in exports was not without its problems. The weight of tradables in GNP fell in each of the three countries, for the output of tradables *for the domestic market* not only did not grow but in fact fell: almost 70 percent in Chile, 40 percent in Uruguay, and 20 percent in Argentina (see

---

6. See chapter 7 for a detailed analysis of the opening up of trade.

7. These coefficients refer to the weight of exports in GNP at 1970 prices. Inasmuch as the prices of exports tended to fall in real terms in respect to 1970, the weight of exports in GNP would have been less if they were calculated at current prices.

Table 5.7.   Southern Cone: Indicators of External Accounts, Historic and
Neoconservative Periods

Country and Period[a]	Annual Growth Rate		Exports as Ratio of GNP	Foreign Debt as Ratio of Exports	Current-Account Surplus as Ratio of Exports
	Volume of Exports	Value of Exports			
Chile					
1950–70	3.0	7.7	15.8		
1971–73	1.8	5.4	13.4	2.7	−28.5
Neoconservative period	10.6	15.2	26.3	2.5	−31.8
Phase I, 1974–76	15.3	23.1	20.5	2.1	−11.5
Phase II, 1977–81	8.9	19.9	26.0	2.2	−42.8
Phase III, 1982–83	6.2	−4.1	32.5	3.8	−37.6
Uruguay					
1950–70	0.0	−0.4	9.4		
1971–74	−0.3	14.6	8.6	2.1	−9.5
Neoconservative period	8.4	12.9	13.1	1.9	−23.0
Phase I, 1975–78	14.6	16.4	11.8	1.6	−20.9
Phase II, 1979–80	3.5	29.3	12.6	1.4	−38.7
Phase III, 1981–83	3.4	−2.8	15.2	2.6	−15.6
Argentina					
1950–70	2.6	2.1	7.6		
1971–75	−3.2	10.7	5.8	1.9	−8.7
Neoconservative period	11.3	14.4	9.1	2.9	−12.1
Phase I, 1976–78	26.1	29.4	8.7	1.6	18.6
Phase II, 1979–80	−6.6	15.2	8.6	2.4	−27.1
Phase III, 1981–83	8.3	−1.1	10.3	4.3	−32.8

Source: CEPAL, on the basis of official data.

Note: Year 1983, preliminary figures.

[a]There are differences between the text and table in the years included in the neoconservative periods and their phases. The text refers to the exact moment when each period can be considered to have begun or ended. The table lists the yearly averages that were, in fact, included in the calculation of the average of each period or phase, which do not necessarily coincide with the exact interval, because the data are available only for annual periods. However, much of the difference is only apparent, for the table lists, for example, the rate of growth for 1974–76 as the average of the *three* years, 1973–74, 1974–75, and 1975–76, and not of the two-year span from January 1974 to January 1976.

chapter 7, tables 7.10, 7.11, and 7.12). This was due to the enormous contraction in domestic demand in phase III and to the implicit policy of "import promotion" during phase II, in which a very serious lag in the exchange rate was generated (least in Uruguay, most in Argentina) and in which tariffs were lowered (to a large extent in Chile, almost not at all in Uruguay).[8]

The other important cost of the phase II policy of outward-oriented growth was the very large increase in foreign indebtedness (capital inflows), which permitted the exchange rate to lag and imports to grow even more rapidly than exports. As a result, ever-increasing deficits were generated in current account, far greater than those that existed at the beginning of these experiences. To be sure, the increase in foreign indebtedness was not limited to the Southern Cone nor does it constitute by itself a negative sign. Indeed, it was only natural to expect that, as the international capital market was reestablished and widened at the end of the sixties and the beginning of the seventies, capital inflows would be greater.

At the beginning of the seventies, foreign savings in Latin America, for example, were 2 percent of GNP; it might be expected that, thanks to the reestablishment and enlargement of international capital markets (petrodollar and Eurodollar), this percentage could be doubled during the second half of the decade. Since exports from the Southern Cone ranged from 10 to 25 percent of GNP, a sustainable level of foreign savings in the second half of the seventies might finance deficits on current account between 16 and 40 percent of exports (Chile and Argentina, respectively; Uruguay's was 30 percent).[9] But in no case was it possible to finance and *sustain* deficits in current account of 50 percent of exports, as were observed in these three countries in the years 1980–81. In other words, the problem was not indebtedness per se but rather the level it had reached, the rate at which it was growing, and the way it was used.

During the bulk of phase I, the level of foreign debt grew at a reasonable rate: in nominal terms, it grew at a rate of 8 percent per year in Chile during 1974–76; 7 percent per year in Uruguay during 1975–78, and 16 percent per year in Argentina during 1976–78. However, from the onset of phase II and particularly from 1979 through the crisis of 1981, the rhythm of indebtedness tripled and even quadrupled: measured in the same fashion, it grew 28 percent per year in Chile during 1977–81; 31 percent per year in Uruguay during 1979–

---

8. These results coincide with firm-level studies, which show that the rate of return to import substitutes was worse than that of exportables in Chile, whereas the reverse was the case in Argentina and Uruguay, especially during phase II. See Petrei and Tybout 1985; Galvez and Tybout 1985; De Melo, Pascale, and Tybout 1985; and Corbo, De Melo, and Tybout 1985.

9. With sustained inflows of foreign capital at 4 percent of GNP and exports at 25 percent of GNP (as was the case in Chile), financial flows could have financed up to a 16 percent deficit in the trade balance (4 percent/25 percent). This was the maximum, for in the course of time interest payments would also increase, so that the trade balance that could be financed by the inflows of foreign capital would slowly decline.

80; and 47 percent per year in Argentina during 1979–80. From any angle you look at it, this rate of growth of indebtedness was unsustainable in the long run, for by the end of phase II the value of exports was growing at much slower and even decelerating rates, whereas interest payments were accelerating. Thus, once the value of exports and the rate of capital inflows fell in 1981 and 1982, these countries were forced to negotiate severe adjustment programs with the International Monetary Fund in order to meet the payments due on external accounts.

So great was their rate of indebtedness that at the end of 1983 the ratio of foreign debt to exports ranged from a low of 3.2 to 1 in Uruguay to a high of 4.9 to 1 in Argentina, well above the average for the region as a whole, especially for Chile and Argentina. The growth rate of debt in these three countries was actually not so different from the other economies of the region.[10] What was difficult—and what made the problem particularly serious—was that, at the beginning of these experiences, the Southern Cone countries were already among the most indebted of South America, at least in relation to their exports.[11]

THE DISTRIBUTIVE IMPACT

Undoubtedly the most frequent criticism leveled at the neoconservative experiences of the Southern Cone is that the distribution of income and wealth became more regressive (table 5.8). Data are limited, but the information that is available (largely wages and employment) clearly confirms the claims. Discussion, therefore, must focus on the causes of such a result. Did income become more regressively distributed because of the specific stabilization policy pursued or because of the neoconservative development strategy itself?

Wages

Real wages fell an average of 20 to 45 percent from those of the period immediately preceding the neoconservative experiences, and they stayed at that level for the next three or four years (table 5.9).[12] Moreover, the worsening

---

10. During the neoconservative period, Chile's foreign debt grew at an annual rate of 17 percent, Uruguay's at 18 percent, and Argentina's at 24 percent, compared to 20 percent in the rest of Latin America during 1975–83.

11. Moreover, interest rates during the first half of the seventies tended to be fixed and low. During the second half of the seventies, loans were made at either variable or much higher rates. Consequently, servicing the same debt-to-export ratio in 1983 was considerably more costly than in 1975.

12. The 20 percent loss is with respect to the lowest levels of the three preceding years; the 45 percent loss takes as a reference point the highest levels of that period, so that the reduction was severe even if we consider the wage improvements during the years of Perón (Argentina) and Allende (Chile) as artificially high.

took place from the very beginning of the experiences. Concretely, it accompanied the price-stabilization policy of wage controls and price liberalization, implemented during phase I in all three countries.

Wage controls were aimed at preventing the incorporation of rampant inflationary expectations into wage contracts, which would have made stabilization difficult and costly. Thus wage readjustments were made in accordance with the inflationary goal (desired inflation) rather than in accordance with the accumulated variation in the level of prices (past inflation). However, in all three cases inflation turned out to be well above what was projected, which necessarily implied an important loss for wage earners. Wage repression was also justified as an instrument to restore the supposed distributive losses suffered by capital in the years immediately preceding the neoconservative experiences and, in this way, to raise the level of savings. (This argument was explicitly expressed in Uruguay.) Whatever the justification, both arguments tended in the same direction—to lower real wages. The policy mechanisms

Table 5.8. Southern Cone: Income Distribution, 1970–1983

	Chile		Uruguay		Argentina	
Year	Index A[a]	Index B[b]	Index A[a]	Index B[b]	Index A[a]	Index B[b]
1970	100.0	100.0	100.0	100.0	100.0	100.0
1971	116.3	113.0	106.3	106.5	98.3	98.8
1972	108.9	105.7	88.3	89.1	81.1	81.9
1973	84.1[c]	82.2[c]	84.2	87.0	84.1	86.4
1974	64.9	63.6	86.4	86.9	97.9	94.5
1975	71.8	65.0			95.9	95.8
1976	71.1	64.2	75.2	73.1	64.4	64.3
1977	73.7	65.7	70.4	69.0	61.4	60.8
1978	77.5	68.7	62.3	61.5	64.2	63.5
1979	81.8	71.6	57.4	57.2	69.2	69.1
1980	86.1	74.1	58.1	57.7	76.9	77.5
1981	92.6	78.5	65.7	64.7	73.2	73.2
1982	99.1	78.5	70.3	69.2	70.4	69.8
1983	97.1	74.4	56.1	53.2	90.8	84.5

Source: CEPAL, on the basis of official data.

Note: Indexes reflect whether the labor share in gross national income improved (greater than 100) or deteriorated (less than 100) with respect to base year, 1970. Preliminary figures for 1983.

[a]Index A = (*RS*) (*O*)/*Y*, where *RS* is real salary, *O* is number of employed, and *Y* is gross disposable income (gross national product adjusted by the effect of the relation of the terms of trade of goods and services).

[b]Same as A, but using the gross national product instead of gross disposable income.

[c]First eight months of year.

Table 5.9. Southern Cone: Real Salaries, Unemployment Rates, Employment Rates, and Real Effective Exchange Rates, 1970–1983 (*percentage*)

	Chile				Uruguay				Argentina			
	RS	U	O	R	RS	U	O	R	RS	U	O	R
1970	100.0	7.1	100.0	100.0	100.0	7.5	100.0	100.0	100.0	4.9	100.0	100.0
1971	123.0	5.7	103.3	68.2	105.2	7.6	101.3	84.9	103.4	5.8	99.1	94.6
1972	96.0	3.7	105.1	67.1	87.2	7.7	100.8	186.2	98.3	6.5	88.0	126.5
1973	80.0a	4.6	104.5	123.6	85.7	8.9	100.3	129.6	104.4	5.3	90.5	106.5
1974	64.8	9.2	100.7	203.7	85.0	8.1	104.2	127.8	117.9	3.7	98.0	78.0
1975	62.1	16.8	93.6	279.0	77.5		105.0	152.5	111.1	3.1	99.3	130.6
1976	63.0	19.4	94.2	224.8	75.6	12.7	108.6	172.3	74.7	4.6	98.7	140.8
1977	71.1	18.6	94.0	206.6	69.9	11.8	112.1	184.7	73.6	3.0	100.7	166.6
1978	75.7	17.9	99.9	161.1	66.9	10.1	109.9	191.6	72.3	2.9	103.5	136.7
1979	82.0	17.7	104.0	154.2	64.8	8.3	112.1	191.6	83.0	2.1	105.0	85.8
1980	89.4	17.4	106.4	124.2	65.1	7.4	119.0	152.0	92.8	2.2	106.5	60.0
1981	97.5	15.6	109.2	94.5	69.9	6.6	122.8	131.0	83.0	4.5	105.8	86.6
1982	97.1	28.2	94.0	106.2	69.7	11.9	118.4	144.4	74.1	4.8	106.7	169.1
1983	86.8	24.5	98.8	143.6	55.3	15.5	113.6	261.5	90.8	4.0	107.6	131.1

Source: CEPAL, on the basis of official data.

Note: RS = real salary index; 1970 = 100. U = unemployment rate, including for Chile persons in the emergency make-work programs (PEM and POJH), who accounted for about one third of the unemployed from 1976 on. O = employment rate (excludes emergency employment programs); 1970 = 100. R = real effective exchange rate index (deflated by salary index); 1970 = 100. Preliminary figures for 1983.

aJanuary–August.

were wage controls, price liberalization, and restricted monetary growth. The repression of the union movement and the mid-seventies recession (except in Uruguay) impeded the speedy recovery of wages, which remained well below historic levels during all of the neoconservative period.

During phase I, tariff reduction was of only secondary importance, affecting mainly redundant protection (in Argentina and Uruguay), and was compensated by the real devaluation in the exchange rate. Thus it does not explain the reduction in wages in phase I, which reinforces our interpretation that the reduction in wages was due to the wage-stabilization policy.

During the second phase, wage readjustments in Chile followed past inflation rather than expected inflation. Given the deceleration in inflation, real wages showed notable improvement, virtually recovering their preneoconservative level by 1981 (table 5.9).[13] In the other two countries, inflation during phase II fell at a slower rate and wage policy was less clearly administered. There was an important recovery of wages in Argentina in 1978–80, but it did not prove sustainable; in Uruguay there was no recovery at all.

Employment

Employment evolved quite differently in the three experiences. In Chile, the employment situation grew systematically worse throughout phase I, unemployment rates tripling their historic average (6 percent). Indeed, even during the boom years of phase II, the unemployment rate remained above its historic maximum (10 percent), tripling the historic average.[14] Unemployment in Ar-

---

13. The unwary observer is apt to believe that automatic cost-of-living escalators, which adjust wages in accordance with the inflation undergone in the period just completed, simply maintain the level of real wages. This is the case only if future inflation is the same as past inflation. But when inflation accelerates, this formula leads to a reduction in real wages; whereas when inflation decelerates, as it did during phase II in Chile, 100 percent readjustment in accordance with past inflation leads to a rise in real wages. For example, if nominal wages are 100 during year t, and inflation in year t is 100 percent, then real wages during year t are approximately equal to 75:100 the first day of the year, 50 on the last (100/200). If nominal wages in year $t + 1$ are fully readjusted to the inflation of year t, they will be 200. This signifies a real wage of 100 (200/200), the first day of $t + 1$. Should inflation in year $t + 1$ decelerate to 50 percent, real wages on the last day of year $t + 1$ will be 67 (200/300). In short, the average real wage in year $t + 1$ will be approximately 83, implying an 11 percent (83/75) increase in real wages between year t and year $t + 1$. If the objective of wage policy is to keep these constant in real terms, it must take into account both future and past inflation. In the case just given, to keep real wages constant (that is, at 75), with an inflation of 100 percent in year t and an expected inflation of 50 percent in year $t + 1$, nominal wages should be readjusted by 80 percent (not 100 percent), real wages thus rising to 90 (180/200) on the first day of year $t + 1$ and falling thereafter throughout year $t + 1$ until they reach 60 (180/300) at the end of year $t + 1$, thus averaging a value of 75 in real terms for the whole of year $t + 1$.

14. Chile's unemployment rates shown in table 5.9 include persons employed in the government's emergency make-work programs (PEM and POJH). If these workers are counted among the gainfully employed, unemployment rates in 1976 would have been about one third less, (double rather than triple the historic average).

gentina showed the reverse behavior. Notwithstanding the stagnation and instability of output, the rate of unemployment remained very low, more or less without change. Indeed, at times it fell below its historic values. Uruguay was in an intermediate position: unemployment seems to have worsened during the first two years, despite the increase in output, but from then on the situation systematically improved until the crisis of 1982–83, when unemployment shot up.

How explain these differences in employment behavior? Those versed in the neoclassical tradition would first look for above-equilibrium wages arising from wage rigidities in the labor market.[15] Yet it is obvious that microeconomic explanations deriving from partial equilibrium analysis should be discarded, inasmuch as real wages suffered a sharp reduction from the very start—far more than output and gross disposable income per worker. Thus if low wages or lower wages were enough to avoid unemployment, as some suggested in explaining the low rate of unemployment in Argentina, the unemployment problem should not have emerged in the other two countries, either.

The differences among the three countries in employment during phase I better lends itself to interpretation in terms of the very different evolutions of their respective outputs, as in the Keynesian macroeconomic spirit. In product market disequilibria, where at the prevailing but inflated level of prices one cannot sell all one wishes, the demand for labor is no longer a function of wage costs but a function of sales.[16] Insofar as sales declined (in Chile) or did not grow (in Argentina) in this first phase, the demand for labor also fell or failed to grow, for, however much real wages had fallen, the opportunity cost of unused machines in factories had fallen even more (to virtually zero). As a result, the prime effect of the fall in wages in this phase was to reduce domestic demand for goods much more than to induce the increased hiring of labor because of its lower cost. This explains why in future years the growth of employment in Chile coincided with increases, and not declines, in real wages.

---

15. In a public address to entrepreneurs in Santiago in 1974, Professor Arnold Harberger tried to explain the dramatic increase in Chilean unemployment the first year after the coup on the basis of what he thought to be a rise in real minimum wages. In fact, unbeknownst to him at the time (because of the authorities' manipulations of the consumer-price index in the last quarter of 1973), official inflation understated real inflation by nearly 50 percent, so that real wages were overstated by one third. Hence, on the basis of official price deflators, real minimum wages appeared to rise, though in fact they had fallen. The point is that he, and anyone versed in the neoclassical tradition, would first tend to explain unemployment in terms of unduly high wages and would find rising unemployment very difficult to reconcile with falling labor costs. On the details of the manipulation of the price index, see Ramos 1975 and Cortázar and Marshall 1980.

16. This explanation obviously is inspired by the disequilibrium, quantity-versus-price-adjusting, Keynesian interpretation of unemployment. See in this regard, chapter 13 of Patinkin 1956, Leijonhufvud 1968, and Barro and Grossman 1971. This interpretation is further developed and applied to the specific case of Argentina and Chile by Cortázar, Foxley, and Tokman 1984; and by Dornbusch 1984 in his comments to Blejer 1984.

Inversely, in Uruguay the price-stabilization-induced fall in domestic consumption was more than made up by strong increases in investment and export volumes, so that GNP grew and employment expanded. That is to say, the unemployment generated in phase I was not so much a symptom of a disequilibrium in the labor market—whose resolution would have required a lowering of real wages—but rather was a result of a disequilibrium in the goods market (overshot prices with depressed sales). The employment problem could not be resolved until the basic disequilibrium affecting the goods market was resolved.

More constructively, it can be affirmed *grosso modo* that the evolution of employment was associated with the level of output. The 11 percent decline in output in Chile between 1973 and 1975 reduced employment by 10 percentage points (table 5.9). The subsequent recovery and expansion of economic activity between 1976 and 1981 increased employment considerably (15 percent), though much less than the 50 percent by which output increased; and when output fell 15 percent in 1982–83, employment fell 10 percent.[17]

Although unemployment grew in Uruguay between 1974 and 1976, the number of employed also increased (4.5 percent per year, well above increases in the working-age population). What occurred is that the rate of labor force participation increased substantially in this period.[18] Thus employment expanded systematically and strongly together with output from the beginning to the end of the neoconservative experience in Uruguay (18 and 30 percent, respectively). Inversely, when output fell 15 percent in 1982–83, employment fell by 7 percent.

This rough association between the evolution of output and employment unfortunately is not at all clear in the case of Argentina, for during the whole of the period, output rose 1.5 percent, whereas employment grew by 8 percent, and unemployment showed no significant changes. It is especially difficult to understand what took place in 1978 and 1980, when output per capita fell (5.0 percent in 1978, 0.5 percent in 1980), while the unemployment rate remained fairly constant.

There seem to be several persuasive explanations for Argentina's rather peculiar employment behavior:

1. The yearly declines in output were not all that severe (at least not as severe as the Chilean ones), and they were perceived as transitory, hence firms may have laid off proportionately fewer workers.

---

17. Though certainly most of this new unemployment was cyclical, the financial crisis in phase III enormously increased the number of bankruptcies. Many of these firms, it is true, simply changed ownership; others, however were dismantled and their equipment sold off separately, at times even as scrap iron. These latter imply an irretrievable loss of jobs and productive capacity (see PREALC 1984).

18. In Chile, on the other hand, the participation rate fell during the first phase, and at least through 1978; thus this explanation is not valid for the Chilean case. See table 5.9 and Meller, Cortázar, and Marshall 1979.

2. Wage employment did fall off sharply in this period, but the decline was more than compensated by the increase in the self-employed, a group that constitutes potential underemployment. Nevertheless, had there been more underemployment rather than unemployment, how are we to explain the fact that in these years firms claimed to have had difficulty in hiring salaried workers? Similarly, if this were the explanation, why didn't self-employment increase in Chile, where the employment situation was even more difficult and where workers had less personal wealth to tide them over? One plausible hypothesis is that, since the unemployed in Argentina tended to come from modern firms, which paid benefits to those laid off, the workers had a capital base to establish themselves in better forms of self-employment.

3. Unlike the case of Chile, public investment remained high in Argentina (as in Uruguay). The reduction in public expenditures was basically limited to current expenditures (especially wages). Thus, public employment, direct and indirect, did not suffer serious reductions.

4. Inasmuch as there was a lot of immigrant labor employed in Argentina at the beginning of this experience, it is possible that unemployment concentrated in these groups, so that the reduction in the demand for labor manifested itself not so much in higher rates of unemployment as in lower rates of immigration.

5. The working-age population was growing at only 1 percent per year in Argentina. (It grew by over 2 percent per year in Chile.)

6. Moonlighting was largely prevalent in Argentina. Thus, as the demand for labor declined, many lost one but not both of their jobs, leaving unemployment rates unchanged.

Concentration of Income and Wealth

Whatever factors explain it, the behavior of employment in no way compensated the fall in real wages, especially during phase I. Indeed, in Chile the deterioration in the employment situation accentuated the fall in real wages. Thus, from the very beginning of the neoconservative experiences, the wage share in national income fell quite sharply.[19] During all of phase I, it remained between one fourth (in Uruguay) and one third (in Argentina and Chile) below its average share in the earlier years of the seventies (table 5.8).

The wage share in income never recovered its historic levels in any of the

---

19. It is important to distinguish between the wage share in gross disposable income and the share in national output. The first is the most pertinent indicator (index A in table 5.8), inasmuch as it measures the participation of labor in that part of national income left after GNP is adjusted for the variations in the terms of trade. As can be observed in the table, this adjustment is especially important in Chile after 1974.

three countries.[20] Nevertheless, the evolution of the wage share was quite different in the three countries during phase II. In Chile in particular, real wages recovered strongly. Moreover, because of the deterioration in the terms of trade, Chilean disposable income grew substantially less than output from 1976 on. In this way, by 1982 the distribution of gross disposable income had virtually returned to its preneoconservative days, whereas labor's share in the distribution of output was still 25 percent below 1970 levels.[21] The recovery in the distribution of income in Argentina was much less. By 1982, the share of labor recuperated from 7 to 10 percentage points of what it had lost during phase I, but it was not until the sharp increase in real wages in 1983 that it approached its share of preneoconservative days. In Uruguay, labor's share remained largely unchanged with respect to phase I; indeed, had it not been for the sharp increase in employment, the distribution of income would have continued to worsen during phase II. And the crisis of 1982–83 led to a further regression in the share of labor in national income.

Not only did the distribution of income worsen during these experiences, but there were signs that the concentration of tangible and financial wealth also did so, especially in Chile. There are seven reasons for this concentration in Chile:

---

20. The data concerning income distribution are quite imperfect, especially those that refer to wages. One cannot assume that the wage income of agricultural laborers or of the self-employed or of laborers in small firms moved the same way as incomes in the larger firms of urban areas, which are the ones typically sampled in such surveys. Nevertheless, given the magnitude of the loss observed and the fact that any biases probably underestimate rather than overestimate wage losses, these observed tendencies can be regarded as largely correct. In any case, these conclusions are corroborated, at least for Chile and Uruguay, by complementary data. In Chile, the survey of expenditures and family consumption shows that between 1969 and 1978 the share in overall consumption of the 60 percent of families with the lowest income fell, whereas the share in consumption of the upper 20 percent of families rose, from 45 percent to 51 percent. Similarly, a study of income distribution in Uruguay shows that between 1973 and 1976 the share in income of the 20 percent of families with the highest incomes grew from 43.5 to 46.7 percent of national income, largely at the expense of the 60 percent of families with lowest incomes. For Chile, see Instituto Nacional de Estadística de Chile 1979. The most complete study on income distribution in Chile in this period is that of Cortázar 1983b. For Uruguay, see Bension and Caumont 1979.

21. The failure of many observers to note the important difference between labor's share in output and labor's share in gross disposable income accounts for the widespread view that, because labor's share in output was so much worse than in 1970, capital's share must have improved correspondingly. The key point is that output remaining in Chile was worth far less in 1983 than in 1970 because of the huge deterioration in Chile's terms of trade. In any case, in no year during the neoconservative period was labor's share in gross disposable income equal to that of 1970, the last year of normalcy in Chile. And labor's cumulative loss over the nine years of the neoconservative experience was 1.33 times one year's gross disposable income, or $26 billion, measured by what it would have earned had its 1970 share in gross disposable income been maintained throughout the neoconservative era. The cumulative loss for labor in Argentina and Uruguay varies according to the base year chosen, but is even worse than in Chile (see table 5.8).

1. Lands and factories intervened in during the previous regime were returned to their former owners.
2. Some 200 firms, some of which had been in hands of the state even before intervention, were sold in the midst of one of the most severe recessions Chile had ever experienced in modern times. The sales were therefore disadvantageous to the state. Once the recession had passed, the market value of these firms grew immensely.
3. A large number of financial institutions were auctioned in similar conditions, without any attempt by the government to sell to people without financial ties to industrial firms. New owners formed several industrial-financial conglomerates, and by 1978, economic conglomerates controlled half the assets of the private banking system and 60 percent of domestic credit (Dahse 1979).
4. Opening up finance to the outside world proved to be partial and selective. Economic conglomerates that controlled the banks thus obtained monopolistic rents of a billion dollars (Zahler 1980).
5. The capital gains tax was eliminated just when, thanks to favorable expectations of future growth and the desire to concentrate wealth, the value of assets shot up remarkably. (Between December 1973 and December 1980, the average value of stocks traded in the stock exchange grew 14 times in real terms.)
6. The private firms created to administer the funds of the new social security system were often linked to the economic conglomerates, so that the social security funds of close to half the labor force were placed at the disposal of these conglomerates.
7. Finally, once the acute financial crisis of phase III broke out into the open, policies were applied with clearly negative redistributive effects. Though the immediate purpose was to keep firms operating to maintain output and employment, the policies taken to meet the financial crisis to a large extent implied socializing private debt, just as in boom times gains had been privatized. The renegotiation of debts at preferential interest rates, the purchase of nonperforming assets from the banks, the sale of foreign exchange at subsidized values for the repayment of foreign debt, and retroactive state guarantees on private foreign debt, all were clearly regressive, and their asymmetry in favor of those who had much wealth (or debt) is quite clear. Paradoxically, with the intervention by the state into the financial system at the beginning of 1983, the bulk of the concentrated private sector once again came to depend on the administrative decisions of the state, much as during the preceding socialist regime.

The tendency to a greater concentration of wealth in Argentina and Uruguay was much less clear. There was some privatization in Argentina of activities on the periphery of the large state enterprises, but almost none in

Uruguay. In the same vein, although the creation of the domestic capital market in Argentina reduced the share of state banks in overall deposits from 50 to 35 percent between 1976 and 1980, the principal gainers were private banks of the interior and small and medium-sized financial institutions, whose share in deposits grew from 12 to 25 percent in those years. With the financial crisis and consequent intervention into the banking system in May-April 1980, the process was reversed, and such deposits were shifted back from the regional private banks to state, traditional, or foreign banks. Thus, the system tended to revert to its starting point.

The liberalization of the financial system in Uruguay also raised the participation of the private sector. Nevertheless, the public sector's share in financial GNP never fell below 50 percent (it was 58 percent at the beginning of the experience); thus, the process of privatization and concentration was necessarily rather modest. Nevertheless, during phase III both Argentina and Uruguay followed redistributive policies on behalf of debtors quite similar to those of Chile; these policies included, in one or both countries, the purchase of risky loans and nonperforming assets from the banks, the renegotiation (*licuación*) of loans at subsidized and preferential interest rates, and the sale of foreign exchange at preferential prices to those indebted in foreign currencies.

In any case, concentration did not lead to an increase in the share of foreigner's assets in any of the three countries. With the exception of Argentinian investments in Uruguay, direct foreign investment was rather low, generally less than 1 percent of GNP. Indeed, foreign firms showed a good deal of reluctance to commit themselves to the neoconservative experiences. There were, in fact, signs of withdrawal, especially in Argentina, for many foreign firms were dedicated to import-substituting activities oriented to internal markets, whose demand was severely contracted during the stabilization and adjustment programs and which were most hurt by the tariff-reduction policy (Ferrer 1981).

In short, in each of the three countries the redistribution of income against wage earners occurred not so much because of the development strategy as such but because of the specific policies chosen to lower inflation or to confront the financial crisis. A clear example is the price-stabilization policy, which was regressive not because reducing inflation requires one to squeeze one group more than the other (labor rather than capital) but because of the specific instruments utilized (wage *controls* and price *liberalization*).

Similarly, the concentration of wealth was largely due to the specific policies chosen to privatize property and to liberalize the economy. Other policies could have been chosen to accomplish these without resulting in such concentration and while retaining the principles of private property and a wider sphere for the market. For example, when lands and firms were returned to their previous owners, these owners could have been charged a capital gains tax; or a tax might have been levied on the inflows of foreign capital, which would have passed on to the government the differential between domestic and international interest rates; or the auctioned banks might have been required to be independent from the productive sectors.

It is thus important to emphasize that, at least from an analytical standpoint, the explicit objectives of the neoconservatives—price stabilization and economic liberalization—did not and do not require a regressive redistribution of wealth or income. It is thus reasonable to conclude that if, nonetheless, the policies followed systematically erred on one side (against labor) or directly aided the concentration of income, it is because in addition to the explicitly stated objectives of stabilization and liberalization there were additional implicit objectives: that labor should be reined in and that wealth and income should be concentrated (a position, however, explicitly formulated only in Uruguay).

CONCLUSIONS

The principal achievements of the neoconservative experiences were raising exports and lowering inflation. The principal costs were distributive.

As far as growth is concerned, the achievements were dissimilar. Uruguay's were moderately successful; Chile's proved to be poor, without any solid and enduring base; and Argentina's were a clear failure. The poor results with respect to growth were in large part due to the initial disequilibrium and the unfavorable international situation (especially the deterioration in the terms of trade, which was only partially and temporarily offset by the massive inflows of foreign capital). Nevertheless, the bulk of the explanation lies with errors in domestic policy, which explain why the initial stabilization policy in Argentina and Chile was excessively restrictive and why it led to a recession; why the adjustment to external disequilibrium in 1982–83 had more severe domestic consequences than necessary (because of the lag in the exchange rate); and why it was accompanied by an acute financial crisis (the result of both excessively high interest rates and the lag in the exchange rate).

While the outward-oriented strategy succeeded in increasing the weight of exports in GNP, this achievement was especially associated with phase I, during which the real exchange rate was high and other export-promotion policies were pursued. In the second phase, because of the lag in the exchange rate and the lowering of tariffs, imports were promoted far more than exports. Thus for the neoconservative period as a whole, the proportion of tradables in GNP actually fell in all three countries.

For much the same reasons, the increase in foreign debt, which had been rather modest during the first phase, accelerated sharply during the second, thanks to financial liberalization, to the great lag in the exchange rate, and to high domestic interest rates. At the same time, the massive inflows of foreign capital made possible the prolonged maintenance of a severely lagged exchange rate, which, in the long run, was not sustainable. Hence, an acute financial crisis, internal as well as external, finally erupted.

The sharply regressive redistribution of income that characterized the neoconservative period was not the inevitable result of the pursuit of price stabilization and economic liberalization objectives as such but rather was due to the specific policies and instruments chosen to achieve them. For there is no theoretical reason why the bulk of the redistributive costs could not have been avoided while pursuing these two objectives. Thus the concentration of income and wealth was the result of a systematic disregard for distributive considerations or, more likely, of a belief in the desirability of concentrating income to raise savings and promote growth.

6

Stabilization and Adjustment Policies

Two immediate economic problems contributed to the political upheavals that gave rise to neoconservative experiences in Chile, Uruguay, and Argentina: one, galloping inflation, and two, disequilibria in their external accounts.

These three Southern Cone countries had long ago learned to live with inflation; indexing was widespread, and most economic agents had come to think in real, and not nominal, terms. Yet the efficacy of these instruments was seriously eroded when these countries were beset by triple-digit inflation. The costs of 600 percent annual inflation in Chile (1973), 300 percent in Argentina (1975), and close to 100 percent in Uruguay (1973), and the fear of hyperinflation, made each of them, especially the first two, assign top priority from the very beginning to an anti-inflationary stabilization policy.

Yet these countries were beset with not only unprecedented rates of inflation but serious disequilibria in external accounts. The deficit in current account at the onset of the new regimes ranged from 20 percent of the value of exports in Chile, through 27 percent in Uruguay, to 37 percent in Argentina; and their debt-to-export ratios were among the highest of Latin America at the time: 1.9 to 1 in Uruguay, 2.3 to 1 in Argentina, and 2.5 to 1 in Chile. Thus they had to tackle two major sources of disequilibrium right from the start.

The purpose of this chapter is to analyze the stabilization and adjustment policies pursued by each; to establish at what cost, in terms of output and income distribution, these disequilibria were corrected; and to determine if these costs were avoidable and, if so, what specific policies were responsible for them. It goes without saying that no policy is ever purely a stabilization or purely an adjustment policy, for internal and external disequilibria often come together. Nevertheless, it is probably fair to say that in the first years, especially in Argentina and Chile, the aim was stabilization subject to a balance-of-payments constraint; whereas in the last years (1981 on) the aim was adjustment subject to an anti-inflationary constraint. Hence, for purposes of simplification, the analysis focuses first on the price stabilization features of the first years and then on the adjustment process of the later years.

INFLATION AS A MONETARY PHENOMENON

The debate concerning the causes of inflation in the Southern Cone traditionally centered in two schools of thought: monetarists and structuralists.[1] Monetarism attributed inflation to an overexpansion of the money supply, normally the result of fiscal deficits. The solution was to correct such maladjustments and slow the expansion of credit. Structuralists, on the other hand, while not challenging the general relation between fiscal deficits, monetary expansion, and inflation, argued that such an expansion was endogenous. That is to say, that the monetary authorities often found themselves forced to increase the money supply in order to minimize the impact both of external disequilibria and of shortfalls in agricultural output on overall output. For example, structuralists argued that the (allegedly) low price elasticity of exports and agricultural output made these economies extremely vulnerable to disequilibria originating in these sectors. Hence the attempt to overcome the negative consequences of such bottlenecks generated pressure to expand credit. The implication of such an approach was to argue that any attempt to eliminate inflation without overcoming structural bottlenecks in the economy would have either only passing success or would lead to recession.

While it is true, as monetarists argued, that in the Southern Cone there has been a very close relation in the long run between the rate of inflation and the growth of the money supply,[2] it is likewise true that in the short run this relation has been quite weak (table 6.1). The failure for this relation to hold in the short run paved the way for the structuralists' arguments that in order to stop inflation it would not be enough to reduce fiscal deficits and slow the growth of money supply. Rather, because the velocity of money could fluctuate in a compensatory fashion given the rigidities and bottlenecks in the economy, a deceleration in the growth of aggregate demand (Mv) could slow either the rate of inflation (the desired objective) or production (not desired).

Possibly because of the greater simplicity of the monetarist model, possibly because of the failure of structuralists to translate their approach into

---

1. This controversy occupied a good part of the debate on inflation through the end of the sixties. The literature is extensive. See, for example, the articles by Campos, Felix, and Grunwald in Hirschman, 1961; "Inflation and Economic Growth" in Baer and Kerstenetzky 1964; and CEPAL 1962.

2. The quantity *identity* states that money (M) multiplied by velocity (v) is equal to prices (P) multiplied by the value of output (Q). Consequently, it is true by definition and by differentiation that $\dot{M}/M + \dot{v}/v = \dot{P}/P + \dot{Q}/Q$. The quantity theory in its traditional and simple form states that v is relatively constant. Consequently, $\dot{M}/M = \dot{P}/P + \dot{Q}/Q$. If we suppose, at least for the short run, that product remains constant, then $\dot{M}/M = \dot{P}/P$ (the better-known expression of the quantity theory). The quantity theory showed excellent explicative power in the period 1950–70 for the three countries. Given the growth in money and product, the theory predicts a rate of inflation for the period of 21 percent in Argentina (it was 24); of 34 percent in Chile (where it was 30); and of 28 percent (it was 29) in Uruguay.

sufficiently operational policy directives, the stabilization policies followed during the fifties and early sixties tended to be monetarist. Because these stabilization programs almost invariably resulted in recession, this approach slowly fell out of grace, only to reappear in the seventies. For one thing, the approach had been enriched theoretically: it was now recognized that velocity (the reciprocal of the demand for money) varied; however, it was argued that it varied not in an unpredictable fashion or in a fashion that automatically compensated monetary growth but rather in a stable or at least predictable way. While it was not at all clear in what way a deceleration in nominal aggregate

Table 6.1. Southern Cone: Money, Prices, and Gross National Product, Annual Growth, 1950–1970 (*percentage*)

Year	Chile			Uruguay			Argentina		
	Money[a]	Prices[b]	GNP	Money[a]	Prices[b]	GNP	Money[a]	Prices[b]	GNP
1950	16.4	15.1	4.8	22.0	−7.1	3.1	23.2	26.0	1.6
1951	32.1	22.6	5.3	−1.3	15.4	8.2	22.7	30.8	3.9
1952	37.0	23.1	3.4	9.0	15.6	−0.4	13.2	41.2	−5.1
1953	53.0	25.0	7.1	12.9	5.8	6.5	25.7	5.0	5.4
1954	47.0	71.0	0.7	7.3	14.5	5.7	19.7	16.0	4.1
1955	63.0	84.2	2.7	5.8	7.9	1.6	18.0	14.3	7.1
1956	38.0	37.5	0.7	11.9	7.4	1.7	16.6	12.5	2.8
1957	25.0	25.0	2.6	8.4	13.7	1.0	13.0	25.9	5.1
1958	33.3	30.8	4.8	20.4	18.1	−3.6	22.8	32.4	6.1
1959	37.5	37.4	6.9	35.0	39.8	−2.8	50.7	100.0	−6.4
1960	18.1	13.6	5.1	40.8	37.2	3.5	34.9	20.0	7.8
1961	27.8	9.0	6.1	25.3	23.4	2.9	17.9	16.7	7.1
1962	25.0	12.9	4.6	7.2	10.8	−2.2	7.1	28.6	−1.6
1963	33.9	44.6	5.1	16.0	21.0	0.5	20.0	22.2	−2.4
1964	41.1	50.0	4.2	70.7	42.4	2.0	38.9	22.7	10.3
1965	55.2	22.2	5.0	56.0	56.7	1.1	32.0	25.9	9.1
1966	51.4	27.3	7.0	70.1	73.3	3.4	30.3	35.3	0.6
1967	28.4	21.4	2.4	51.1	89.3	−4.1	34.9	28.3	2.7
1968	30.1	23.5	3.0	86.5	125.4	1.6	32.8	15.3	4.3
1969	24.0	28.6	3.5	69.2	21.0	6.1	16.9	8.8	8.6
1970	58.1	33.3	3.6	31.3	16.3	4.7	12.2	12.2	5.4
1950–1970	37.7	30.3	4.2	29.5	29.4	1.8	24.3	23.8	3.7

Sources: International Monetary Fund, *International Financial Statistics,* May 1976; and *Statistical Yearbook* 1980; CEPAL 1978.

[a]M1 (bills and coins in circulation plus demand deposits).

[b]Index of consumer prices.

demand would divide itself in the short run between a slower rate of inflation and a recession,[3] it was argued that a recession could be avoided to the extent that inflation was correctly anticipated. Second, and possibly more decisively, given the urgency to combat triple-digit inflation, it seemed quite unconvincing to attribute such high inflation to structural factors or to insist that it was indispensable to eliminate such in order to prevent runaway inflation.

Given the neoconservatives' preference for the market and their aversion to administrative controls, it is not at all surprising that these countries initially adopted a monetarist approach to price stabilization and, more specifically, the monetarist approach for a closed economy. Over time, with the increased opening of the economy, the monetarist approach was modified; the key policy instrument would shift from control of the money supply to control of the exchange rate. In any case, throughout the entire experience, the prevailing spirit was that of minimizing administrative intervention in the market.

PHASE I: MONETARISM FOR A CLOSED ECONOMY

Its Logic

The quantity identity in its dynamic form offers a good starting point to explain the stabilization policy of phase I in the three neoconservative experiences of the Southern Cone: $\dot{M}/M + \dot{v}/v = \dot{P}/P + \dot{Q}/Q$. If one wants to slow inflation, one needs to slow the growth in nominal aggregate demand (Mv). Nevertheless, the relative impact on prices and production of such a deceleration depends on inflationary expectations.[4] If such expectations are fairly uniform among economic agents and if these expectations coincide with the inflationary goal implicit in monetary policy, the deceleration in nominal aggregate demand will fall exclusively on prices (precisely what is desired). On the other hand, to the extent that there is a significant difference between the expected inflation and that consistent with monetary and fiscal policy, the deceleration in nominal aggregate demand will also fall on production (precisely what we want to avoid).

In short, however high inflation might be, it is theoretically possible to bring it down without a fall in output.[5] Problems emerge if there are rigidities,

---

3. Friedman himself states that this is the single most important problem to be resolved in modern macroeconomics (Friedman 1970).

4. To be sure, the demand for money does not depend solely on inflationary expectations but rather, among other things, on money's alternative uses. The creation of an internal capital market, for example, would give rise to highly liquid financial instruments that pay high interest rates, which would affect the demand for money. At the same time, the supply of money is not easy to control.

5. Sargent (1981) makes this point quite explicitly in arguing that the costs of reducing inflation are proportional not to the rate of past inflation (the theory of inflationary mo-

especially of expectations, for these will slow timely adjustments to the new conditions that economic policy is trying to establish. In such cases, stabilization policies end in recession, but this is not because it is inevitable; rather, it is a sign of failure, a failure to harmonize the expectations of economic agents with the inflationary goal implicit in the fiscal and monetary policies the government is carrying out (see Díaz-Alejandro 1981; Dornbusch 1982).

In the three neoconservative experiences, serious efforts were made to avoid the formation of "erroneous" inflationary expectations. During the first phase, efforts centered in the labor market, for should inflationary expectations based on past inflation come to be incorporated into labor contracts, wage movements would become terribly rigid. A government that fails to harmonize the inflation expected in wage contracts with that implicit in its economic policy is confronted with the following dilemma: either ratify the erroneous expectations, easing monetary and fiscal policy at the cost of its stabilization program; or persist in stabilization goals and the consonant restrictive economic policy at the cost of a recession.

We may call this the neoclassical variant of recession (as opposed to the neo-Keynesian one), inasmuch as unemployment and recession would be due to a rise in real labor costs. In other words, unemployment would be a reflection of a disequilibrium in the labor market and not, as in neo-Keynesian models, of a disequilibrium in the goods market. Thus, for neoconservatives, any stabilization program that aims at avoiding recession and unemployment must necessarily attempt to harmonize wage readjustments with the inflationary goal set by the government. This means wage controls, for the market, left to itself, cannot adjust wages to coming inflation, inasmuch as it cannot know in advance the seriousness with which the government intends to apply its stabilization program. Any doubt as to this would inevitably create rigidities in expectations and lead to recession.

For reasons of this sort (among others), neoconservatism in the Southern Cone justified the use of administrative controls on wages.[6] However, such

---

mentum) but rather to expected inflation (rational expectations). Thus should the public believe that there has been a change in the rules governing fiscal and monetary policy (in short, a permanent change in the regime) and not solely a change of policy within those rules (a transitory change), the cost of reducing inflation can be quite low. He cites as specific examples the hyperinflations that were abruptly stopped after the First World War in Germany, Austria, Hungary, and Poland, and in which recession was either slight or nonexistent.

6. This is not to suggest that there were not other motives behind wage controls. For example, in Uruguay many argued explicitly that wages ought to fall in the short run in order to increase profit margins and thus raise the heretofore low levels of savings and investment. It is also possible that some believed that real wages had exceeded equilibrium levels during the periods of Perón in Argentina and Allende in Chile (the periods immediately preceding the onset of neoconservatism). In point of fact, this was not the case in Chile, since real wages had already fallen by over 15 percent with respect to 1970 levels in the last year of Allende. This argument is possibly somewhat more plausible in Argentina, since real wages grew 11 percent

doubts as to the ability of the market to adjust rapidly in transition situations did not lead to the adoption of similar interventionist measures in other markets (for example, the goods or financial markets).[7] In these latter markets, there was confidence (misplaced, as we will soon see) that competition would assure rapid and converging adjustments, so that any disequilibria in such markets would be quite transitory. In short, neoconservative stabilization policy focused on avoiding neoclassical recession and unemployment but failed, given the high inflation, to consider the possibility of neo-Keynesian, demand-deficient, recession and unemployment.

The Policies

Inasmuch as inflation was considered to be fundamentally a monetary phenomenon, the key instrument in reducing it was the control of the money supply. However, in order to avoid or minimize recessive costs, control of the money supply had to be accompanied by wage controls. Moreover, a deceleration in the growth of monetary variables required a reduction in the fiscal deficit, all the more so given the magnitudes of these deficits at the beginning of the neoconservative experiences (between 4 and 25 percent of GNP). This implied an increase in the prices of public services, increased taxes, reductions in current expenditures (principally wages), and, in Chile, a decline in public investment. According to the monetarist framework, such measures were the sine qua non of a price-stabilization program. Nevertheless, this program was accompanied by two other measures, which proved to be of paramount importance in the evolution of these economies.

First, from the very beginning the three countries faced serious external disequilibria, which required real devaluations (in Chile and Uruguay) or the maintenance of a high real exchange rate (in Argentina, which had recently devalued). Nevertheless, it is important to note once again that a recession is not required in order to improve the trade balance; what is required is to reduce domestic spending and to switch output toward tradables by means of devaluation or appropriate commercial policy. Such a policy would substitute (not simply reduce) imports, promote exports, and switch domestic spending from tradables to nontradables. Distributive neutrality would require that all factors share proportionally in the ensuing decline in disposable national income. The

---

between 1970 and 1975, whereas per capita output grew only 8 percent. Nevertheless, even had wages exceeded equilibrium, the need for adjustment would have been minimal, given the small magnitudes involved. Finally, there is no doubt that union power was looked upon with great suspicion, for both political and ideological reasons: unions had been an important base of support for the preceding governments in Argentina and Chile, and they were thought to be incipient instruments of monopolistic control. Therefore, neoconservatives tended to believe that wages had been artificially raised over a long period of time.

7. The control of the exchange rate was justified for another reason: the need to have some reference price to which all other prices could freely adjust.

worsening in the terms of trade, which Argentina and Uruguay experienced from the very beginning and Chile as of the end of 1974, thus required some decline in real wages, though far less than what actually took place.[8]

Second, there existed a widespread system of price controls in the three countries. As a result, relative prices were severely distorted (either creating downward pressure on food prices relative to industrial goods, or repressing inflation, or both).[9] For these reasons, price controls were eliminated in all three countries, radically and abruptly in Chile, gradually in Uruguay, and erratically in Argentina.

It is thus evident that the policy pursued in these three countries from the very beginning did not limit itself solely nor even principally to the fight against

Table 6.2. Chile: Monetary and Basic Macroeconomic Indicators, 1973–1983

	Annual Growth Rate				Public-Sector Surplus as Ratio of GNP
Year	Nominal Devaluation	Money[a]	Prices[b]	Gross National Product	
1973	455.0	259.1	441.0	−5.6	−24.7
1974	649.5	314.6	497.8	1.0	−10.5
1975	490.3	239.2	379.2	−12.9	−2.6
1976	165.8	216.0	232.8	3.5	−2.3
1977	64.9	156.7	113.8	9.9	−1.8
1978	47.0	81.2	50.0	8.2	−0.8
1979	17.7	60.0	33.4	8.3	1.7
1980	4.7	62.6	35.1	7.8	3.1
1981	0.0	−6.0	19.7	5.7	1.7
1982	30.5	9.4	9.9	−14.3	−2.3
1983[c]	54.9	26.6	27.3	−0.8	−3.8

Source: CEPAL, on the basis of official data; International Monetary Fund, International Financial Statistics.

[a]M1 (bills and coins in circulation plus demand deposits).

[b]Index of consumer prices.

[c]Preliminary figures.

---

8. In no case did the deterioration in the terms of trade imply a loss greater than the equivalent of 6 percent of GNP. Therefore, a similar decline in real wages should have maintained income distribution. However, inasmuch as the wage decline was far in excess of this, other factors explain most of the fall in real wages.

9. The repressed inflation in Chile at the end of 1973 was so severe that there was a general shortage of products—not so much because output had declined but because there was an excess of money, which was capable of buying far more than the economy was able to produce at the prevailing controlled prices.

inflation; rather, in differing degrees, each country made serious attempts to restore equilibrium in the external sector and correct the heavily distorted system of relative prices.

The Results

Thanks to the restrictive monetary, fiscal, and wage policies, the external disequilibrium notably improved during this phase as inflation was reduced (tables 6.2, 6.3, and 6.4). As might have been expected, the sizes of the fiscal deficit, monetary growth, and inflation were correlated in this period (figures 6.1, 6.2, and 6.3). Acceleration in the rate of inflation in the period preceding the neoconservative experience was accompanied by large fiscal deficits and very strong monetary growth. After the onset of the neoconservative stabilization policy, decelerations in inflation coincided with lower deficits and rather modest monetary expansion, but this relationship was quite loose in the short run.

The costs of the stabilization policy were a sharp fall in real wages in all three countries, a severe recession in Chile, and stagnation in Argentina. Uruguay's growth, as noted earlier, was due to the very strong increase in public

Table 6.3.   Uruguay: Monetary and Basic Macroeconomic Indicators, 1973–1983

Year	Annual Growth Rate			Gross National Product	Public-Sector Surplus as Ratio of GNP
	Nominal Devaluation	Money[a]	Prices[b]		
1973	55.4	63.5	97.0	0.4	−1.2
1974	39.0	80.0	77.2	3.1	−3.8
1975	89.1	50.1	81.4	5.9	−4.3
1976	47.7	67.9	50.6	4.0	−2.1
1977	39.9	45.3	58.2	1.2	−1.3
1978	28.9	53.0	44.5	5.3	−0.9
1979	29.3	99.5	66.8	6.2	0.0
1980	15.7	34.9	63.5	5.8	−0.3
1981	18.7	8.3	34.0	1.9	−1.5
1982	36.2	19.8	19.0	−9.7	−9.1
1983[c]	148.3	11.1	51.5	−4.7	−3.9

Source: CEPAL, on the basis of official data; International Monetary Fund, International Financial Statistics.

[a]M1 (bills and coins in circulation plus demand deposits).

[b]Index of consumer prices.

[c]Preliminary figures.

investment and exports, which more than compensated the decline in domestic consumption. Moreover, important as was the reduction in inflation, it was considerably less than might have been expected given the sharp reduction in labor costs (in all three) and effective demand (in Argentina and Chile). If not excessive demand or cost pressure, what kept inflation from decelerating more rapidly during phase I?

In Argentina and Chile, at any rate, prices appear to have risen not so much because of excess cost or demand but rather because of the price decisions of producers in anticipation of a demand for goods that never materialized. For that reason, the increase in prices in the first year of Chile's neoconservative experiment, for example, exceeded the increase in money supply by 50 percent.

It is reasonable to suppose that, in periods of accelerating inflation, the velocity of money will rise because of inflationary expectations, so that the growth of prices will be greater than that of monetary expansion. Yet in these two cases, prices rose not because of the inflationary expectations of the public (demand was in fact sluggish) nor because of cost pressure from labor costs (which fell sharply)[10] but because of the inflationary expectations of producers.

Table 6.4.   Argentina: Monetary and Basic Macroeconomic Indicators, 1973–1983

	Annual Growth Rate				Public-Sector Surplus as Ratio of GNP
Year	Nominal Devaluation	Money[a]	Prices[b]	Gross National Product	
1973	14.6	86.3	61.2	3.6	−4.7
1974	−5.3	93.0	23.3	6.2	−5.3
1975	311.2	90.5	182.5	−0.8	−10.3
1976	282.5	399.4	443.2	−0.5	−7.2
1977	191.1	176.2	176.1	6.4	−2.8
1978	95.2	142.8	175.5	−3.0	−3.2
1979	65.5	131.4	159.5	7.1	−2.7
1980	39.5	115.8	100.8	1.1	−3.6
1981	175.0	53.9	104.5	−6.2	−8.1
1982	360.3	195.7	164.8	−5.3	−7.0
1983[c]	350.2	361.7	343.8	2.8	−11.0

Source: CEPAL, on the basis of official data; International Monetary Fund, International Financial Statistics.

[a]M1 (bills and coins in circulation plus demand deposits).

[b]Index of consumer prices.

[c]Preliminary figures.

10. To be sure, costs are not made up solely of wages; imported inputs, capital costs, and entrepreneurial services also weigh in. Because of the real devaluations then effected, the

Moreover, once an inflationary process reverses itself, an inverse relationship is normally expected between monetary expansion and inflation: that is to say, expectations of decelerating inflation should increase the demand for money so that prices grow less rapidly than the growth of money supply. This did not take place in either Argentina or Chile—quite the contrary. In phase I, although inflation slowed, it continued to advance at a rate well in excess of the growth in money supply. Consequently, the increase in prices exceeded the expansion of the money supply by over 100 percent in Chile and by 25 percent in Argentina.

Moreover, the neoconservatives' implicit assumption that inflationary expectations express themselves solely or principally in the labor market is rather

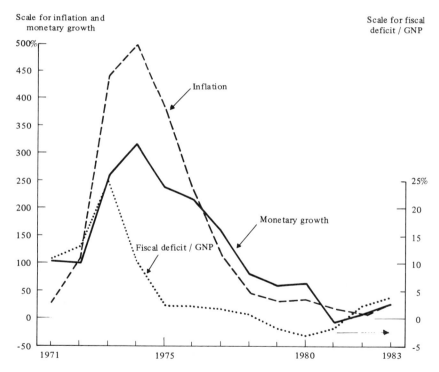

Figure 6.1   Chile: Inflation, Monetary Growth, and Fiscal Deficit, 1971–1983 (percentage)

relative cost of imported inputs did rise. But the relative weight of imports in GNP (of the order of 10 percent) was far less than that of labor (unquestionably above 50 percent), so that the sharp reduction in labor costs dwarfed the relative increase in the cost of imports. In effect, capital and entrepreneurial margins rose not because of demand or cost pressure but because of firms' margin to set prices in the absence of significant external competition.

doubtful, at least from a theoretical point of view. The validity of this assumption is brought further into question if one takes into account that policy also attempted to bring about a real devaluation, which implied raising the relative prices of tradables, and to raise the relative prices of goods heretofore controlled (generally speaking, foodstuffs) by liberalizing the price system. Moreover, the public could not know how much of the nominal devaluation would be real and how much would be nominal (purely inflationary); nor could it know how long the policy of price liberalization would last (indeed, Argentina restored price controls within the year) .

It is therefore easy to understand why producers set their prices not in accordance with current demand, wage costs, and costs of imported inputs but in accordance with what they expected these to be in the future. What is pertinent for such future values is the expected cost of labor, the expected cost of importing (expected devaluation), the expected course of real interest rates,[11] the evolution of public-service prices, the evolution of prices heretofore controlled, expectations about other producers' prices, and so on. Finally, inasmuch as these entrepreneurs faced little competition, especially at the beginning of phase I, they fixed prices in accordance with their own inflationary expectations, be they erroneous or not.[12]

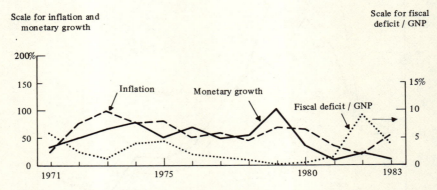

Figure 6.2   Uruguay: Inflation, Monetary Growth, and Fiscal Deficit, 1971–1983 (percentage)

---

11. High interest rates affected not only inflationary expectations but production costs as well, pressuring prices upward, at least in the short run. Thus, rather than inducing the sale of inventories, high interest rates and consequently increased financial costs tended to be passed on in prices (see Cavallo 1977).

12. Referring to Frenkel 1979 and Ramos 1977, Foxley 1983 pointed out: "Double or three-digit inflation, as observed in Argentina, Chile, and Uruguay before and during the first years of the stabilization program, provides the kind of environment where imperfect information, uncertainty about future inflation, and the high risk attached to them become deter-

To the extent to which inflationary expectations significantly exceeded the inflation implicit in monetary and fiscal policy, the deceleration in nominal aggregate demand fell on output (something undesirable) and not only on prices, showing monetary and fiscal policy to be too tight. There were three results of prices overshooting their equilibrium: (1) there was too little money for the prevailing price level (that is, real interest rates were too high); (2) real wages proved to be too low; and (3) output and employment, especially in industry, fell well below the productive capacity of the country (in other words, there was a demand-deficient recession).[13]

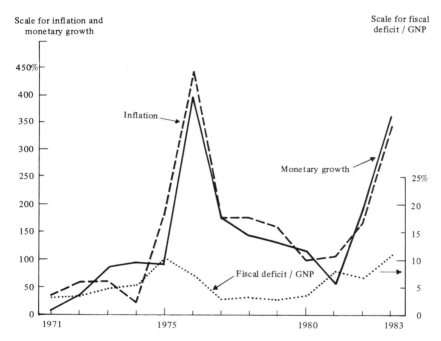

Figure 6.3   Argentina: Inflation, Monetary Growth, and Fiscal Deficit, 1971–1983 (percentage)

mining elements in price decisions by firms. Markups become a function of expected inflation scaled up by an uncertainty and risk premium. During the period of high inflation, maximum uncertainty, and market disequilibrium, prices exhibit some autonomy not only from demand but also from cost increases" (p. 147).

13. Farmers had fewer possibilities of setting their prices in accordance with their inflationary expectations, either because farm goods are perishables subject to high storage and conservation costs or because farming is a more competitive sector. Hence the expected improvement in agricultural prices was also weakened.

Had the divergence between the inflationary expectations of the public and the inflation implicit in economic policy been quickly closed, the contraction in internal demand would have been harmless. Unfortunately, inflationary expectations adjusted quite slowly, thereby prolonging and worsening the recession. National income was redistributed toward producers, which served to cushion their loss of sales due to their high prices.[14] In short, what producers lost by virtue of lower sales they made up via higher prices and margins, thus slowing the movement to equilibrium and worsening income distribution.

The recession in Chile was further aggravated by a sharp fall in public-sector investment and external demand (volume of exports did not grow enough to compensate the very severe decline in its terms of trade). The cumulative effects of reduced consumption (via wage reductions), investment, and internal demand resulted in a very sharp economic contraction: GNP per capita fell 13 percent between 1973 and 1976.

In contrast, the restrictive effects of stabilization policy were compensated in Argentina and more than compensated in Uruguay by very sharp increases in public investment and in the volume of exports. Thus demand was reoriented from domestic consumption to investment and exports. Unemployment in Argentina and Chile was therefore not caused by unduly high or rigid wages (the neoclassical cause of unemployment) but by insufficient aggregate demand.[15] Demand proved insufficient, notwithstanding high inflation, because of rigidity in producers' inflationary expectations, thus accounting for the sluggish deceleration in inflation—much less than that implicit in government policies—and giving rise to neo-Keynesian demand-deficient unemployment.

In short, the effort to simultaneously balance external accounts and stabilize as well as correct relative prices made the possibility of reducing inflation without inducing a recession less and less likely. It is not that recession is inevitably a consequence of the pursuit of these objectives. Rather, it was the pursuit of both goals simultaneously with similar sets of instruments, without considering the repercussions on other objectives, that jeopardized the success of the stabilization policy. Hence deceleration in nominal aggregate demand fell not only on prices, as was desired, but on the level of economic activity, which obviously was not desired.

---

14. To be sure, this situation cannot be maintained in the long run, at least in competitive markets, because a firm can improve its profits by lowering its prices and thus increasing sales. Nevertheless, in periods of recession, with prices in disequilibrium, this effect operates slowly, for each firm tends to see the demand of its products as much less elastic to price than what it really is. For a detailed explanation of this point, see Ramos 1980.

15. Unemployment was less severe in Argentina than in Chile, since its output did not fall but simply stagnated. In addition, Argentina's foreign labor force took the brunt of the job losses, self-employment increased, and moonlighting decreased.

PHASE II: THE MONETARY APPROACH
TO THE BALANCE OF PAYMENTS

Its Logic

Producers' inflationary expectations during phase I thus limited the degree to which money supply could be decelerated without incurring an excessively severe recession. This limitation led to a new approach to stabilization,[16] focusing on the exchange rate rather than on monetary policy. Devaluations of ever-declining percentages were made according to a preannounced program, and money supply adjusted passively and automatically to the balance of payments.

The immediate and central objective of exchange-rate policy was control of inflation. By bringing inflationary expectations rapidly into line with the inflationary goal implicit in the preannounced devaluation, it was hoped that both an overvalued exchange rate and recession would be avoided.[17] The announcement and implementation of this policy change, it was believed, would demonstrate clearly to economic agents the seriousness with which the government intended to pursue its anti-inflationary goal. Since devaluation was programmed to decelerate, inflation could be expected to quickly equal that rate.[18] Should things work out this way, the overshot level of prices and the disequilibria it brought about could be corrected without any further costs in output. At the same time, the real rate of exchange would be maintained.

Exchange policy was expected to influence the behavior of prices not only through expectations but, more directly, by limiting the prices of tradable domestic products to that of the imports they competed with. For by this time, the three economies had substantially opened up imports (removed barriers or lowered tariffs), so that domestic prices had a ceiling—the international price of the imported goods plus transport, tariffs, and retailing costs. This ceiling is the so called law of one price. Given the relatively free flow of imports, it was believed that, regardless of inflationary expectations, the price of domestic goods would converge to this price.

At the same time, the liberalization of the domestic capital market had

---

16. A good introduction to the monetary approach to the balance of payments, especially its implications for price stabilization in the context of the Southern Cone, can be found in Blejer 1984 and the comments to that paper, especially those by Dornbusch 1984, Harberger 1984, Lerdau 1984, and Williamson 1984.

17. This point is expressly recognized by Sjaastad (1982), one of the foremost proponents of the monetary approach to the balance of payments in the Southern Cone and its exchange-rate stabilization approach.

18. Strictly speaking, the rate of inflation would fall to the algebraic sum of the devaluation and the rate of international inflation.

created substitutes for money, which made it increasingly difficult to control the supply of money. Monetary control was further complicated by the opening up of financing to the outside world. Money growth began to be explained largely by exchange operations and not, as in the past, by the expansion of internal credit or treasury financing. The loss of control of the money supply was a further argument on behalf of the new exchange policy.

The monetary approach to the balance of payments provided the underlying theoretical basis for this policy change. According to this view, differences in the amount of money demanded and supplied are resolved principally through the balance of payments and not by changes in production. For example, given a certain demand for monetary balances, when the supply of internal credit contracts, the domestic interest rate rises. Two adjustment mechanisms then automatically come into play to resolve this difference. If the capital account is open, capital comes in, increasing international reserves until the supply of money equals the demand for money and the initial monetary restriction determines not the amount of money on hand but only its composition between internal and external credit. On the other hand, if the capital account is closed, the increase in domestic interest rates lowers the demand for goods, reducing imports, producing a surplus in the trade balance, and augmenting reserves. At the same time, higher interest rates eventually lower the price of internal goods, generating a further surplus in trade balance and increasing reserves. Thus the supply of money expands to the level being demanded.

That changes in the level of output have little to do with resolving disequilibria is a central assumption that the monetary approach has in common with the quantity theory of money. It is this assumption that distinguishes this approach from most others. To be sure, the speed with which the law of one price equalizes internal and external rates of interest and the prices of domestic and imported goods is critical in determining whether adjustment takes place principally via product or via monetary adjustments. The high degree of international liquidity available in the second half of the seventies made interest-rate "equalization" plausible; the lowering of trade barriers in the Southern Cone made product-price "equalization" plausible.[19]

Thus rather than attempting to resolve domestic disequilibria by opening the economy to great amounts of foreign capital, a prudent course would have limited its entry to the amount demanded had domestic interest rates been at equilibrium. For, to the extent that the high rate of interest of domestic credit signaled disequilibria in other markets (as I argue in chapter 8), any attempt to satisfy this abnormal demand for credit via capital inflows would lead to excess levels of foreign indebtedness.

---

19. Equalization of interest rates should take into account a surcharge to cover country risk and the additional cost that domestic financial intermediation might entail. Equalization of prices should take into account the cost of shipping, tariffs, and additional domestic retailing costs.

The Policies

Domestic inflation was expected to equal international inflation plus the rate of devaluation. To accomplish this, domestic prices should have approximated international prices. Unfortunately, early in phase II there emerged a gap between domestic and international prices—which persisted even after taking into account transport, tariff, and trade costs. Thus until internal prices equaled external prices, the domestic inflation goal should have been *less* than international inflation plus devaluation. This point, critical though it was, tended to be overlooked by policymakers in the Southern Cone.

To be sure, they did not attempt to fix exchange rates immediately, for as long as inflation continued to be high and the internal factors contributing to monetary expansion continued to persist, fixing the exchange rate was unsustainable. For example, if $M1$ was 10 percent of GNP and if a public deficit of 5 percent of GNP was expected, money growth would have to be at least 50 percent—an inflation rate of that order of magnitude could be expected. Hence, it would have been reckless for the government to devalue less than 40 percent a year (implying 10 percent external inflation).

On the other hand, once the public-sector deficit was eliminated, there would be no reason why (according to this approach) the exchange rate could not be fixed—indeed, once the deficit was eliminated, this approach dictated that the exchange rate *ought* to be fixed. The method used was to devalue at diminishing rates (in order to affect expectations) according to a preannounced schedule (generally for six months). This policy was begun in Chile in mid-1976 and in Argentina and Uruguay toward the end of 1978. Once the fiscal deficit was eliminated in Chile (in 1979), the exchange rate was fixed at thirty-nine pesos to the dollar, exactly as this approach would suggest (although Chile's inflation at the time was 33 percent). The fiscal deficit was also eliminated in Uruguay in 1979, but the authorities there preferred not to fix the exchange rate yet, for domestic inflation was still 60 percent (whereas international inflation was only 10 percent).

At the same time, given the extensive international liquidity available, the three Southern Cone countries increased their financial opening to the outside world in the hopes of achieving an even more rapid convergence of internal and external rates of interest. Trade was further opened by lowering tariffs (a great deal in Chile, less in Argentina, almost nothing in Uruguay) to stimulate competition and further press domestic prices to converge rapidly toward external ones.

The Results

While the phase II stabilization program was in effect, both Chile (in 1981) and Uruguay (in 1982) managed to lower inflation to international rates. This reduction was especially spectacular in Chile, where five years earlier inflation had exceeded 200 percent. Inflation was almost halved in Argentina; nevertheless it never fell below 100 percent a year.

Argentina's inability to control its public deficit would seem to explain why it was unable to make further headway on this plane. Its deficit was never less than 3 percent of GNP, and in 1980, the year of lowest inflation (100 percent), its deficit once again began to grow, closing at 4 percent of GNP.[20] This fact could not fail to have a negative influence on the credibility of its exchange policy. For as Rodríguez (1983) has argued, it is very hard to believe that the announced policy of devaluing at a rate of 1 percent per month between July 1980 and May 1981 could be long sustained while inflation was five times that and the expected public deficit was 6 or 7 percent of GNP (a fact that alone implied some 80 percent inflation).

While an important component of growth was simply a cyclical recovery, in any case the growth in output in this period in all three countries was well above that experienced during phase I. In Argentina, output per capita grew more than 2 percent per year in 1979 and 1980, compared to −0.9 percent per year in 1976 through 1978. In Chile, it recovered and grew 6 percent per year in the five years, 1977 through 1981, compared to a fall of over 4 percent per year between 1974 and 1976. And in Uruguay it grew more than 5 percent per year in 1979 and 1980, versus a 3.6 percent annual growth in the four years, 1975 through 1978. In other words, the phase II stabilization policy did not bring on recession, at least not in its first years.

Inflation, however, fell much slower than the deceleration in the rate of devaluation, creating a problem that would become increasingly more serious in the course of time. The price of domestic goods relative to imported goods rose by 50 percent in Argentina between 1978 and 1980, 30 percent in Chile between 1976 and 1981, and 30 percent in Uruguay between 1978 and 1981 (table 6.5 and figures 6.4, 6.5, and 6.6). Indeed, the loss of competitiveness was even greater than these figures suggest, for during this period tariffs were lowered, especially in Chile, further cheapening imports relative to their domestic substitutes. Moreover, since real wages recovered somewhat during phase II in Argentina and Chile, it is likely that costs rose by even more than the lag in the exchange rate.[21] Once one adjusts for both of these phenomena, the

---

20. The data in table 6.4 to which the text refers (public surplus as share of GNP) is the central government's deficit. If provincial governments' deficits were included—and these are important in Argentina—the deficit would increase by over 50 percent.

21. This does not imply, as some observers have argued, that the loss in competitiveness was largely due to this increase in real wages, for both the relative rate of change as well as the level of wages is important in determining cost competitiveness. Wages that rise to normal levels obviously have less impact on competitiveness than wages that rise above normal levels. Since all throughout phase II, real wages remained well below their historic levels (and labor costs even more so, given the reductions in employers' social security contributions), it is doubtful that their partial recovery of historic levels significantly impeded the desired

increased relative cost of domestic goods with respect to international goods during phase II exceeded 50 percent in Uruguay and 100 percent in Argentina and Chile (index B, table 6.5).[22]

Table 6.5.   Southern Cone: Real Effective Exchange Rates, 1970–1983

	Index A			Index B		
Year	Chile	Uruguay	Argentina	Chile	Uruguay	Argentina
1970	133.2	110.5	144.6	80.5	62.9	166.6
1971	122.4	101.7	137.2	54.9	53.4	157.6
1972	128.4	125.7	155.2	54.0	117.1	210.8
1973	142.8	107.5	148.5	99.5	81.5	177.4
1974	124.5	103.6	126.9	164.0	80.4	130.0
1975	133.4	119.3	194.1	224.6	95.9	217.6
1976	116.0	127.1	127.9	181.0	108.4	234.6
1977	112.4	126.1	164. 9	166.3	116.2	277.6
1978	130.2	122.9	148.8	129.7	120.5	227.7
1979	116.4	103.9	111.7	124.1	120.5	143.0
1980	100.0	100.0	100.0	100.0	100.0	100.0
1981	89.8	95.8	125.8	76.1	82.4	144.3
1982	105.1	110.8	163.2	85.5	90.8	281.7
1983	111.2	136.8	150.0	115.6	164.5	218.4

Source: CEPAL, on the basis of official data; methodology explained in CEPAL 1983.

Note: Index A = exchange rate deflated by wholesale prices. Index B = exchange rate deflated by domestic wages. Base year = 1980. Lower rates indicate cheaper imports in domestic currency and more expensive exports. Year 1983, preliminary figures.

deceleration in inflation. If, as the argument of such observers implies, there is a tight relation between wage and price movements, the real effective exchange rate should have evolved in much the same way had the exchange rate been deflated by the evolution of wholesale prices or by that of wages; or, what amounts to the same thing, wholesale prices should have evolved much the same as wages (their principal cost). The evidence of the evolution of wholesale prices and wages in the neoconservative period clearly contradicts both of these propositions: table 6.5 shows the evolution of the effective exchange rate deflated both by wholesale prices (index A) and by domestic wages (index B).

22. To be sure, had the lag in the exchange rate been compensated by an equivalent improvement in the terms of trade, no problem would have emerged. The higher cost of domestic production would have been compensated by the increase in the international price of exports, thus maintaining their competitiveness. While there was a certain improvement in the terms of trade of Argentina in this period, it was far from sufficient to compensate the strong increase in costs. Indeed, in Chile the terms of trade worsened, so that the problem was accentuated rather than relieved. In Uruguay, the terms of trade remained virtually constant. What did rise in this period were capital inflows. To lose competitiveness by allowing the exchange rate to revalue on the basis of a transitory, once-and-for-all, increase in capital

That this loss in competitiveness was due to a lag in the exchange rate is a fact. And that, in turn, the maintenance of an increasingly overvalued exchange rate would not have been possible without the sudden and largely unsustainable surge in capital inflows is also true. Yet why didn't such capital inflows give rise to concomitant increases in capacity-augmenting investment, which would have increased competitiveness, rather than financing consumer imports, which weakened competitiveness? In short, why did the exchange rate lag and become increasingly overvalued?

The following hypotheses are pertinent in explaining why inflation exceeded devaluation plus international inflation by so large a margin and for so long:

1.   The law of one price pertains directly and exclusively to tradables, and in the three Southern Cone countries, these made up only half of GNP. It is

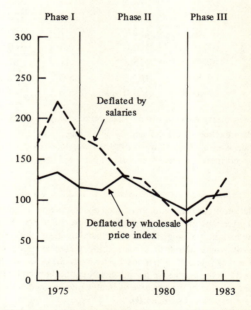

Figure 6.4   Chile: Real Effective Exchange Rates, 1974–1983 (1980 = 100)

inflows, which subsequently had to be repaid with interest, was, as pointed out earlier, an especially perverse form of Dutch disease. To maintain competitiveness, policymakers should have either controlled capital inflows or devalued the exchange rate (which itself would have probably slowed the inflows).

quite likely that many activities related to commerce, to import distribution, to the financial system, and to construction experienced an excessive demand during this period, which raised the prices of certain nontradables. Moreover, inasmuch as important disequilibria persisted in the economy, there was still some margin within which producers (especially industrialists) thought they could set their prices without losing much of their domestic market. Thus, to the extent to which the producers of tradables set prices according to their historic relation to the prices of nontradables, the rising prices of nontradables brought on by excess demand led to increases in the prices of tradables, even in the absence of excess demand.

2. Initially, an excess margin of protection seems to have existed for import substitutes; that is to say, some tariffs were partially redundant. Hence, reductions in tariffs did not in and of themselves bring about a proportional reduction in domestic prices.

3. High transport costs (especially for products with little value-added per unit volume) or high financial costs (especially imports with low turnover) provided natural protection, so that domestic prices did not equal international prices but rather equaled international prices plus the cost of transport plus financial costs and tariffs. The prices of many domestic goods could, therefore, vary widely within a broad range of prices, the lower

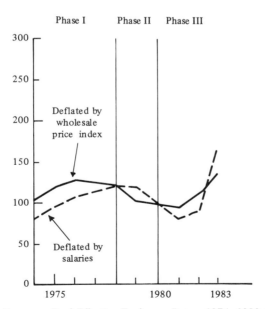

Figure 6.5   Uruguay: Real Effective Exchange Rates, 1974–1983 (1980 = 100)

limit of which was given by the price at which the goods could be imported from abroad, the upper by the price at which they could be exported.[23]

4. It is reasonable to expect, especially in the initial stages of trade liberalization, that small-scale importers set their price not equal to international prices plus tariffs (price equals cost) but rather equal to domestic prices or a bit less. In this way, price convergence took place, but *upward* to domestic prices and not downward to international prices.

5. In a later stage, many importers introduced differentiated products that heretofore had not existed in the domestic market (for example, whiskey). Although the imported product took away part of the domestic market from the local product (for example, the local alcoholic beverage), it did not affect the price of the local product in any significant fashion. In-

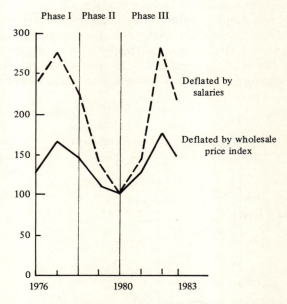

Figure 6.6   Argentina: Real Effective Exchange Rates, 1976–1983 (1980 = 100)

23. For example, a product that sells for $100 in New York could cost $110 in the Southern Cone, once transport costs are added. With a tariff of, say 18 percent, its domestic price would be $130. On the other hand, the selling price in New York of the same Southern Cone export could be no more than $100. This implies that its domestic price would be no more than $90. Indeed, it would have to cost even less if the United States placed a tariff on the good. Hence, the price of the domestic good could fluctuate between $90 and $130 without being exported nor facing the competition of comparable imported goods.

asmuch as the domestic product was but an imperfect substitute of the imported good, it would have required a very substantial reduction in its price to avoid the loss of important segments of the market, for the imported good was attractive because of its quality, or variety, or indeed its novelty, but certainly not solely because of its price.[24]

6.   Many goods were imported by producers of the domestic goods with which they competed. To the extent to which these producers controlled the domestic market, they controlled the price of both the domestic and the imported product, so that domestic prices continued to remain above international prices plus transport costs plus tariffs so long as there was insufficient competition in importing and distribution (Corbo, De Melo, and Tybout 1985). Competition was fully achieved solely in relatively standardized products with high turnover, such as television sets, radios, portable cassettes, and nonsophisticated clothes.

The above reasons explain why domestic prices remained above international prices plus tariffs plus transport costs for some time. Nevertheless, given enough time and enough competition, the convergence of domestic prices and international prices would eventually have had to take place. The point simply is that such an adjustment can be quite slow and costly. And it was precisely the slow downward adjustment in prices and inflation in the Southern Cone that made it increasingly likely that governments would find themselves forced to abandon their exchange policies.

Obviously, the loss in competitiveness that the large exchange-rate lag implied had very serious consequences on the balance of payments, inasmuch as exports were discouraged and imports encouraged. Nevertheless, the more pernicious effects of the lag in exchange rates were not noted or felt at once. One effect, the deficit in current account, could be financed for a while through the heavy affluence of external credit, because the cost of foreign credit was much less than that of domestic credit and, indeed, was negative when expressed in local currency during most of phase II precisely because of the lag in the exchange rate. Nevertheless, capital inflows of 5 and 10 percent of GNP were clearly not sustainable in the long run, for they bore no relation to the country's capacity to pay. Yet the increasing lag (revaluation) of the exchange rate could be maintained only as long as strong capital inflows continued, and these were clearly transitory. Hence the greater the lag in the exchange rate, the less confidence there was in the maintenance of the exchange-rate policy, thus requiring extraordinarily high domestic interest rates (3 or 4 percent real per month) to attract foreign capital and to impede capital flight.

---

24. Moreover, thanks to the strong inflow of capital and the consequently high aggregate demand, domestic output tended to rise notwithstanding its loss of market share.

PHASE III: FORCED ADJUSTMENT
TO EXTERNAL DISEQUILIBRIUM

Its Logic

A price-stabilization policy is never absolutely necessary, for inflation can be lived with if one so chooses. However, in the case of external disequilibria, adjustments need to be made whether a country wants to or not. In the particular instance of the Southern Cone countries, it would be fair to say that there was no deliberately chosen policy to adjust to external disequilibrium (except for the first few months of this phase), but rather adjustment was forced on them by events.

High domestic prices and high real domestic interest rates steadily sapped internal demand. In addition, firms could not indefinitely pay real interest rates of the order of 20 percent per year, while the economy grew at only modest rates, without risking insolvency and jeopardizing the entire domestic financial system. Because of firms' desire to postpone such a crisis, the demand for credit became increasingly inelastic. This, together with the waning confidence in the exchange-rate policy, raised real annual interest rates to 26 percent in Argentina, 40 percent in Uruguay, and 58 percent in Chile, the year before maxidevaluations were finally effected.

Thus it was finally recognized that a real depreciation was indispensable to correct the external disequilibrium. Discussions centered on the means: either raise the price (in domestic currency) of international goods to that of domestic goods via a devaluation or lower the price of domestic goods to that of international ones via a deflation, exchange policy standing pat.[25] The two approaches were perfectly equivalent in theory, yet in practice they entailed different risks.[26] Devaluation could set off inflationary expectations, giving rise to an

---

25. The issue was more complicated in Chile, for not only had the exchange rate been fixed as of 1979, but by law wages had to be readjusted 100 percent in accordance with past inflation. Thus a problem of two numeraires arose. Since a devaluation requires that real wages fall, at least in terms of tradables, in Chile devaluation would need be accompanied by deindexing wages as well, otherwise inflation would have had to increase greatly to effect the needed change in the price of tradables relative to wages. A debate arose regarding what loss real wages would need to suffer in relation to all goods, tradables and nontradables alike, as well as what loss would need to be incurred by profit margins, domestic financial services, and managerial incomes, all of which, like labor, were relatively nontraded factors.

26. During transition, there is asymmetry in theory as well. The option of automatic adjustment or deflation would be limited by the fact that nominal interest rates can never be negative, inasmuch as the mere holding of money pays a zero nominal rate of interest. This built-in inflexibility in the nominal rate of interest implies that deflation automatically increases real rates of interest, for nominal rates of interest are necessarily positive. So if domestic prices actually fell because of deflation, real interest rates and financial costs would rise. Hence, deflation would create its own brake in the form of real interest rates, which would tend to force part of the monetary contraction on output rather than on prices. More-

upward spiral in inflation rather than a once-and-for-all shift in relative prices. Deflation, on the other hand, ran a very high risk of severe recession, especially given the needed correction in relative prices (30 to 50 percent). It is difficult to imagine that the required deceleration in nominal aggregate demand could be absorbed immediately and completely by a sharp deceleration in domestic prices. Rather, it should have been expected that at least some of the deceleration in nominal aggregate demand would fall on production, leading to recession, whose severity would be in direct relation to the rigidity in inflationary expectations.

The Policy

Policymakers in all three countries preferred to bide their time, maintaining their exchange policy rather than devalue, for they feared that devaluation would lead to an explosive resurgence of inflation. And, after all, lower inflation was one of their principal achievements. Hence, they placed their hopes on what was called automatic adjustment; that is to say, that the deceleration in monetary growth would rapidly lower inflation to a rate less than that equal to the rate of devaluation plus international inflation. This option entailed simply maintaining the exchange policy. If the balance of payments went into deficit, monetary growth would automatically slow. Whether this would have an impact on output as well as on prices is another question. The hope was that the brunt if not the whole of the impact of the deceleration in nominal aggregate demand would fall on inflation rather than on production and in this way lead to a real devaluation.

The Results

The ensuing deceleration in nominal aggregate demand indeed lowered the rate of inflation in all three countries (tables 6.2, 6.3, 6.4). Nevertheless, the real devaluation achieved by this means (deflation) was not at all important (a few percentage points per semester)—much too slow to significantly correct the large exchange lag accumulated in the course of the foregoing years. In short, the bulk of the contraction in nominal aggregate demand fell not on prices, as desired, but on output. To be sure, imports were thus sharply and "automatically" curtailed, reducing current-account deficits but at the cost of severe recession in all three countries (tables 6.6, 6.7, and 6.8).

The severity of the recession increased the pressure by domestic producers on the governments to abandon the policy of minor (or zero) periodic and preannounced devaluations and to replace it with a massive devaluation to

over, this problem would be more serious the greater the absolute fall in prices required. I believe that Arellano and Cortázar (1982) were the first to note this asymmetry, and, to their further merit, to point it out before either option was adopted by Chile or Uruguay.

correct prices quickly. This pressure became irresistible once it became clear that the only way each government could maintain its exchange policy without an even more severe recession was if foreign capital continued to flow in in massive proportions. This, of course, was not to be the case. The very decline in internal output, the deceleration in exports, and the increasing signs of internal financial crises eroded what confidence there was left among foreign creditors as to the capacity of these countries to serve their foreign debt.

The die was then cast. Notwithstanding astronomical domestic interest rates the year before the maxidevaluations, inflows of capital were sharply curtailed: these fell 30 percent in Argentina in 1981, almost 80 percent in Chile in 1982 and over 100 percent in Uruguay in 1982 (tables 6.9, 6.10, 6.11). It is difficult to exaggerate the adverse impact that such a shift in net capital flows implied. Indeed, once interest and other factor payments were deducted from net capital flows, the three countries, instead of receiving resources from the rest of the world as in the past—and as befits developing countries—became net exporters of resources in the year they were forced to devalue (see tables). The variation in net resources transferred from the year before to the year of the

Table 6.6.   Chile: Indicators of External Accounts, Historic and Neoconservative Periods

| Period | Annual Growth Rate | | | Tradables as Ratio of GNP | Foreign Debt as Ratio of Exports | Current-Account Deficit as Ratio of Exports |
	Value of Exports	Volume of Exports	Terms of Trade			
Historic						
1950–70	7.7	3.0	67.0			
1971–73	5.4	1.8	81.0	43.3	2.7	29.0
Neoconservative						
1974	59.0	18.0	88.0	44.4	1.9	13.0
1975	−21.0	9.0	55.0	41.7	2.6	27.0
1976	31.0	19.0	59.0	42.7	1.9	−5.0
1977	8.0	7.0	54.0	42.4	2.0	22.0
1978	13.0	8.0	49.0	41.4	2.3	38.0
1979	58.0	24.0	55.0	40.9	1.8	26.0
1980	29.0	15.0	52.0	40.1	1.9	34.0
1981	−8.0	1.0	45.0	40.0	2.8	88.0
1982	−9.0	9.0	40.0	40.1	3.7	49.0
1983[a]	4.0	0.0	41.0	41.4	3.8	23.0

Source: CEPAL, on the basis of official data.

[a]Preliminary figures.

maxidevaluation was the equivalent of a deterioration in the terms of trade of 25 percent in Argentina, 40 percent in Uruguay, and over 50 percent in Chile (see tables). In 1981, for example, Chile imported 67 percent more than the amount brought in by its export earnings because of the positive effect of the net transfer of resources; but in 1982, because the net transfer of resources was negative, Chile imported only 78 percent of the value of its export earnings (figures 6.7; figures 6.8 and 6.9 show similar instances in Uruguay and Argentina). Such was the impact of the shift in capital flows on the net transfer of resources.

Not only was there no longer any confidence in the sustainability of the exchange policy but, once capital flows were curtailed, resources (reserves) had finally been run down to finance the deflation. Given the lag in the exchange rate, the unprecedented reduction in capital flows, and the severe internal recession and accompanying domestic financial crises, there was no alternative other than to abandon the policy of automatic adjustment with a preannounced exchange rate and to proceed to a massive devaluation.

Massive devaluations were followed by sharp increases in the rate of inflation in all three countries. Nevertheless, the intensity of such inflation was considerably less than the devaluation, so that competitiveness tended to be

Table 6.7.   Uruguay: Indicators of External Accounts, Historic and Neoconservative Periods

| Period | Annual Growth Rate | | | | | |
	Value of Exports	Volume of Exports	Terms of Trade	Tradables as Ratio of GNP	Foreign Debt as Ratio of GNP	Current-Account Deficit as Ratio of Exports
Historic						
1950–70	−0.4	0.0	104.0			
1971–74	15.0	−0.3	115.0	35.3	2.1	10.0
Neoconservative						
1975	−23.0	−11.0	80.0	34.9	1.9	36.0
1976	32.0	32.0	79.0	34.0	1.6	12.0
1977	43.0	41.0	85.0	35.5	1.6	21.0
1978	14.0	6.0	89.0	34.1	1.4	15.0
1979	23.0	−3.0	97.0	32.1	1.4	30.0
1980	8.0	−10.0	95.0	33.5	1.4	47.0
1981	10.0	15.0	89.0	31.2	1.8	28.0
1982	−17.0	−6.0	88.0	29.7	2.8	15.0
1983[a]	3.0	11.0	88.0	29.7	3.2	7.0

Source: CEPAL, on the basis of official data.

[a]Preliminary figures.

Table 6.8.   Argentina: Indicators of External Accounts, Historic and Neoconservative Periods

Period	Annual Growth Rate		Terms of Trade	Tradables as Ratio of GNP	Foreign Debt as Ratio of GNP	Current-Account Deficit as Ratio of Exports
	Value of Exports	Volume of Exports				
Historic						
1950–70	2.1	2.6	109.0			
1971–75	10.7	−3.2	119.0	43.6	1.9	−9.0
Neoconservative						
1976	32.0	32.0	93.0	42.9	1.8	−14.0
1977	43.0	41.0	89.0	42.9	1.5	−17.0
1978	14.0	6.0	90.0	41.9	1.7	−25.0
1979	23.0	−3.0	98.0	42.3	2.1	6.0
1980	8.0	−10.0	110.0	40.2	2.8	48.0
1981	10.0	15.0	100.0	38.9	3.3	43.0
1982	−17.0	−6.0	89.0	40.9	4.8	28.0
1983[a]	3.0	11.0	86.0	42.3	4.9	21.0

Source: CEPAL, on the basis of official data.
[a]Preliminary figures.

Table 6.9.   Chile: Capital Transfers and Their Impact on the Economy, 1980–1983

Item	1980	1981	1982	1983[a]
Net capital inflows (millions of U.S. dollars)	3,341	4,941	1,032	595
Interest and other factor payments (millions of U.S. dollars)	1,028	1,595	2,035	1,801
Net transfer (capital inflows minus factor payments; millions of U.S. dollars)	2,313	3,345	−1,003	−1,206
Net transfer as share of exports (percent)	38.8	66.8	−21.6	−26.1
Variation in terms of trade (percent)	−5.0	−14.0	−11.0	2.3
Added importing capacity as result of improved terms of trade and net transfer (percent)	33.8	52.8	−32.6	23.3
Growth in volume of imports (percent)	13.4	8.0	−34.8	−14.9
Growth of GNP (percent)	8.0	5.7	−14.3	−0.8

Source: CEPAL, on the basis of official data.
[a]Preliminary figures.

Table 6.10.   Uruguay: Capital Transfers and Their Impact on the Economy, 1980–1983

Item	1980	1981	1982	1983[a]
Net capital inflows (millions of U.S. dollars)	811	494	−182	−11
Interest and other factor payments (millions of U.S. dollars)	100	74	197	288
Net transfer (capital inflows minus factor payments; millions of U.S. dollars)	711	420	−379	−299
Net transfer as share of exports (percent)	46.6	24.7	−24.7	−21.2
Variation in terms of trade (percent)	−2.0	−6.0	−1.8	−10.3
Added importing capacity as result of improved terms of trade and net transfer (percent)	44.6	18.7	−26.5	−31.5
Growth in volume of imports (percent)	16.1	−10.6	−19.4	−25.8
Growth of GNP (percent)	6.0	1.9	−9.7	−4.7

Source: CEPAL, on the basis of official data.
[a]Preliminary figures.

Table 6.11.   Argentina: Capital Transfers and Their Impact on the Economy, 1980–1983

Item	1980	1981	1982	1983[a]
Net capital inflows (millions of U.S. dollars)	2,176	1,520	1,686	−13
Interest and other factor payments (millions of U.S. dollars)	1,607	3,932	5,054	5,922
Net transfer (capital inflows minus factor payments; millions of U.S. dollars)	569	−2,412	−3,368	−5,935
Net transfer as share of exports (percent)	5.8	−22.2	−36.7	−63.9
Variation in terms of trade (percent)	12.0	−9.0	−11.0	−2.6
Added importing capacity as result of improved terms of trade and net transfer (percent)	17.8	−31.2	−47.7	−66.5
Growth in volume of imports (percent)	40.0	−12.0	−44.0	−2.2
Growth of GNP (percent)	1.1	−6.2	−5.1	3.1

Source: CEPAL, on the basis of official data.
[a]Preliminary figures.

restored and the real exchange rate experienced sharp improvement (table 6.5).[27] To be sure, thanks to the recession, the quantum of imports fell so sharply that by 1983 the deficit in current account in all three countries was sharply reduced (in Chile, from almost 90 percent of the value of exports in 1981 to just slightly above 25 percent in 1983; in Uruguay, from almost 50

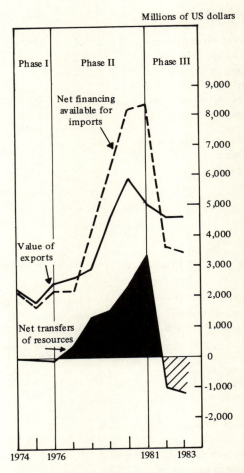

Figure 6.7   Chile: Value of Exports, Net Transfers of Resources, and Net Financing Available for Imports, 1974–1983

27. I stress this point because many other observers, notwithstanding their recognition that there was an important lag in the exchange rate that needed correction, argued that a devaluation would be ineffective, believing it would very rapidly be wiped out by a similar rise in the rate of inflation. To be sure, a devaluation *could* set off a new inflationary spiral. Yet this need be so only if the starting point was one already in equilibrium, for then any attempt to

percent in 1980 to 4 percent in 1983; and in Argentina, from well over 40 percent in 1980 and 1981 to somewhat over 25 percent in 1983). Moreover, all three countries moved from severe deficits in their balance of trade in 1980 and

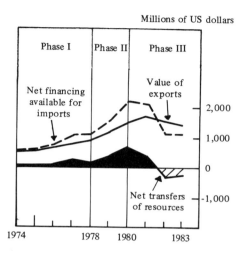

Figure 6.8   Uruguay: Value of Exports, Net Transfers of Resources, and Net Financing Available for Imports, 1974–1983

improve the trade balance via devaluation would soon be limited by a fully utilized productive capacity, thus leading to a price rise, and a rapid elimination of any balance-of-trade improvement. However, deflation would prove similarly useless if starting from equilibrium, for lower prices would raise foreign and domestic demand, and prices would rise, wiping out the deflation and the transitory gains in competitiveness and in the balance of trade. However, either a devaluation of the exchange rate or deflation can be effective if the starting point is in *disequilibrium*, in which domestic prices are above international ones, for the resolution of this disequilibrium requires a *real* depreciation. Whether this is best achieved by raising the prices of international goods to those of comparable domestic ones (devaluation) or lowering the prices of domestic goods to international levels (deflation) is another matter. Either way is theoretically feasible, if the starting point is in disequilibrium. Thus this whole debate was rather bizarre, for it was premised on a continuing equilibrium, whereas a lag in the exchange rate implied precisely the contrary; namely that domestic prices were above international, and equilibrium, levels. Similarly, despite the fact that no special efforts were made to defend wages, real effective devaluation was achieved. Between 1980 and 1981, the real effective exchange rate rose 63 percent in Argentina, whereas real wages fell "only" 20 percent; between 1981 and 1983, Chile showed a 24 percent improvement in competitiveness versus an 11 percent decline in real wages; and in the same period, Uruguay's competitiveness showed a 43 percent improvement versus a 21 percent decline in real wages (table 6.5). Moreover, the improvement in the exchange rate is far greater if the devaluation is deflated by the rise in consumer prices or wages. This lends further credence to the argument (generally from proponents of the devaluation) that there was room to reduce profit margins, costs of financial services, and managerial returns, so that wages need not assume the bulk of the loss.

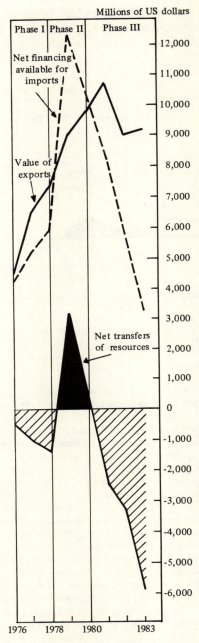

Figure 6.9   Argentina: Value of Exports, Net Transfers of Resources, and Net Financing Available for Imports, 1976–1983

1981 to important trade surpluses in 1983. Once again, these improvements were almost exclusively based on the extraordinarily sharp reduction in the quantum of imports during the ensuing recessions (55 percent in Argentina in 1981 and 1982; 50 and 40 percent, respectively, in Chile and Uruguay in 1982 and 1983). A recession is, of course, an extraordinarily rapid method of lowering imports, but it does so at the cost of a severe contraction in output. Consequently, in the two or three years of phase III, output fell well over 10 percent in the Southern Cone countries (as opposed to 4 percent in the rest of Latin America), and unemployment sharply increased.

Finally, notwithstanding the fact that inflows of foreign capital were sharply curtailed in these years, the level of foreign debt was still extraordinarily high by the end of 1983. The ratio of foreign debt to the value of all exports of goods and services ranged from 3.2 to 1 in Uruguay to 4.9 to 1 in Argentina, comparing quite unfavorably with 2.6 to 1 for the rest of Latin America. To be sure, the Southern Cone countries were among the most highly indebted countries of Latin America when the neoconservative experiences began, which makes it all the more remarkable that they did not slow their indebtedness in the course of the eight to ten years of considerably strong export growth and seeming allegiance to the principles of strict financial discipline. That they should be among the most indebted countries of the region in 1983 certainly does not speak well of their policies of economic and financial liberalization.

Financial liberalization, especially, seems to have heightened rather than reduced their dependence on foreign savings and consequently made them more vulnerable to swings in the international economy, for now they had to be prepared to offset unexpected movements in capital accounts as well as in their terms of trade. If their debt had been more modest, financial liberalization might have given them the freedom to cope with the external disequilibrium they faced in later years. But financial liberalization in the face of high debt and major domestic disequilibria (evidenced by unduly high interest rates) served to accentuate rather than attenuate unexpected movements in their external accounts. Consequently, rather than gaining degrees of freedom, these countries lost them. Adjustment was thus largely forced upon them, rather than being deliberately chosen. The overindebtedness of phase II thus eventually led to the capital reversals and overadjustment of phase III.

A CRITICAL ASSESSMENT

The stabilization and adjustment programs pursued by the neoconservatives in the Southern Cone had important costs: sharp recession and reduction in real wages. The questions naturally arise whether, first, such costs in reduced output could have been avoided and, second, if not avoidable, could their burden have been more equitably shared?

These questions can be addressed at two levels. The first, and in a sense the easier, is whether in theory such costs need be paid; the second, and subtler, is whether in practice—given the initial conditions, the multiplicity of problems, and the state of macroeconomic knowledge—better alternatives were known and available and not taken. To the extent that the reader's interest, as mine, lies principally in lessons to be drawn for the future and not simply in an economic history of Southern Cone neoconservative economies, then the theoretical question is the more interesting. Nevertheless, I will pursue both answers, though emphasizing the theoretical approach.

When speaking of costs, one must sharply distinguish two types of stabilization policies: those that are intended principally to overcome internal disequilibria (inflation or recession) and those designed to overcome external disequilibria (deficits in the balance of payments). The most important distinction between the two is that the former need not be faced—inflation can be lived with indefinitely—whereas the latter cannot be put off. The balance of payments is a binding restriction rather like a budget restraint. Adjustment to it is, therefore, unavoidable.

The Costs of Stabilization Policies

Precisely because inflation can be lived with, depending solely on the country's tolerance, there is no reason, at least in theory, why an anti-inflationary stabilization policy need reduce output. To be sure, recession is all too often the unwanted result of an anti-inflationary stabilization policy, but it is not inevitable. On the contrary, to the extent that inflation is "too much money chasing too few goods," it is far from obvious why reducing inflation should entail producing fewer goods.

Recession would thus seem to be a failure of policy design or implementation. For in the ultimate analysis, inflation "merely" requires simultaneously decelerating by like amounts (or as close to it as possible) the growth in the nominal values of the principal variables in the economy (exchange rate, interest rate, wages, and so on). But it requires neither major (real) changes in the values of most variables nor reductions in output or its rate of growth.

To be sure, it is both theoretically and empirically necessary that a decline in the rate of inflation be accompanied, sooner or later, by a deceleration in monetary growth and a reduction in the fiscal deficit. But a stabilization policy will be successful only to the extent to which the remaining principal variables—prices, wages, exchange rates, interest rates—decelerate at the same time. Theoretically, the mere announcement of the deceleration in the inflation rate could be enough to assure that the remaining variables adjust instantly and in this way harmonize their behavior with the programmed monetary and fiscal policy and the projected inflationary goal. In practice, however, inflationary expectations do not adjust instantaneously. For one thing, the public normally is rather skeptical. It wants to see results first, before believing that inflation is going to fall as fast as the government projects. Because of this inertia in the adjustment of expectations, the level of prices normally remains above the level consistent with the economic policy in being—thus leading to recession.

Moreover, it is often the case (and was the case in the neoconservative experiences) that in addition to wanting to lower inflation, policy also aims at correcting distorted relative prices—the exchange rate, the prices of public services, and the prices of agricultural products in relation to industrial goods. Unfortunately, private agents often view an increase in these heretofore repressed prices as an indicator of probable inflation and not simply the expression of a needed corrective adjustment in relative prices. Thus their inflationary expectations exceed the inflationary goal implicit in economic policy, giving rise to a demand-deficient recession.

Hence while it is certainly true that to reduce inflation money supply must be controlled and the fiscal deficit reduced, no stabilization policy worth the name can be based on these instruments alone if it wishes to avoid recession. Stabilization policy must harmonize, or guide, or control, though certainly not repress, the movements of *all* the principal economic variables (prices, wages, exchange rate, interest rate, and so on) in such a way that they are compatible with the rate of inflation implicit in the monetary and fiscal policy being programmed. If some variables adjust more rapidly than others, a recession will ensue, with serious distributive consequences (at the expense of those variables that adjusted their prices downward more rapidly). Thus traditional monetarist stabilization programs failed in countries with persistent inflation (in the 1950s in Latin America and later the Southern Cone) because they controlled monetary expansion and the fiscal deficit but failed to affect expectations. Hence the deceleration in aggregate nominal demand fell on output and not just on prices.

Southern Cone neoconservatives in the 1970s were aware of the problems of expectations but, as noted earlier, at first identified this principally with the labor market. They chose wage controls along with traditional restrictive monetary and fiscal policies. Had all other variables (interest rates and the price of goods) quickly fallen into line, their stabilization program would have succeeded, with no fall in output, employment or wages. Their fatal error was in neglecting producers' inflationary expectations, supposing that competition would quickly bring these into line. The fact is that competition proved too weak to do this—especially in a situation of multiple disequilibria (prices just having been freed and relative prices having suffered important changes). Rather, the uncontrolled inflationary expectations of producers led to overblown prices and recession.

Could this have been avoided? Could distorted or repressed prices not have been freed gradually and guided to equilibrium? Contrariwise, if gradualism seemed inappropriate for such high inflations, might it not have been worthwhile to have considered a shock stabilization program, along the lines of that followed in postwar Germany, and including monetary reform to curb expectations all along the line? We will never know whether such alternatives (gradual but simultaneous deindexing of wages, prices, and interest rates along with restrictive monetary and fiscal policies; or a shock program with monetary reform) would have been more successful. What can be said is that these alternatives focus on controlling expectations all along the line, and not exclusively in the labor market (phase I) or the exchange market (phase II), and that they were under discussion at the time.[28]

Finally, even if recessions were unavoidable, there certainly is no theoretical reason why their costs should have been distributed so unequally—and *systematically*—against labor. To be sure, not all inflation is inertial (or expectations driven); at times wages or other relative prices do get out of line, and ending inflation then does require correcting this relative price, implying a change in income distribution. But there is no theoretical reason for this to have been systematically at the expense of wages. Rather, the distributive costs fell so sharply on labor because of the specific policy measures chosen, especially during phase I: freeing prices while controlling wages. Failures in achieving the targeted inflationary goals thus led to overblown prices, unemployment, and losses in real wages.

The Costs of Adjustment Programs

Whereas stabilization programs need have no cost, adjustment policies have an unavoidable cost. Adjustment to an external disequilibrium requires that the quantum of goods available to the country (domestic expenditure) decline in order to be able to meet its foreign commitments. This is unavoidable. What is avoidable (since it is unnecessary for reducing expenditure, though unfortunately it often accompanies adjustment processes) is a decline in output. The optimum adjustment would maintain the rate of growth of output but reorient it from domestic to foreign usage. Exports would increase and imports would decline, the latter being substituted, as needed, by domestic production. And in

---

28. In Chile, monetary reform was being openly considered as part of a shock stabilization program by opposition economists before Allende's fall. Balassa (1984) also reports that he suggested such a program in a confidential memo to Chilean authorities in 1974. A critique of overblown prices in Chile (Ramos 1973) argued the need for guiding the prices of goods to equilibrium to avoid a recession and for not relying simply on market forces. (While I therefore correctly predicted a recession if policies were not changed, in fairness to the truth, I also thought inflation would come down much faster because of that same recession. So this book has benefited from hindsight. Indeed, the coexistence of a strong recession and triple-digit inflation started me out on a search that has ended with this book.) Finally, Southern Cone neoconservatives might have followed the Brazilian stabilization program of the mid-sixties, which was far less costly but which sacrificed ideological purity by using interventionist mechanisms for a time (see Foxley 1980).

the course of time, the output of tradables would expand in relation to nontrada-bles. Thus while adjustment inevitably implies a slower growth or a worsening of the standard of living, it does not require a decline in output. By this standard, Southern Cone adjustment was unduly costly. The decline in output was around 10 percent in the first two years after maxidevaluations, well in excess of the 4 percent fall in output brought on by adjustment programs in the rest of Latin America.

Why were Southern Cone adjustment programs so costly? In a word, because they were shock programs. Unlike a price-stabilization program, in which a shock policy may be efficient, especially in dealing with hyperinfla-tion, there is no efficient shock adjustment to an external disequilibrium, for efficient adjustment implies changes in real, not simply nominal, values. Thus gradualism is essential: efficient adjustment requires not just that the output of nontradables decline, which can be done quickly, but that the output of trada-bles rise, and this is necessarily a slow process; not just that the volume of imports be reduced, which can be as fast as desired, but that exports and import substitutes increase, and this is again necessarily a much slower process.

Given the magnitude of the disequilibrium by phase III and the brief time in which to close it, Southern Cone adjustment was thus anything but efficient. It was based almost exclusively on expenditure reduction (controlling demand and so slowing output, which can be speedy) rather than on "expenditure switching" (shifting supply and production, which is necessarily slow). This, of course, is the worst of all possible adjustments. For in phase II, neoconser-vative policymakers violated the basic principle of recession-minimizing ad-justment; namely, of *equalizing the costs on the margin of saving or generating foreign exchange by expenditure-switching and expenditure-reducing pol-icies.*[29] Their underemphasis of switching policies, especially of transitory,

---

29. To give more meat to this seemingly innocuous truth, I suggest three clear implica-tions for alternative adjustment programs: (1) Because expenditure-reducing policies act more rapidly than expenditure-switching policies, one would be justified in pursuing policies of super switching, both to discourage imports and to encourage exports. Because they would be transitory, these policies (additional tariffs and additional export-promotion subsidies) would be selective, focusing on those goods with the highest short-run price elasticity. (2) A more efficient adjustment program would also imply equalizing the incentives (or costs) of saving foreign exchange via import substitution and of generating it via export promotion. Given the incentive structure prevailing in the Southern Cone, especially in Argentina and Uruguay (high tariffs with few export-promotion subsidies), it would presumably have been easier to acquire additional foreign exchange through greater export promotion than through further import substitution (which, in all likelihood, had been pushed close to the limit of diminishing marginal returns in preneoconservative days). (3) Since resources released from the production of nontradables via expenditure reduction are not as rapidly absorbed in the production of tradables, the reduction of expenditures in nontradables (public works and housing, especially) could be limited to the speed at which the expansion of tradables took place. This is in contradistinction to the orthodox adjustment programs effected by neoconser-

selective super switching, was no doubt a reflection of their legitimate preference for long-term policies and their consequent disdain of selective or discretionary policies (even when reserved for the short run, as here, to deal with
massive disequilibria).

In the first two years of their adjustment programs, the approximate cost
for the three countries to improve their trade balance by sixteen billion dollars
(accumulated) was thirty-five-billion dollars in output.[30] In short, by relying
too heavily on expenditure-reducing policies, Southern Cone adjustment programs sacrificed $2.20 of output to save $1 of foreign exchange. A costly form
of adjustment, indeed.

CONCLUSIONS

The anti-inflationary stabilization programs in the Southern Cone followed two
approaches, each of which focused on, and controlled, some (but not all) of the
principal economic variables of the economy. During the first phase, efforts
were centered on direct control of the money supply and wages. Such controls
together with natural market forces were expected to rapidly bring internal
prices into line with the programmed inflationary goal. During the second
phase, efforts centered on controlling the movements of the exchange rate, and
by this means decelerate the growth of prices. In both cases, inflation was
reduced substantially. Nevertheless, the cost was high, inasmuch as the free
variable, prices, adjusted far more slowly than the controlled variables, thus
generating important disequilibria.

In the first phase, the principal disequilibrium emerged in the market of
goods. Prices (freed) shot up far more than wages (controlled), thus avoiding
neoclassical unemployment but giving rise to a severe, neo-Keynesian demand-
deficient recession in Chile and to stagnation in Argentina. Only Uruguay was
spared, thanks to its high public investment and to growth in external demand.

---

vatives, in which nontradables were cut back sharply, whether or not the resources so released
were absorbed by an expansion of tradables. For example, in the first years of adjustment in
the three countries, the production of nontradables fell sharply—construction alone fell 30
percent—with no absorption by tradables of the factors released (indeed, the output of
tradables fell more than 10 percent). The reason for this is that the opportunity cost of
construction and like expenditures is quite low in adjustment-program transitions—on the
order of a four-dollar sacrifice in output to a one-dollar gain in foreign exchange (that is, the
reciprocal of the marginal propensity to import).

30. The benefits are assumed to be the improvement in the trade balance during each of
the first two years of the adjustment program in relation to the base year (this increased some
$5.5 billion in the three countries during their first year of adjustment and $10 billion in the
second year, thus giving a total accumulated savings or generation of foreign exchange of
about $16 billion in the two years). The cost is assumed to equal the 3.5-percent-a-year growth
that failed to materialize plus the reduction in output that did take place (equaling $35 billion
for the two years after the maxidevaluations).

Whether a stabilization-policy-induced recession is avoidable or not, there certainly is no reason why this loss must be distributed unequally. Yet the belt tightening during phase I was quite uneven in all three countries. Income was sharply redistributed against wage earners, as can be seen by the very sharp fall in real wages (much sharper than the decline in the growth of national income) and, in the case of Chile, was further accentuated by an unprecedented increase in the unemployment rate, leaving it two to three times above historic rates. The uneven distributive cost of the stabilization policy was the result of the specific policy instruments applied during phase I—that is, the policy of allowing inflationary expectations to operate freely in the goods market while controlling wages and pursuing a tight monetary policy. Such expectations led producers to set prices well above that consistent with macroeconomic policy. In this way, prices overshot equilibrium and proved to be far above what wage costs alone would have led them to be.

In the second phase, the principal disequilibrium emerged in the market for foreign exchange, since domestic inflation declined much more slowly than the rate of devaluation. This lag in the exchange rate was in turn the result of the slow convergence of domestic prices and interest rates to international ones at a rate well below that which might have been expected had the law of one price been effective. Contrary to what was expected, the initial tendency was for prices of goods and interest rates on international loans to converge to domestic prices and interest rates and not to their long-run or international values (their cost). In short, initial convergence was not downward toward international prices and costs but upward toward domestic ones.

The lag in the exchange rate during phase II finally led to a serious disequilibrium in the balance of payments, eventually giving way to a sharp recession. Initially, recessionary symptoms were hidden by the unusually strong inflows of foreign capital, which expanded demand more than enough to offset the loss in competitiveness. The strong but unsustainable surge in capital inflows thus made possible the prolonged maintenance of an overvalued exchange rate; but once such flows slowed, a sharp recession proved inevitable. The failure of domestic prices to decelerate at a rhythm similar to the rate of devaluation, and the dependence of the exchange-rate policy on unsustainable levels of capital inflows, rendered ever less believable the continuation of the exchange policy and the stabilization program based on it. Such a growing lack of confidence finally made the abandonment of the exchange policy inevitable. Massive devaluations became necessary in order to close the huge gap between domestic and foreign prices.

In any case, while the second phase lasted—that is to say, up until the maxidevaluations—the distribution of income did begin to recover the loss incurred (fully in Chile, partially in Argentina and Uruguay). Such an improvement took place because employment (in Chile and Uruguay) and real wages (in Argentina and Chile) tended to rise. Real wages recovered sharply in Chile, since they were readjusted in accordance with past inflation, while current inflation was rapidly decelerating.

Capital inflows proved to be highly procyclical. During the period of programmed devaluations, capital inflows were sufficiently strong so as to minimize, indeed to more than compensate, the negative effects on output of a lag in the exchange rate, and so to maintain strong aggregate demand. Inversely, however, once doubts were created as to the country's capacity to service its debt, capital inflows diminished sharply, forcing exceptionally rapid and strong adjustment to external disequilibria. Thus not only was there overindebtedness (excessive capital inflows) in phase II, as can be seen by the extraordinarily high level of the ratio of debt to exports in all three countries, but there was overadjustment in phase III. For in this last phase, all three countries were forced to adjust their economies not only to continuing external disequilibria but to the procyclical reduction in capital inflows. Although it would normally be desirable to draw on additional capital inflows to soften and prolong the adjustment experience, so that adjustment could take place via an expansion of tradables and not simply via a reduction of output, the three Southern Cone countries were so heavily in debt that capital flows ceased to be a variable they could draw on. Rather, it became a variable to which they were forced to adjust.

A devaluation (that is to say, a switching policy) taken earlier or of greater magnitude might have succeeded in reducing imports at a lower cost in output. By the time devaluation was forced upon these countries, the large disequilibrium and the slowed capital inflows meant that the devaluation was less effective (and given the briefer time available, much less effective) than it might otherwise have been. Even then, recession might have been less acute had these countries, in anticipation of the relative sluggishness with which output initially responds to devaluation, pursued a temporary super switching policy on selective price-elastic products. Super switching would have equalized on the margin the costs of expenditure-reducing and expenditure-switching policies. In fact, the countries relied too heavily on expenditure reduction, sacrificing $2.20 of output for each $1 of foreign exchange saved.

In short, the neoconservative stabilization and adjustment programs in the Southern Cone proved to be very costly and inequitable. What is worse, much of this was avoidable had neoconservatives not been so strongly enamored of any number of questionable assumptions: that the key rigidity in the economy was in the labor market; that competition was strong enough to assure rapid convergence to equilibrium; that discretionary policies are to be avoided under almost any circumstances and at almost any cost; and, more generally, that market clearance is rapidly achieved via price adjustment, whereas output adjustment is a relatively exceptional and transitory phenomenon.

7

Trade Liberalization

One of the main neoconservative criticisms of the development model followed by the Southern Cone countries since the 1930s was directed at their strategy of actively promoting industrialization based on import substitution (or inward-oriented growth).

LOGIC AND COSTS OF PAST STRATEGY

This strategy emerged as a practical response to the Great Depression, and only later did it acquire its intellectual grounding.[1] The collapse of the prices and volume of exports forced these countries to intervene heavily in their external sector, devaluing strongly in addition to imposing high tariffs and quantitative controls on imports. These policies not only helped overcome the Great Depression but changed the role of the industrial sector from a passive one, dependent on the growth of exports, to an active one—the main dynamic sector of the economy (see Díaz-Alejandro 1980). The difficulty of importing manufactured goods from industrial countries during the Second World War provided a new impetus to industrialization based on import substitution. Thus the industrial sector became a substantial part of the economy, and exports came to be a relatively low proportion of product.

Once the war was over, the existence of an important industrial sector encouraged the transformation of quantitative import controls and tariffs into deliberate development policy instruments. Nevertheless, the intellectually plausible position on behalf of active industrial promotion degenerated in many cases into the indiscriminate promotion of all forms of manufacturing: "to each activity the protection it needed" to produce domestically, without taking into

---

1. Among the earliest formulations and rationales for industrialization based on import substitution in Latin America is the classic 1950 ECLA study, produced under the hand of Raul Prebisch. An excellent summary of the issues can be found in Hirschman 1968.

account the costs (usually implicit and indirect) to the community as a whole.[2]

Such a social evaluation of tariff protection was in fact rarely carried out. Rather, tariffs tended to be justified on the grounds that the protected activity created jobs and saved foreign exchange. This argument, though appealing at first sight, is, on reflection, spurious, since all activities create jobs and save foreign exchange in one way or another. The real issue, of course, is whether the protected activity creates more jobs or saves more foreign exchange per unit of investment than other activities. Yet this issue was rarely addressed in the Southern Cone.

This disregard of opportunity costs was the great deficiency in indiscriminate protection. And that is why its benefits became increasingly dubious as industrialization moved from the stage of easy substitution of final-consumption goods to stages requiring mass-production techniques, heavy doses of capital per unit of labor, or changing and sophisticated technologies.

The costs of indiscriminate protection were neither direct nor immediately perceptible, yet they were quite real and significant. The resources transferred to protected sectors ultimately came from the export sector, whose potential dynamism, especially in the case of nontraditional exports, was thereby frustrated. To the extent such protection succeeded in reducing the demand for imports, it was possible to balance external accounts with a low exchange rate (fewer pesos per dollar). The combination of a high tariff with a low exchange rate was thus the equivalent of a higher exchange rate combined with a tax on exports. Hence, though the transfer mechanism was indirect, in the final analysis, the cost of indiscriminate protection was shouldered by the export sector in the form of this implicit tax (high industrial tariffs and a low exchange rate).

This "tax" might have made sense had it been limited to those goods based on intensive use of the Southern Cone's natural resources (copper, beef, wool, and wheat) or had its purpose been to affect the international price of these goods. For in that case it either would have ceased to pay a quasi rent to the traditional sector or it would have improved the country's terms of trade. But the policy's cost fell on all exports and thus was especially detrimental to nontraditional exports (those not based on a land-derived or natural-resource-derived rent). These nontraditional exports tended to be industrial exports, whose supply, moreover, was likely to be more elastic to price.

---

2. The close relation between industrialization and development is not enough to justify the active promotion of industrialization, since this can be the effect or concomitant, more than the cause, of development. Its promotion can only be justified if there are factors that induce the market to undervalue its benefits. For example, Prebisch (1950) pointed out that there was a secular tendency toward the deterioration of the terms of trade of primary goods with respect to industrial goods. If this is so, future comparative advantage would shift toward manufacturing activities, justifying a protective tariff that would make that future advantage current. In a similar vein, Lewis (1954) argued that, due to underemployment, rural labor was cheaper than urban labor, even though both had the same social cost. Hence, protection in favor of manufacturing was justified to compensate this artificially higher cost of labor for industry, which made manufacturing seem less profitable than that it really was.

To be sure, tariff protection can be justified if it brings social benefits not adequately produced by the market: higher employment (if the market wage is greater than labor's opportunity cost) or externalities associated with the technological dynamism of a sector (like the manufacturing sector and its important linkages to the rest of the economy). Protection for these reasons, however, need not be high. For example, an urban wage 50 percent higher than the social value (or opportunity cost) of labor would justify an industrial tariff of approximately 20 percent. Since labor typically represents less than one-third of costs, the 50 percent over-pricing of urban labor affects only 33 percent of the final cost; in short, it raises product price by less than 20 percent.[3] Moreover, since other imperfections tend to favor industry over agriculture—for example, subsidized credit generally goes to industry—even this level of protection would have to be revised downward.

In any case, it is beyond question that the tariff structure in the Southern Cone in the preneoconservative period obeyed no such redeeming logic. Rather, tariff levels and differentiation seem to have corresponded to the "needs" of each sector and to its power to pressure the government on its behalf. The average level of effective protection was quite high, with huge sectoral dispersion, that included rates of up to 1,300 percent in Argentina, 740 percent in Chile, and 609 percent in Uruguay (table 7.1). The differentiation was dissimilar among countries and was subject to no conceivable principle of social justification. Many activities with low nominal protection but that used highly protected inputs ended up with negative effective protection: for example, clothing in Chile, where, because of protection, domestic textile prices were much higher than international prices (see table). For this reason as well, agriculture and many manufactures intensive in labor, ended up with protection that was negative or below average, thus transferring resources to capital-intensive sectors that made little use of economies of scale, and that were, thus less efficient.[4] It is not strange then that the only activities capable of exporting under such conditions were a few traditional, rent-generating sectors engaged in primary production and highly intensive in an abundant natural resource (copper, beef, wheat, or wool).

In short, it is probable that the deliberate policy of import substitution in the thirties helped the Southern Cone countries come out of the Great Depression more quickly and helped them widen their industrial base. Nevertheless, it is also probable that, because they kept looking inward, toward their relatively

---

3. The more labor intensive the activity, the higher the tariff should be. Nevertheless, studies suggest that effective protection was higher, the more capital intensive the sector (See Nogués 1982 and Corbo and Meller 1977.

4. For example, Nogués (1982) found that in Argentina effective protection was negative in labor-intensive exportables; however, less labor-intense industries whose products competed with products from developed countries were favored by strong effective protection. Similar results were found for the Chilean industrial sector by Corbo and Meller 1977. Table 7.1 shows that effective protection was low in the agricultural sector, normally much more unskilled-labor intensive than manufacturing.

small, narrow, and static domestic markets, they failed to take advantage of the great boom in world trade in the postwar period. So instead of specializing and eventually exporting manufactures, as other countries did, they looked toward their own markets, overdiversifying and therefore spreading themselves too thin, while their exports continued to be those few rent-generating activities on which their comparative advantage had been traditionally based.[5]

THE NEOCONSERVATIVE DIAGNOSIS

The foregoing diagnosis, it is fair to say, was shared by economists of various persuasions in the Southern Cone. All agreed that the tariff structure was in need of rationalization and simplification, that import substitution had reached

Table 7.1.   Southern Cone: Rates of Effective Protection by Product (*percentage*)

Product	Chile 1967	Uruguay 1976	Argentina 1969
Agriculture and forestry	−7		−10
Processed food	365	−9	−10
Textiles	492	89	400
Footwear	34	80	147
Clothing	−2		35
Lumber	−4		1,300
Furniture	−5		43
Paper	95	10.1	
Printing	−15		−1
Leather	18		6
Rubber	304	262	384
Chemicals	64	−19	180
Iron and steel	35		103
Metals	92	283	137
Machinery	76		105
Electric material	740	609	195
Domestic appliance	384		195
Transport equipment	*a*		299
Bicycles	555		307

Source: Chile: World Bank 1979; Uruguay: Mezzera 1981; Argentina: Nogués 1981, 1982.

*a*Prohibited.

---

5. Thus in 1970, copper accounted for 78 percent of Chile's export earnings, wool and beef for 72 percent of Uruguay's, and beef and wheat for 56 percent of Argentina's.

a stage of rapidly diminishing returns, and that more outward-oriented strategies should be launched.[6] But how far outward the economies should look, whether this outward orientation should begin within the region and then move beyond or move out all at once, and whether to achieve this by subsidizing exports, lowering tariffs, or raising the real effective exchange rate via devaluation, were questions there was little agreement on.

In any case, Southern Cone neoconservatives, while differing among themselves as to the speed, the most appropriate instruments, and their sequence, unequivocally supported an outward-oriented growth strategy from the start. Their aim was to use the international economy to stimulate greater domestic efficiency and competition by means of a growth strategy based on comparative advantage, specialization, and economies of scale.

To this end, an exchange rate was to be established geared to the promotion of both exports and import substitutes. Quantitative controls on imports and excessively high tariffs were to be reduced. Because of the large external disequilibrium, these policies were not put into practice simultaneously but in two phases: phase I centered on keeping a high exchange rate and promoting exports; phase II centered on reducing tariffs and using the exchange rate to achieve price stabilization. This latter mix would result in an increasingly overvalued exchange rate and, in effect, in import promotion, so long as strong capital inflows persisted.

PHASE I: EXPORT PROMOTION

Policy was aimed mainly at transforming exports into a dynamic growth sector (in Chile and Uruguay) or at raising the efficiency of this sector through foreign competition (in Argentina). In all three cases, this implied raising the scant weight of exports in GNP: 13 percent in Chile, 1971–73; 9 percent in Uruguay, 1971–74, and 6 percent in Argentina, 1971–75 (tables 7.2, 7.3, and 7.4).

Moreover, as a result of the combination of high tariffs and low exchange rates, the volume of exports had been either increasing quite slowly or decreasing: 1.8 percent per year in Chile, 1971–73; −0.3 percent per year in Uruguay, 1971–74; and −3 percent per year in Argentina, 1971–75. The external problem was greater for Argentina and Uruguay because their terms of trade were deteriorating, whereas Chile's were rising. Nevertheless, at the beginning of

---

6. In fact, Argentina began an export-oriented policy in the late sixties, raising industrial exports to almost $1 billion by 1974 and growing at an average annual rate of 31 percent between 1965 and 1974. Similarly, Chile adopted a more outward-oriented strategy during the Frei period (1965–70), industrial exports growing at 17 percent per year, though from a far smaller base than Argentina's. (This policy was ended under Allende, 1970–73.) Uruguay too, in the late sixties, began to experiment with mechanisms to promote nontraditional exports; manufactured exports grew at a rate of 18 percent per year between 1965 and 1973, though, as with Chile, taking off from a very small base.

Table 7.2. Chile: Basic Indicators of the External Sector, 1971–1983

Indicator	1971	1972	1973	1974	1975	1976	1977	1978	1979	1980	1981	1982	1983[a]
Coefficients													
Exports/GNP	13.8	12.2	14.3	16.7	20.9	24.0	23.4	23.4	26.8	28.7	27.5	34.8	33.2
Tradables/GNP	43.7	43.7	42.6	44.4	41.7	42.7	42.4	41.4	40.9	40.1	40.0	40.1	41.4
Current-account-surplus/exports	−17.8	−48.1	−19.7	−12.9	−27.1	5.4	−21.8	−37.8	−26.1	−33.9	−88.4	−48.6	−26.6
Terms of trade[b]	80.6	75.5	84.7	88.3	55.4	59.3	54.1	48.6	54.7	51.6	44.6	39.8	40.7
External debt[c]	2.8	3.0	3.6	4.4	4.7	4.5	5.2	6.7	8.5	11.1	15.6	17.2	17.5
External debt/exports	2.5	3.1	2.5	1.9	2.6	1.9	2.0	2.3	1.8	1.9	2.5	3.7	3.8
Growth rates													
Volume of exports	9.0	−12.2	10.1	18.0	9.2	18.7	7.4	5.8	26.8	15.3	−7.7	10.8	1.6
Value of exports	−9.4	−13.0	48.7	59.1	−21.0	31.3	7.9	13.0	57.1	29.2	−16.1	−7.3	−0.9
Volume of imports	2.7	2.2	4.1	11.0	−24.9	−6.5	31.5	15.2	20.6	13.4	8.0	−34.8	−14.9
Value of imports	6.0	8.1	25.2	43.5	−13.3	−3.4	45.0	26.1	44.1	34.6	17.7	−39.2	−19.2

Source: CEPAL, on the basis of official data.

[a]Preliminary figures.
[b]1970 = 100.
[c]Billions of dollars.

Table 7.3. Uruguay: Basic Indicators of the External Sector, 1971–1983

Indicator	1971	1972	1973	1974	1975	1976	1977	1978	1979	1980	1981	1982	1983[a]
Coefficients													
Exports/GNP	7.8	9.4	8.0	9.1	10.7	12.7	13.3	13.2	12.5	12.6	13.7	15.0	15.9
Tradables/GNP	35.5	35.5	35.3	35.0	34.9	34.0	35.5	34.1	32.1	33.5	31.2	29.7	29.7
Current-account-surplus/exports	−28.7	13.5	4.4	−27.3	−35.9	−11.8	−21.2	−14.5	−30.4	−46.9	−27.5	−15.3	−4.0
Terms of trade[b]	102.2	109.9	139.8	106.4	80.4	78.6	84.7	89.1	96.6	94.5	89.1	87.5	78.5
External debt[c]	0.6	0.8	0.7	1.0	1.0	1.1	1.3	1.2	1.7	2.1	3.1	4.3	4.5
External debt/exports	2.4	2.2	1.8	1.9	1.9	1.6	1.6	1.4	1.4	1.4	1.8	2.8	3.2
Growth rates													
Volume of exports	−16.7	18.0	−14.4	17.3	24.3	24.1	5.7	4.3	0.6	6.3	7.1	−1.2	4.3
Value of exports	−12.9	38.8	16.9	22.0	10.2	26.4	16.1	12.9	30.8	27.8	11.4	−9.6	−10.1
Volume of imports	−7.5	−15.6	22.1	18.3	−2.7	0.1	27.2	3.2	29.1	16.1	−10.6	−19.4	−25.8
Value of imports	−5.2	−7.7	31.1	61.6	14.2	4.3	29.7	6.1	55.0	42.6	−2.1	−24.4	−28.7

Source: CEPAL, on the basis of official data.

[a]Preliminary figures.
[b]1970 = 100.
[c]Billions of dollars.

115

Table 7.4. Argentina: Basic Indicators of the External Sector, 1971–1983

Indicator	1971	1972	1973	1974	1975	1976	1977	1978	1979	1980	1981	1982	1983[a]
Coefficients													
Exports/GNP	6.0	5.8	6.4	5.8	5.2	6.9	9.1	10.0	9.1	8.1	9.8	9.9	9.8
Tradables/GNP	42.9	43.5	44.4	44.0	43.1	42.9	42.9	41.9	42.3	40.2	38.9	40.9	42.3
Current-account-surplus/exports	−18.4	−9.7	18.9	2.6	−36.8	14.3	17.1	24.5	−5.8	−48.3	−43.4	−27.5	−27.4
Terms of trade[b]	108.1	117.3	141.8	128.7	97.1	93.1	88.9	89.9	97.6	110.3	100.2	89.1	86.8
External debt[c]	4.5	5.8	6.2	8.0	7.9	8.3	9.7	12.5	19.0	27.2	35.7	43.6	45.5
External debt/exports	2.1	2.5	1.7	1.7	2.3	1.8	1.5	1.7	2.1	2.8	3.3	4.8	4.9
Growth rates													
Volume of exports	−12.1	−1.2	13.5	−3.3	−10.7	31.9	40.5	6.0	−2.8	−10.3	14.5	0.7	9.8
Value of exports	−0.2	9.5	60.8	23.1	−23.2	31.8	42.9	13.6	22.6	7.8	9.7	−16.9	4.0
Volume of imports	3.8	−3.0	1.1	12.9	−5.8	−23.0	27.5	−0.6	52.1	40.2	−11.9	−44.1	−2.2
Value of imports	9.0	−0.9	18.5	58.3	7.4	−19.8	35.8	5.3	76.8	49.1	−10.1	−44.7	−4.8

Source: CEPAL, on the basis of official data.
[a]Preliminary figures.
[b]1970 = 100.
[c]Billions of dollars.

the neoconservative experiences, all three countries registered acute disequilibria in external accounts: the current-account deficit amounted to 20 percent of the value of exports of goods and services in Chile (1973), 27 percent in Uruguay (1974), and 37 percent in Argentina (1975).

The Measures

Under the former policy of import substitution, the level of imports had been reduced to an absolute minimum. It is not strange, then, that in the beginning trade liberalization focused on export promotion. The instrument used to carry this out was a high exchange rate (Chile and Uruguay raised their exchange rates via devaluation; Argentina maintained its high exchange rate, reached by a recent sustantial devaluation). To be sure, what is relevant for maintaining the competitiveness of exports and import substitutes is not the variation in the nominal exchange rate but the variation in the real effective exchange rate (that is, the variation in the nominal rate adjusted by the differential between internal and external inflation).[7]

Inasmuch as all three countries substantially decreased real wages in the first phase, the competitiveness of tradables, both exportables and import substitutes, improved all the more:[8] the real effective exchange rate (adjusted by wages) rose 33 percent in Uruguay, 40 percent in Argentina, and 200 percent in Chile (table 7.5, index C). Were it not for the large deterioration in real wages, the real exchange rate would have improved much less in the three countries, despite the strong nominal devaluation (table 7.5 and figures 6.4, 6.5, 6.6).

In this first phase, most of the quantitative controls on imports were also eliminated, and Argentina and Chile reduced their tariffs significantly (from 94 to 44 percent and from 94 to 35 percent, respectively). It seems, however, that a

---

7. Unless otherwise stated, the real effective exchange rate used in the text is the nominal exchange rate divided by the domestic wholesale-price index (the best internal price indicator of tradable goods) and multiplied by a weighted wholesale-price index of the main trading partners of the country (the best indicator of the international prices of tradable goods). For a detailed description of the methodology, see CEPAL 1983.

8. Since wages represent the main domestic component of costs, variations in the exchange rate adjusted by this variable reflect variations in the relative *costs* of internal production with respect to external production (for simplicity, we suppose that costs of external production are constant). This indicator is better than the price deflator, since internal prices not only reflect variations in costs but also variations in profit margins or lags in the adjustment of inflationary expectations. As the evidence suggests that these latter phenomena took place during this period, deflating by wages provides a better measure of variations in domestic productive costs with respect to international products. There is an important exception to the above. To the extent that internal financial costs—which were always higher than external ones—vary inversely with wages, the above indicator exaggerates variations in the real exchange rate. Even though the internal real rate of interest was higher in phase I than in phase II, the amount of the debt was much higher in phase II. Thus it is not obvious that financial costs varied in inverse relation to wages.

Table 7.5. Southern Cone: Real Effective Exchange Rates, Preneoconservative and Neoconservative Periods

Period	Chile				Uruguay				Argentina			
	Years	Index[a]	Index B[b]	Index C[c]	Years	Index[a]	Index B[b]	Index C[c]	Years	Index[a]	Index B[b]	Index C[c]
Preneoconservative	1970–73	128.0	68.2	63.1	1970–74	111.3	114.4	78.7	1970–75	151.1	199.7	176.7
Neoconservative[d]												
Phase I	1974–76	124.6	122.2	189.9	1975–78	119.8	129.9	104.3	1976–78	147.2	195.3	246.6
Phase II	1977–81	109.8	101.0	119.2	1979–80	102.0	109.9	110.3	1979–80	105.9	113.9	121.5
Phase III	1982–83	108.2	102.0	100.6	1981–83	114.5	125.4	112.6	1981–83	146.3	169.8	214.8

Source: CEPAL, on the basis of official data; International Monetary Fund, International Financial Statistics.

Note: Year 1983, preliminary figures.

[a]Real effective exchange rate adjusted by the difference in the variation between the internal and external wholesale-price index.
[b]Real effective exchange rate adjusted by the difference in the variation between the internal and external consumer-price index.
[c]Real effective exchange rate adjusted by the nominal salary.
[d]There are differences between the text and the table in the years included in each phase. The text refers to the exact moment when each phase can be considered to have begun and ended. The table lists the yearly averages that were, in fact, included in the calculation of the average of each phase, which do not necessarily coincide with the exact interval, because the data are available only for annual periods. However, much of the difference is only apparent, for the table uses the real effective exchange rate for each phase, including both the beginning and end years. Thus, for example, the data for Phase I in Chile (1974–76) are the average of the three variations, 1973–74, 1974–75, and 1975–76, and not of the two-year span from January 1974 to January 1976.

118

great part of the reduction affected only redundant levels of protection, since the effective protection required had decreased substantially in the sixties and seventies.[9] Moreover, the rise in the exchange rate and the fall in real wages in this period compensated to a large extent the tariff reductions for the bulk of activities. For this reason, few complaints were heard from entrepreneurs during this phase, for, as will be seen, imports made no significant inroads. Hence, the main effect of trade liberalization during this phase was to increase exports.[10]

Aside from the rise in the real exchange rate and the reduction of tariffs, two additional measures encouraged exports: the first was indirect: an internal recession, especially in Chile and Argentina, induced a search for foreign markets in which to sell national production; the second was direct: export promotion policies in Argentina and Uruguay included the reduction of special levies on traditional exports. For years, Argentina and Uruguay had maintained special taxes on these exports (beef, wool, cereals) representing up to 50 percent of their value (Anichini, Caumont, and Sjaastad 1977). These taxes had a clear distributive aim—namely, to extract the quasi rents deriving from devaluations from sectors with strong natural comparative advantages, whose productivity was thereby well above that of other exports and hence which did not require further incentives to expand production. In addition, since these products were wage goods, every devaluation raised the cost of living and pressured wages upward. Hence taxes on such exports had also served to keep their internal prices below their prices in international markets.

Before the beginning of the neoconservative experiences, both Uruguay and Argentina had established various incentives in favor of nontraditional exports, especially industrial exports; these were maintained in Argentina and augmented in Uruguay during a good part of this first phase. Such instruments were particularly effective when accompanied by a high and stable exchange rate, as was the case during phase I. In the Argentinian case, for example, the effective exchange rate of promoted sectors such as basic metals and machinery and transport was 50 percent higher than the nominal exchange rate, whereas the effective exchange rates of traditional exports such as wheat and corn were significantly lower than the nominal rate (table 7.6). Hence the effective exchange rate of promoted sectors was about double that of traditional exports until 1977, when these special incentives for nontraditional exports began to be

9. Analysts agree that there was much redundancy in tariff protection at the sectoral level, so that it was foreseeable that tariff reductions in the first phase would not affect the bulk of activities, even without an increase in the real exchange rate. For Argentina, see Sourrouille and Lucángeli 1983 and Canitrot 1982; For Chile, see Ffrench-Davis 1980 and Cortés 1981.

10. Since tariffs were not eliminated but simply reduced, and since the rise in the effective exchange rate promotes both exports and import substitutes, some purists refer to this phase as one of a reduction in the antiexport bias of previous policies rather than one in which trade opened up. So be it.

Table 7.6. Argentina: Effective Exchange Rates by Product, 1973–1977

Year and quarter	Wheat	Corn and Sorghum	Prepared Meat	Processed Food	Basic Metals	Machinery and Transport	Nominal Exchange Rate
1973							
Second	5.51	6.90	5.99	11.60	11.53	13.06	5.00
Third	5.49	4.45	6.05	11.22	11.53	13.06	5.00
Fourth	5.49	5.32	6.05	11.22	11.53	13.06	5.00
1974							
First	5.47	5.29	6.46	11.18	10.90	13.38	5.00
Second	5.47	5.29	7.50	11.19	10.89	13.38	5.00
Third	5.47	7.54	7.50	11.19	10.89	13.38	5.00
Fourth	5.47	6.07	7.50	11.19	10.89	13.38	5.00
1975							
First	5.42	6.02	11.17	13.35	13.19	16.50	10.00
Second	14.09	14.09	17.34	25.14	20.72	28.51	26.00
Third	20.09	20.09	28.28	46.48	34.47	58.24	36.40
Fourth	32.95	32.95	59.40	74.60	84.94	86.14	60.89
1976							
First	55.17	55.17	93.45	119.45	113.68	155.57	140.20
Second	88.36	108.35	173.33	235.30	219.81	269.29	140.20
Third	119.38	119.38	190.95	253.67	246.26	295.66	140.20
Fourth	258.94	229.02	235.82	292.94	284.78	339.18	274.50
1977, first quarter							
January	276.08	244.18	251.43	312.33	303.63	361.63	292.50
February	295.12	261.02	268.77	333.87	324.57	386.57	312.50
March					349.70	416.50	336.50

Source: World Bank 1977.

Note: Effective exchange rate is the nominal exchange rate adjusted by export taxes and subsidies on the product.

reduced and incentives were centered on the exchange rate alone. And in Uruguay as late as 1977, 60 percent of industrial credits (at highly subsidized interest rates) were for exports.

The Results

During the first phase, the volume of exports increased substantially in all three countries (tables 7.7, 7.8, 7.9): 26 percent per year in Argentina (1976–78) and 15 percent a year in Chile (1974–76) and Uruguay (1975–78). Even though part of this growth in exports represented a recovery from recent declines, the bulk of it was an increase over former levels.

In Chile and Uruguay, this increase was centered mainly on nontraditional exports, especially manufactures, that were operating with underutilized capacity (see tables 7.7 and 7.8). Its value quadrupled in three years (1974 through 1976) in Chile and quintupled in five years (1974 through 1978) in Uruguay. Thus at the end of the first phase, nontraditional exports represented 20 percent of the value of total exports in Chile and close to 50 percent in Uruguay, versus 5 and 20 percent, respectively, at the beginning of the neoconservative experience. In Argentina, where taxes on traditional exports had been eliminated and incentives to nontraditional exports had been partially reduced, the growth of traditional exports was even stronger. Nevertheless, the growth of nontraditional exports was also very strong (in 1976–78 their value increased 70 percent, and industrial exports alone grew 140 percent). At the same time, the destination of exports was widely diversified, for nontraditional exports gained entry to new markets. Hence, during this first period, the share of nonoil-exporting developing countries' markets in Chilean exports grew from 16 to 31 percent, while that of Uruguayan exports grew from 21 to 35 percent (see International Monetary Fund, *Statistical Yearbook* 1982).

For reasons earlier adduced, the opening of trade during this first phase proved to be a greater spur for exports than for imports. The volume of imports grew only slightly in Argentina (1 percent per year) and even decreased in Chile (−6 percent a year); there was a strong growth only in Uruguay (9 percent a year), but even here the growth of imports was less than that of exports (whose volume grew 15 percent per year in the same period).[11] Even consumption goods, those most protected in the past, registered an increase in import volumes only in Argentina (33 percent); but as the initial base was quite low, even here the absolute increase was of little significance (eighty million dollars more in 1978, the end of phase I, than in 1975).

Thus at the end of phase I the policy of trade liberalization and of outward-

---

11. Volume of imports is the most pertinent indicator of the effect of domestic policies, since countries cannot change the price of imports—and since oil prices skyrocketed during this period. (Throughout the text, volume and quantum are used interchangeably, even though quantum is the more precise concept.)

Table 7.7. Chile: Value, Volume, and Composition of Exports and Imports, 1971–1983 (*percentage*)

Item	1971	1972	1973	1974	1975	1976	1977	1978	1979	1980	1981	1982	1983[a]
Export growth													
Value	-9.4	-13.0	48.7	59.1	-21.0	31.3	7.9	13.0	57.1	29.2	-16.1	-7.3	-0.9
Volume	9.0	-12.2	10.1	18.0	9.2	18.7	7.4	7.9	24.3	15.3	-7.7	10.8	1.6
Value of nontraditional goods				157.7	99.5	29.0	30.1	26.1	57.7	33.6	-15.9	-1.8	8.0
Value of industrial goods		-31.1	8.5	225.1	34.4	33.1	20.7	24.6	59.2	25.2	-31.2	-12.8	-10.8
Nontraditional exports/total exports	8.1		4.9	7.9	19.9	19.5	23.5	26.3	26.4	27.3	25.5	25.5	27.3
Import growth													
Value	6.0	8.1	25.2	43.5	-13.3	-3.4	45.0	26.1	44.1	34.6	17.7	-39.2	-19.2
Volume	2.7	2.2	4.1	11.0	-24.9	-6.5	31.5	15.2	20.6	13.4	8.0	-34.8	-14.9
Volume of consumer goods				-10.5	-40.0	-12.8	79.5	26.9	9.3	36.8	23.5	-48.6	-31.3
Volume of durable consumer goods				23.1	-56.6	-2.2	336.2	26.9	19.0	38.2	45.0	-57.4	-44.7
Imports of durable consumer goods/total imports			8.1	8.3	4.5	4.8	15.3	16.6	15.4	18.1	22.6	16.1	12.9

Source: CEPAL, on the basis of official data. Banco Central de Chile, 1983.

[a]Preliminary figures.

122

Table 7.8. Uruguay: Value, Volume, and Composition of Exports and Imports, 1971–1983 (percentage)

Item	1971	1972	1973	1974	1975	1976	1977	1978	1979	1980	1981	1982	1983[a]
Export growth													
Value	−12.9	38.8	16.9	22.0	10.2	26.4	16.1	12.9	30.8	27.8	11.4	−9.6	−10.1
Volume	−16.7	18.0	−14.4	17.3	24.3	24.1	5.7	4.3	0.6	6.3	7.1	−1.2	4.3
Value of nontraditional goods				77.8	31.9	60.5	13.1	26.7	29.3	13.8	11.4	21.6	−24.0
Value of industrial goods	−8.6	15.9	5.2	100.0	43.0	58.9	29.0	22.7	30.6	6.9	2.7	−4.1	−15.0
Nontraditional exports/total exports			19.8	28.8	34.5	43.8	42.6	47.9	47.3	42.1	41.7	50.5	47.6
Import growth													
Value	−5.2	−7.7	31.1	61.6	14.2	4.3	29.7	6.1	55.0	42.6	−2.7	−24.4	−28.7
Volume	−7.5	−15.6	22.1	18.3	−2.7	0.1	27.2	3.2	29.1	16.1	−10.6	−19.4	−25.8
Volume of consumer goods				19.8	−30.8	−35.1	53.7	26.5	66.1	97.6	32.4	−62.6	−57.5
Imports of durable consumer goods/total imports			7.1	6.3	4.1	2.7	3.4	4.3	5.3	8.3	12.3	6.6	2.4

Source: CEPAL, on the basis of official data; International Monetary Fund, Statistical Yearbook.

[a]Preliminary figures.

Table 7.9. Argentina: Value, Volume, and Composition of Exports and Imports, 1971–1983 (percentage)

Item	1971	1972	1973	1974	1975	1976	1977	1978	1979	1980	1981	1982	1983[a]
Export growth													
Value	-0.2	9.5	60.8	23.1	-23.2	31.8	42.9	13.6	22.6	7.8	9.7	-16.9	4.0
Volume	-12.1	-1.2	13.5	-3.3	-10.7	31.9	40.5	6.0	-2.8	-10.3	14.5	0.7	9.8
Value of industrial goods	9.0	47.2	86.2	31.4	-25.6	34.7	37.4	27.1	11.8	8.7	-6.6	2.9	-26.5
Import growth													
Value	9.0	-0.9	18.5	58.3	7.4	-19.8	35.8	5.3	76.8	49.1	-10.1	-44.7	-4.8
Volume	3.8	-3.0	1.1	12.9	-5.8	-23.0	27.5	-0.6	52.1	40.2	-11.9	-44.1	-2.2
Volume of consumer goods		13.6	-28.7	68.4	-9.9	-52.2	94.2	44.5	193.3	132.6	-19.4	-78.0	-39.2
Imports of consumer goods/total imports	3.2	3.9	2.6	3.3	3.1	1.9	2.9	4.3	8.0	14.2	14.2	5.2	5.3

Source: CEPAL, on the basis of official data; International Monetary Fund *Statistical Yearbook* 1980.
[a]Preliminary figures.

oriented growth had significantly increased the weight of exports in GNP: from 13 to 20 percent in Chile, 1973–76; from 7 to 10 percent in Uruguay, 1974–78; and from 4 to 9 percent in Argentina, 1975–78 (tables 7.10, 7.11, 7.12). Moreover, the cost (increase) in imports, especially those competitive with national production, was almost insignificant: the weight of consumer-goods imports in all imports increased only in Argentina, and then only slightly (3 to 4 percent). Thus, the first phase of trade liberalization was a success, at least in terms of the objectives proposed. A different issue, of course, is whether the growth of nontraditional exports was worth the major decline in production for Chile's and Argentina's domestic markets and whether Uruguay's export incentives were worth the implied sacrifice in fiscal income.

PHASE II: TARIFF REDUCTION

Due to the sharp spurt of exports during the first phase of the neoconservative experiences, initial external disequilibria were substantially reduced. Current-account surpluses were achieved in both Argentina and Chile; and although in Uruguay the current account still registered a deficit, the gap was reduced from 27 to 15 percent between 1974 and 1978. Hence the objective of exchange policy in the three countries began to shift from achieving external equilibrium to slowing inflation. External equilibrium was now to be achieved by capital movements; in other words, the monetary approach to the balance of payments came to dominate policy thinking.

Table 7.10. Chile: Share of Tradables, Exportables, and Importables in Gross National Product, Neoconservative Phases (*percentage*)

Phase	Tradables/ GNP	Exportables/ GNP	Importables[a]/ GNP	GNP	Importables[a]
I					
Beginning	42.6	12.8	29.8	100.0	100.0
End	42.7	20.4	22.3	94.6	70.8
II					
Beginning	42.7	20.4	22.3	94.6	70.8
End	40.0	20.0	20.0	127.2	85.4
III					
Beginning	40.0	20.0	20.0	127.2	85.4
End	41.4	33.2	8.2	115.8	31.9

Source: CEPAL, on the basis of official data.

Note: Year 1983, preliminary figures.

[a]Goods that substitute for imports, estimated as the difference between tradables and exportables and that are a proxy for tradables destined for the domestic market.

Table 7.11.   Uruguay: Share of Tradables, Exportables, and Importables in Gross
National Product, Neoconservative Phases (*percentage*)

Phase	Tradables/ GNP	Exportables/ GNP	Importables[a]/ GNP	GNP	Importables[a]
I					
Beginning	35.0	6.7	28.3	100.0	100.0
End	34.1	10.0	24.1	118.4	100.8
II					
Beginning	34.1	10.0	24.1	118.4	100.8
End	33.5	9.3	24.2	132.7	113.5
III					
Beginning	33.5	9.3	24.2	132.7	113.5
End	29.7	15.9	13.8	116.4	56.8

Source: CEPAL, on the basis of official data.

Note: Year 1983, preliminary figures.

[a]Goods that substitute for imports, estimated as the difference between tradables and exportables and that are a proxy for tradables destined for the domestic market.

Table 7.12.   Argentina: Share of Tradables, Exportables, and Importables in Gross
National Product, Neoconservative Phases (*percentage*)

Phase	Tradables/ GNP	Exportables/ GNP	Importables[a]/ GNP	GNP	Importables[a]
I					
Beginning	43.1	4.0	39.1	100.0	100.0
End	41.9	8.6	33.3	102.3	87.1
II					
Beginning	41.9	8.6	33.3	102.3	87.1
End	40.2	6.9	33.3	110.0	93.7
III					
Beginning	40.2	6.9	33.3	110.0	93.7
End	42.3	11.3	31.0	100.8	79.9

Source: CEPAL, on the basis of official data.

Note: Year 1983, preliminary figures.

[a]Goods that substitute for imports, estimated as the difference between tradables and exportables and that are a proxy for tradables destined for the domestic market.

During the first phase, none of the three countries had resorted to massive foreign indebtedness to resolve their external disequilibrium. Now that they did, international capital markets were enjoying great liquidity and were offering it to all comers. Hence, at least for most of phase II, it was feasible to make this shift in objectives and instruments. That this policy modification was maintained for such a long period after inflation was slowed (and despite the growing lag in the exchange rate) reveals both the high priority given to price stabilization and the dogmatic belief that current prices were always equilibrium prices. Of course, it was possible to persevere in this approach for such an extended period only because of the heavy external indebtedness that characterized phase II.

Lowered and uniform tariffs also characterized phase II, for the aim was to raise the weight not only of exports in GNP but also (necessarily) of imports. Which imports were to be promoted? Basically, those goods in which the country enjoyed a comparative *dis*advantage and that were thus too costly to produce at home. Protection was not given according to the needs of producers, since this favors the less-efficient activity. Rather, protection tended to favor all producers with equally effective protection.[12] At the same time, the average level of protection was also reduced, since it was considered excessive. Reduced and uniform tariffs implied that the imports promoted would be those whose domestic substitutes had enjoyed the highest effective protection: manufactures more than agricultural goods (since the latter had negative effective protection) and, within manufactures, final goods.

The Measures

Two measures characterized trade liberalization in this phase. First, tariffs were reduced—strongly in Chile, significantly in Argentina, only slightly in Uruguay.[13] Second, the real effective exchange rate was reduced. Thus exports became more expensive and imports cheaper, the latter pressuring domestic prices downward. Both measures thus tended to promote imports.

It was thought that few discrepancies between social and private (market) benefits could require the tariff levels of the past (table 7.1), which, it was believed, had been made largely for private gain. This assumption was no doubt correct, even though it is difficult to determine whether Chile's final level (10 percent) was too low or Uruguay's aim (35 percent) too high. The three coun-

---

12. Not all discriminatory protection is inefficient. To the extent that it closes differences between social and private rates of return, it is probable that such discrimination is justified. The inefficient, differentiated protection in the Southern Cone, however, provided for an adequate private rate of return, even though the social rate of return was low or nonexistent.

13. Chile left the Andean Pact in October 1976 both because it wanted to offer more favorable conditions to foreign investors than those allowed by the other countries of the subregion and because it wanted a lower tariff than that required by the Pact.

tries' tariff liberalization concurred in the direction of the change (reduction) but differred not only with respect to the final level but with respect to the degree of differentiation and the speed of achieving its final levels. Chile reduced tariffs from 94 percent in 1973, to 35 percent in 1976, to 10 percent in 1979; Argentina reduced nominal tariffs, especially industrial protection, from 94 percent in 1976, to 44 percent in 1978, and to 35 percent in 1981, but did not foresee reaching its final goal of 15 percent until 1984; Uruguay initiated its program in 1980 and projected finishing it at the end of 1985 with a 35 percent tariff.[14]

Likewise, the three countries intended to make effective protection more uniform, but only Chile completely eliminated tariff differentiation on goods, regardless of whether these were final, intermediate, or capital.[15] Uruguay planned to have a uniform tariff by the end of 1985. By contrast, the goal of the Argentinian program consisted of a differential tariff, fluctuating between a minimum of 10 percent and a maximum of 40 percent.

The second key decision in this phase affecting the opening up of trade was the shift in the objective of exchange policy. During the first phase, policy had been aimed at the achievement of a balance in the external accounts, keeping the real effective exchange rate high. Had this exchange policy been maintained, the reduction in tariffs would have required a compensatory *increase* in the exchange rate. Thus, more than promoting imports generally, tariff reductions would simply have favored the importation of products that had previously been highly protected and could thus have led to greater specialization but not to a generalized increase in imports beyond export capacity.

However, with the adoption of the monetary approach to the balance of payments in this phase, financial liberalization was accelerated, and capital inflows surged. Thus capital movements were assigned responsibility for attaining balance-of-payments equilibrium, whereas the exchange rate aimed at price stabilization. Such a reorientation was possible only because of international liquidity and financial liberalization. Had domestic inflation rapidly decreased, adjusting itself to the variation in the exchange rate, no major problems would have arisen. Yet, for reasons analyzed in the previous chapter, the law of one price was never achieved. Thus a growing exchange-rate lag emerged: internal prices increased much more rapidly than the exchange rate plus international inflation. As noted earlier, this lag took place in all three countries—not only in Argentina and Uruguay, where tariff reduction was modest or insignificant, but also in Chile, where tariffs had been drastically reduced and thus where the downward pressure of tariff reductions on domestic prices might have been expected to be strong.

In any case, tariff reductions were followed, not by a compensatory in-

---

14. The average nominal tariffs are a weighted average. For Chile, see Ffrench-Davis 1980; for Uruguay, see Mezzera 1981; for Argentina, see Sourrouille and Lucángeli 1983.

15. The sole exception was automobiles, which enjoyed privileged treatment.

crease in the real exchange rate, but by a fall (table 6.5). Simultaneously, at least in Argentina and Chile, wages tended to recuperate. Both factors increased the loss of competitiveness of national production and determined that this second phase would be characterized as one of "import promotion," financed not by the expansion of exports (which could have been permanent) but by a surge in capital inflows (which, at those strong rhythms, necessarily had to be transitory).

Thus, in this phase, internal production was subject to three types of pressure, each of which reduced the cost of imported goods in relation to their equivalent domestic counterpart: (1) tariff reductions (especially in Argentina and Chile), (2) a lagged exchange rate (in all three), and (3) a recovery in wages (especially in Argentina and Chile).

The Results

As a result of the tariff reductions and the exchange-rate lag, imports, especially of consumer goods (formerly highly protected), increased enormously in all three countries, much more than output and income (tables 7.2, 7.3, 7.4). In the two years of phase II in Argentina (1979 and 1980), the volume of imports more than doubled and the volume of consumer-good imports increased almost seven times. In the five years of Chile's phase II (1976 through 1981), the volume of imports increased 2.25 times and imports of consumer goods increased 4 times. On the other hand, in Uruguay, where the lag in the exchange rate was much less, the volume of imports increased "only" 50 percent during this phase (1979 and 1980); nevertheless, even here consumer-goods imports more than tripled.

The fact that the marginal propensity to import consumer goods was very high (even in Uruguay, where no significant tariff reduction had taken place) shows the magnitude of the latent demand for products whose importation had been formerly prohibited. This suggests that the greater variety of goods available arising from the lifting of nontariff barriers was as important in stimulating consumption of imports as was the price reduction arising from tariff reductions.[16] The volume of consumer-goods imports tripled in only two years in Uruguay, which had almost no tariff reduction; and the greatest increase took place not in Chile—which had the steepest tariff reduction—but in Argentina, where, in spite of less-intense tariff reduction, the volume of consumer-goods imports increased almost seven times.

The loss of competitiveness and of domestic market was not noted imme-

---

16. The greater access to consumer credit may also have affected this outcome. Nevertheless, it must be borne in mind that its cost (interest rate) was always very high and, in general, it was also available for buying domestic goods. This credit explanation would only be pertinent, then, for those imported goods (like automobiles) in which the credit in dollars was available at relatively low interest rates.

diately (at least not as a generalized phenomenon), since the strong capital inflows of the first years of this phase led to an expansion of overall demand. Because of this income effect, output of most sectors recovered or expanded.

The clearest example of the dominance of the income effect, at least in the short run, can be seen in the evolution of manufacturing output in Chile: it fell in 1974–75 despite the absence of significant price pressure from imports, whereas it grew briskly in 1976–81 because of high or growing demand (fueled by capital inflows), notwithstanding the negative price effect arising from reduced tariffs (see Vergara 1980, and Corbo and Pollack 1982). Indeed, during this latter phase, Chile's industrial output increased at an average rate of almost 7 percent per year, though not industrial employment.[17] The slow recovery of employment was probably due to the greater competition brought on by the opening up of trade. Since variable costs consist largely of labor costs, the need to reduce costs implied (notwithstanding record low levels of real wages) reduced employment. While low wages may have induced a long-run movement toward investment in labor-intensive operations, in the short run there was no input of significance that could be cut down other than labor.

Nevertheless, there were important differences within the manufacturing sector and also among countries. The loss of competitiveness in relation to imports was so important in Chile that thirteen sectors, representing 38 percent of industrial output, did not recover their 1969 levels of production even by 1981, the year of maximum production (table 7.13). The output of many important subsectors, such as textiles, clothing, and footwear, stagnated at levels close to the worst moments of the 1975 recession (a third of their domestic market was lost to imports). On the other hand, other subsectors were favored by the combined effect of the opening of trade and the exchange-rate lag, either because the cost of imported inputs was reduced or because imports pressured down (though slowly and partially) the overblown prices of domestic industrial products, thus raising real wages and so aggregate demand.

The increase in aggregate demand in Chile more than compensated for the contractionary effect of the exchange-rate lag and tariff reduction. Manufacturing output grew at an average rate of 5 to 7 percent a year (according to revised

---

17. Using the official statistics, which keep constant the relation between gross value of production and value-added, industrial growth was 6.9 percent per year in this period. This assumption is challenged by Meller, Livacich, and Arrau 1984, whose estimates suggest a growth rate of 4.2 percent per year. Even then, this is considerably faster than the growth in industrial employment, which seems not to have grown at all. Estimates on manufacturing employment vary enormously, from −2.9 percent per year during 1976–81, according to INE's industrial establishments survey, to 2.0 percent per year for the same period, according to INE's household employment survey. The first figure is more relevant for our purposes, inasmuch as its source derives from the same establishments whose output is taken as representative of industrial output. Yet even the maximum figure is still well below the rate of growth of output. This is all the more intriguing since through most of this phase output was just recovering. Hence output and employment would have been expected to have grown at similar rates. See, on this point, Meller 1984.

and official statistics, respectively) not only during the years of recovery, 1976 through 1978, but also in 1979 and 1980. Nevertheless, to the extent that aggregate demand was based on massive inflows of foreign capital, which could not be sustained in the long run, this overall net expansionary effect could only be transitory. Once capital inflows decelerated at the end of 1981, aggregate demand collapsed, and industrial output fell 22 percent in 1982.

Table 7.13.   Chile: Industrial Production by Product, 1976 and 1981 (*1969 = 100*)

Product	1976	1981
Food products	108.6	133.1
Beverages	109.0	159.5
Textiles	71.6	91.2
Clothing	61.2	80.1
Leather except footwear	69.9	69.7
Footwear	70.0	70.0
Lumber	98.7	188.2
Furniture and accessories	78.2	215.1
Paper	99.9	124.9
Printing and publishing	68.5	114.1
Industrial chemicals	58.0	55.4
Other chemicals	113.1	133.1
Petroleum refining	110.8	128.0
Petroleum derivatives	65.4	82.5
Rubber products	76.0	95.7
Plastics	81.2	122.2
Ceramics	64.1	71.8
Glass	101.5	150.1
Other nonmetallic minerals	56.5	115.7
Basic iron and steel	61.0	94.1
Nonferrous basic metals	166.9	195.1
Metal products	68.1	93.1
Nonelectric machinery	67.8	44.4
Electric equipment	80.9	229.7
Electronic equipment	74.7	195.5
Electric appliances	87.3	228.3
Transport materials	49.6	94.6
Professional scientific equipment	51.7	53.5
Miscellaneous	105.9	228.7
Total industry	95.4	129.3
Internal demand	100.0	154.8
National product	100.0	146.7

Source: Sociedad de Fomento Fabril; CEPAL 1983.

A similar phenomenon seems to have taken place in Argentina (table 7.14). Despite the fact that in this phase, tariff reductions affected mainly the industrial sector, overall output recovered 5 percent between 1978 and 1980 because of a 17 percent increase in domestic demand. What is surprising is that half of the increase in domestic demand and up to two-thirds of the demand for industrial products was satisfied by imports. This shows how strong the elasticity of imports was to income, to price (due to the exchange-rate lag), and to the removal of nontariff barriers. Thus, although average industrial output grew, the contractionary effect of the loss of competitiveness was greater than the expansionary effect of growing domestic demand in sectors such as paper, textiles, clothing, and leather products, whose production fell below 1978 levels (table 7.14).

Although tariff reduction could have favored the exports of sectors that had previously suffered from negative effective protection, the fact that both Argentina and Chile suffered a steep decline in the exchange rate meant that this potential stimulation was mitigated or altogether nullified. In any case, these sectors could have been less damaged, since output was likely to be restructured in favor of activities with heretofore less-effective protection.

As could have been foreseen, between 1976 and 1983 manufactures, which previously enjoyed the greatest effective protection within tradables, declined significantly as a portion of GNP in both countries: in Chile, from 26 to 20 percent; in Argentina from 27 to 24 percent (table 7.15). A detailed and more disaggregated study of Chile shows that within the industrial sector a recomposition took place in favor of those subsectors more intensive in natural resources or skilled labor, sectors that had received a relatively lower level of

Table 7.14.   Argentina: Industrial Production by Product, 1978 and 1980 (*1970 = 100*)

Product	1978	1980
Food, beverages, tobacco	101.5	102.5
Textiles, clothing, leather	94.4	92.3
Lumber and furniture	94.3	104.1
Paper, printing, publishing	108.7	101.9
Chemicals, rubber, plastic	113.1	128.0
Glass and nonmetallic minerals	109.4	112.9
Basic metals	121.1	128.0
Machinery and equipment	118.5	130.8
Total industry	108.3	114.1
Internal demand	100.0	117.0
National product	100.0	108.3

Source: Canitrot 1982.

effective protection in the past.[18] That is why subsectors like meat and fish processing, alcoholic beverages, basic metals, paper, and lumber expanded more rapidly than the industrial average during the neoconservative experience, even surpassing by wide margins their previous historic maximums.

Nevertheless, the growing lag in the exchange rate decelerated the growth of export volumes, so that by the end of phase II these had come to a virtual standstill in Chile and were actually falling in Argentina, thus helping generate massive deficits in current account. These deficits reached close to 50 percent of the total value of exports in Argentina and Uruguay (1980) and 90 percent in Chile (1981). Obviously, such gaps could be maintained only through huge inflows of foreign capital, yet these inflows could not be sustained indefinitely without like increases in the capacity to service such debt. And, because of the lagging exchange rate, export volumes were decelerating, not accelerating. Hence, once capital inflows were cut back, these countries had no other resort

Table 7.15.   Southern Cone: Share of Tradables in Gross National Product, 1970–1983, Selected Years (*percentage*)

Country	Agriculture	Mining	Manufactures	All Tradables
Chile				
1970	7.5	10.1	26.0	43.6
1974	7.3	11.5	25.6	44.4
1981	7.1	11.1	21.8	40.0
1983[a]	7.8	13.2	20.4	41.4
Uruguay				
1970	12.9		23.0[b]	35.9
1974	11.2		23.8[b]	35.0
1981	10.1		23.4[b]	33.5
1983[a]	11.0		18.7[b]	29.7
Argentina				
1970	13.2	2.3	27.0	42.5
1976	13.7	2.2	27.0	42.9
1980	12.7	2.5	25.0	40.2
1983[a]	15.3	2.8	24.2	42.3

Source: CEPAL, on the basis of official data.

[a]Preliminary figures.

[b]Includes mining.

18. See Willmore 1982. Corbo and Pollack 1982 also concluded that "the sectors more protected in 1967 were those in which import substitution was more rapidly reversed. At the same time, in those sectors highly intensive in labor, the relative contribution of exports to the change in production has been more important" (p. 78).

than to devalue massively, in an effort to recover the loss of competitiveness suffered during phase II.

AN EVALUATION OF TRADE LIBERALIZATION

Whether the external sector could or should have become the engine of growth in the economies of the Southern Cone cannot be answered solely on the basis of the experiences of these last few years. There is no doubt that, since the end of the Second World War, the three countries had suffered from serious external restrictions, which to a large extent explained their slow growth. By the mid-seventies, not much more could be done along the lines of further import substitution. It was reasonable then to expect—regardless of the development strategy adopted—that, from then on, efforts to overcome foreign exchange restrictions in the Southern Cone would increasingly shift toward export promotion. Indeed, even before the advent of the neoconservative experiences, important steps had already been taken in that direction. Hence neoconservatism reinforced, and provided theoretical justification for, processes already initiated.

Trade liberalization aimed at raising the weight of exports in GNP, which necessarily implied raising the weight of imports as well. Imports would grow as fast as exports because of the policy of export promotion, whereas tariff reduction would largely affect the composition of imports. Such a scheme, correctly applied, would largely promote the importation of goods formerly protected in excess (goods whose internal production was inefficient because they required relatively scarce resources or scales of production greater than those allowed by the domestic market).

Due to the marked preference of neoconservatism for rules and general policies, it is not surprising that the key instruments for outward-oriented growth were the exchange rate (expected to increase) and trade barriers (programmed to decline); while selective instruments (quotas, export taxes, subsidies) were to fall into disuse. In practice, such criteria were adhered to only during the first years. In phase II, because of the largesse of international liquidity, the objective of exchange-rate policy switched from achieving external equilibrium (a high exchange rate) to fostering price stabilization (which risked a low exchange rate). This policy indiscriminately promoted all imports rather than simply modify their composition. The ever-more-pronounced lag in the exchange rate could be maintained only with an accelerated increase in external debt. Once this source of funds was exhausted, a general crisis developed in the balance of payments, the financial sector, and overall production, signaling the end of the neoconservative experiences.

Trade liberalization was thus accompanied by sharp ups and downs in aggregate demand, enormous variations in the real exchange rate, and different measures of financial liberalization, making it difficult to evaluate its effect per se. Nevertheless, it is worthwhile analyzing in greater detail the principal cost commonly attributed to trade liberalization—namely, the decline in industrial production.

To begin with, all of this loss took place during the recessions of phases I and III, which were induced by stabilization and adjustment policies. In other words, the immediate cause was deficient aggregate demand, not low tariffs. The pressure of tariff reductions was slight in phase I, both because devaluations were strong and because tariff reductions affected mainly levels of redundant protection; in phase III, because, although tariffs were lower, exchange rates were severely devalued. Moreover, in phase III, expenditure-reducing adjustment was so strong that import volumes collapsed, falling far more than domestic output. Imports, in fact, grew strongly only during phase II; yet the growth of aggregate demand (made possible, to be sure, by capital inflows) more than nullified their effect on domestic production.

Second, if, as argued in chapter 6, much of the demand-deficient recession of phase I was due to overblown prices (especially industrial prices), it is reasonable to assume that in phase II domestic demand (and so sales) would not have grown as strongly had the prices of industrial goods not come down (relatively) and real wages risen. Certainly, then, the pressure of lower tariffs on the overblown prices of domestic goods need have accounted for part of the increase in the sales and output of these goods during phase II, and did not simply serve to displace domestic production by imports.

Third, the displacement effect of trade liberalization—and no doubt it did substitute for much domestic production—can be decomposed into the three factors at play in phase II (tariff reductions, the exchange-rate lag, and wage policy), all of which tended to reduce the price of imported goods relative to domestic production:

1. Tariff reductions in Chile, 1976–79, lowered the cost of imports (cost, insurance, and freight plus tariff) 19 percent—from 135 to 110, (since tariffs fell from 35 to 10 percent). In Argentina, 1978–81, tariff reductions lowered the cost of imports 6 percent—from 144 to 135. (Uruguay's tariff-reduction program had not advanced significantly in phase II.)
2. The exchange policy programmed devaluations at a decreasing rate, which, because domestic inflation far exceeded the rate of devaluation, lowered the cost of imports with respect to domestic products. In Argentina the reduction in cost competitiveness due to the exchange-rate lag was between 32 percent (measured with respect to the wholesale-price index) and 49 percent (measured by the consumer-price index); in Chile it ranged from 28 to 32 percent; in Uruguay, between 20 and 32 percent.[19]
3. Wages tended to adjust according to past inflation, especially in Chile and

---

19. For example, in Argentina the real effective exchange rate (deflated by the wholesale-price index) fell from 147 to 100 between phase I and 1980, which implied a 32 percent decline in the cost of the imported product relative to the domestic product. If we use the consumer-price index as a deflator, the decline is from 195 to 100, that is to say, 49 percent (see table 7.5).

to a lesser extent in Argentina. In periods of decreasing inflation, as in phase II, wage adjustments thus raised the purchasing power of workers. Thus the competitiveness of the domestic production of tradables declined and the prices of imports in relation to the prices of domestic products decreased another 21 percent in Argentina and 36 percent in Chile. (There was no major effect in Uruguay, since real wages did not vary significantly during phase II.)

The relative weight of each of these three factors in explaining the loss of competitiveness and product substitution and displacement can be determined and decomposed as follows:

1. Imports were much cheapened with respect to domestic products during phase II: 60 to 70 percent in Argentina and Chile; 20 percent in Uruguay.
2. The lag in the exchange rate was by far the main factor in the cheapening of imports. It was two to six times more important than tariff reductions in Chile and Argentina, respectively, and it accounted for all of the loss of competitiveness in Uruguay (which made no significant tariff reduction). If we also consider the effect of wage policy, the impact of tariff reductions in cheapening imports is even less.
3. The exchange-rate lag was not related to tariff reduction. Even though it might have been assumed that the lower the tariffs, the greater the pressure of external prices on domestic prices and the lesser the lag in the exchange rate, this was not the case. It is true that Chile, whose tariff reductions were greater, had less of an exchange-rate lag than Argentina. Yet Uruguay, which had no significant tariff reduction at all, experienced the smallest exchange-rate lag of the three. This suggests that the cost or displacement effect of tariff reductions was far less than at first appears.

CONCLUSIONS

The main success of trade liberalization consisted in substantially raising the growth of exports, especially during phase I. Fears of a presumed low elasticity of exports to price, or of entrepreneurial sluggishness in penetrating international markets, proved to be baseless. On the contrary, on receiving adequate incentives, entrepreneurs were able to increase their participation in traditional export markets as well as to penetrate new ones.

To be sure, a good part of this export effort would not have been possible without existing productive capacity, the result of the former policy of import substitution. Nevertheless, in the absence of the incentives established during the neoconservative experiences (reduction in the antiexport bias of previous policy), it is likely that exports would have continued to grow at the scant rates characteristic of the postwar period. The incentives provided, especially during phase I, mobilized this underutilized export potential. These incentives were a stable and high exchange rate (in real terms) and, in Argentina and Uruguay, an active export promotion policy. Nontraditional exports, especially, proved to be elastic to price and quite sensitive to appropriate incentives, at least so long as the world economy was not in recession.

The failure of trade liberalization took place in phase II, when imports flooded the domestic market. This occurred in all three countries, regardless of differences in tariff liberalization (almost nil in Uruguay, modest in Argentina, and important in Chile). Hence, the strong growth in imports cannot be attributed solely to tariff reduction, nor to the speed with which the reduction took place, nor to its discriminatory or uniform character. Imports responded, at least in the short run, largely to fluctuations in aggregate demand (the income effect), which was all the more volatile because demand was fed and starved by capital movements. Imports responded far less to changes in the competitiveness of domestic products (the price effect).

In any case, the loss of competitiveness was quite important. Yet it was due far more to the lag in the exchange rate than to tariff reduction. Tariff reduction was steep only in Chile, and even there it explains only one-third of the loss of competitiveness of domestic goods. Thus, if tariff reduction had been accompanied by a compensatory increase, and not a fall, in the exchange rate (as is in fact posited by standard economic theory), overall competitiveness could have been maintained despite the reduction in tariffs. To be sure, the maintenance of a high real exchange rate would have implied the need to reduce capital inflows or at least to have channeled a far greater proportion of them toward investment in tradables (thus increasing these countries' relative capacities to service their debts). The impact of the lag in the exchange rate is exemplified by the paradoxical fact that the weight of tradables in GNP was higher at the beginning of the neoconservative experience than at the end or even than in its heyday—the phase II booms (table 7.15).

The elimination of quantitative restrictions on imports, virtually the only direct trade liberalization measure applied in Uruguay, increased the volume of imports, since many were products for which there were only imperfect domestic substitutes. Their entry, even with high tariffs, took away significant segments of the domestic market and reflected a pent-up differentiated demand, which is not very sensitive to price. The fact that Uruguay's imports increased in like magnitude as those of Argentina and Chile—even without significant tariff reduction—suggests the importance of the impact of the lifting of non-tariff barriers, and not just tariff reductions, in explaining increased imports.

Financial Liberalization

Financial repression was one of the most characteristic elements of the economies of the Southern Cone and among those most severely criticized by neoconservatives. It was inconceivable for these theorists that the central mechanism for determining the allocation of resources—the capital market—should be controlled not by the forces of supply and demand but by the discretional authority of the government. For this reason, the creation of a domestic capital market and its opening to the outside world made up part of their package of basic structural reforms right from the beginning. Ironically, the end of the three neoconservative experiences was accompanied, if not brought on, by the collapse of the very financial system they had created.

Ever since the Great Depression, the countries of the Southern Cone had established increasing controls over the financial system. Selective credits at preferential interest rates—often negative in real terms—were created to promote the development of sectors and activities considered to be of the highest priority. Exchange controls were placed on capital movements in order to avoid capital flight and to render possible the maintenance of a low rate of exchange and so to cheapen imported foodstuffs and intermediate inputs. Moreover, a good part of the banking system not only belonged to the state but was administered in highly discretional form, so that credit was often assigned according to political rather than economic criteria.

THE NEOCONSERVATIVE DIAGNOSIS

In addition to its basic stance against intervention, neoconservatives (most notably, McKinnon 1973) criticized domestic financial repression for the following reasons:

1. Low and negative rates of interest were thought to explain why savings were so low in Chile (17 percent) and Uruguay (10 percent), and why they

138

depended so heavily on the public sector in Argentina (table 5.4), since low rates provided little or no incentive for individuals to sacrifice current consumption.

2.   Artificially low interest rates encouraged self-financing and discouraged financial intermediation, thus segmenting the market between those with access to cheap credit and those without access. Those with access were induced to initiate projects with low rates of return and to overmechanize or build unnecessary capacity. But capital-scarce activities with high rates of return were forced to borrow at the overblown interest rates of informal credit channels or were condemned to expand only to their limits of self-financing. (Even so, the capital-scarce activities with good investment opportunities hurt by segmentation were likely to be small- and medium-sized firms on the verge of modernizing, rather than, as some thinkers favorable to financial liberalization believed [see Galbis 1977], large firms already using modern technology).

3.   The volume and variety of financial assets were severely limited. The proportion of $M2$ in Southern Cone GNP at the beginning of the neoconservative experiences (20 percent) was well below that in the industrialized countries (60 percent) and in some fast-developing underdeveloped countries (60 percent in Taiwan, 33 percent in South Korea and Mexico; see McKinnon 1979). Moreover, the variety of financial instruments, especially for medium- and long-term debt, was quite limited.

The majority of economists was aware of these problems and concurred with the need to reduce financial repression. However, only the neoconservatives à outrance thought that the solution was to leave the financial system wholly and entirely in the hands of the market. Those from other schools of thought believed that some form of control was indispensable, for the financial market is not like any other market. They argued that financial activity is intrinsically fragile, subject to abrupt and discontinuous changes (vicious and virtuous circles): critical levels of confidence (or lack of confidence) regarding the future ability to service one's debts tend to reinforce themselves. The liquidity problems of firms, for example, can lead to generalized insolvency if not attended to in timely fashion by the economic authorities. It was further pointed out that, given the relatively small size of the Southern Cone economies plus the fact that there tend to be important economies of scale in financial activities, it was altogether likely that, if left to itself, the financial sector could come under the control of a relatively few economic conglomerates—with all the vices and defects that an oligopolistic allocation of credit entails.

As for capital inflows, neoconservatives were one in insisting on the merits of an extensive financial opening to the outside world. A less-developed country could then augment domestic savings with foreign savings and so speed up growth rates. Nevertheless, neoconservatives did differ among themselves as to the optimal sequence of liberalization in different markets. Some, such as

McKinnon (1973) and Frenkel (1982) argued that liberalization of trade and the creation the domestic capital market should come first, and only later—and gradually—financial liberalization. They feared that, should financial liberalization come early, interest rates would tend to converge before the prices of goods. Thus investment would increase, but it would be misallocated inasmuch as relative prices would still be distorted. Others believed that such a risk was worth taking, since heavy inflows of capital could be expected to offset the initial contractionary effects of the devaluation, helping avoid a recession and so generating confidence in the overall liberalization process.

THE POLICIES

Domestic capital markets were created in each of the three countries by the first or second year of its neoconservative experience (Chile 1975, Uruguay 1976, and Argentina 1977).[1] Uruguay chose to accompany this with a wide financial opening to the outside world but a timid trade opening, whereas Chile liberalized trade first and only gradually opened up its capital account.

Chile's policy was conditioned by its very high inflation and, therefore, its perceived need to assure control over the money supply. Moreover, the reluctance of the international banks to lend to Chile during the first years following the coup (for political as well as economic reasons) really made no other alternative possible. Argentina followed a middle road, controlling capital inflows during the first phase of its price-stabilization program (1976–78) and increasingly opening up financially during the second phase, once its stabilization efforts came to center on controlling the exchange rate.

The creation of a domestic capital market included the following principal measures: (1) freeing interest rates; (2) eliminating or dramatically reducing qualitative and quantitative controls over credit (for example, control by sector, activity, type of collateral, size of firm, final use); (3) reducing the barriers to entry for new banks, financial intermediaries, and foreign banks (especially in Argentina and Chile); (4) easing banking regulations concerning minimum capital requirements, ownership concentration, financial-industrial conglomerates, and reserve requirements; and (5) in Chile, returning or auctioning to the private sector most of the banks that had been placed under state control under Allende. Financial opening to the outside world included (1) authorization of domestic bank accounts denominated in foreign currency and (2) the progressive reduction of time limits on the inflows and outflows of capital and of

---

1. For an extensive and detailed treatment of the process of financial liberalization in Argentina, Chile, and Uruguay see, Frenkel 1980, Sourrouille and Lucángeli 1983, Ffrench-Davis and Arellano 1981, and Wonsewer and Saráchaga 1980. Firms' responses to financial liberalization in each of the three countries are analyzed in Petrie and Tybout 1985, Galvez and Tybout 1985, and De Melo, Pascale, and Tybout 1985.

amount limits on inflows. These limits were important in Argentina and Chile, especially through 1978.

Argentina first prohibited the entry of foreign capital for periods of less than 180 days, later raising it to one year (August 1977) and two years (November 1977). Moreover, borrowers were obliged to deposit the equivalent of 10 to 20 percent of the foreign credit in domestic currency and at zero interest, all of which raised its effective cost to borrowers. These restrictions (which were levied only on private-sector borrowing) were justified as necessary to maintain control over the growth of the money supply. However, once the price-stabilization policy (in mid-1978) shifted from controlling money supply to controlling the exchange rate, these restrictions were gradually eased. Indeed, to meet the heavy drain on reserves, even the inflow of very short-term capital was permitted as of mid-1980.

Chile, on the other hand, maintained the prohibition on capital inflows for periods under two years almost to the end (mid-1982), for it feared that unrestricted financial liberalization would bring in so much capital—given the huge differentials between domestic and international interest rates—that the stabilization program could be jeopardized. In any case, Chile did tend to increase access in the course of time. At the beginning, only nonfinancial enterprises could borrow; then banks were allowed to borrow up to certain limits—which were later substantially raised.

Even though the three countries established different sets of restrictions, capital inflows to the three did not differ much. In the final analysis, such inflows depend not only on the demand for credit (what the country wants and allows) but on its supply (what international banks are willing to lend under the conditions). Similarly, one really effective restriction was the limit imposed on external borrowing by the public sector. Argentina and Uruguay increased the public sector's foreign indebtedness substantially right from the very beginning, whereas Chile discouraged it almost to the very end.

THE RESULTS

The final objective of the policy of financial liberalization was to raise the level of domestic savings, increase investment, and improve resource allocation. The key policy instrument for this in the domestic plane was the freeing of interest rates. This was expected to encourage savings, equalize interest rates between formal and informal credit segments, and lower the costs of financial intermediation to increase the volume and variety of financial instruments. The freer flow of international capital was expected to raise investment further and move domestic interest rates closer to international ones.

The effects of liberalization proved to be dramatically different from expected effects. No doubt some of the unsatisfactory results were due not to financial liberalization itself but to unfavorable external conditions. Yet, as I will spell out shortly, a large part of the failures can be attributed to the questionable decision to pursue financial liberalization along with, rather than after, price stabilization (both its initial tight-money variant and its later variant of fixing or preannouncing the exchange-rate devaluation). This error, along with others committed in the process of financial liberalization, grew out of the neoconservatives' grossly simplified or mistaken assumptions as to the workings of the economy. The principal seven results were an increase in the financial sector as a portion of GNP, lower national savings in GNP, increased foreign debt, a drop in investment as a portion of GNP, increased interest rates, a permissive regulatory environment, and erratic stock prices. Summaries of these results are given below.

First, as expected and desired, the financial sector strongly increased its share in GNP, rising by at least two percentage points. More importantly, there was a remarkable increase in the proportion of GNP held in the form of time and savings deposits and of credit to the private sector. These increased from threefold to over tenfold between the onset of the neoconservative experience

Table 8.1.   Chile: Share of Savings and Financial Sector in Gross National Product, 1970–1983 (*percentage*)

Year	Gross Domestic Savings[a]	Gross National Savings[a]	Foreign Savings[b]	Financial Sector[a]
1970	23.4	21.6	1.7	11.5
1971	20.8	17.8	2.9	11.1
1972	15.2	10.4	4.8	10.7
1973	14.3	9.5	4.8	10.1
1974	25.8	25.3	0.5	12.0
1975	14.0	8.5	5.6	13.8
1976	13.6	15.4	−1.9	13.8
1977	14.4	10.7	3.7	13.4
1978	16.5	11.6	4.8	13.7
1979	19.6	13.7	5.9	14.4
1980	23.9	17.9	6.0	15.2
1981	23.9	11.3	12.6	15.9
1982	9.6	1.0	8.6	17.8
1983[c]	11.2	6.5	4.7	16.5

Source: CEPAL, on the basis of official data, Banco Central de Chile 1983.

[a]Computed in national currency. Financial sector is value-added generated by financial institutions, insurance, real estate, and indirect services to firms.

[b]Computed using deficit in current account in 1970 dollars converted to current dollars using implicit deflator of U.S. GNP.

[c]Preliminary figures.

and the peak values achieved before the final crisis and demise of the neoconservative experiences (tables 8.1 through 8.6).

Notwithstanding the wide variety of financial instruments generated by the liberalization of capital markets, the bulk of these were of very short-term duration (thirty days and less). High interest rates on such short-term depostis, plus strong inflation and future uncertainty, made it very difficult subsequently to generate longer-run instruments attractive to depositors and borrowers. Hence, the domestic capital market was never really anything other than a market in quasi money. It was only toward the end of phase II that significant long-term instruments were offered, but their interest rates ranged between 12 percent and 18 percent real per year, and they never became more than a small fraction of overall credit. The market for long term bonds was virtually nonexistent.

Second, despite the remarkable increase in time and savings deposits, the proportion of GNP actually saved (that is, income not consumed), was actually lower during the neoconservative period than in the years immediately preced-

Table 8.2.   Uruguay: Share of Savings and Financial Sector in Gross National Product, 1970–1983 (*percentage*)

Year	Gross Domestic Savings[a]	Gross National Savings[a]	Foreign Savings[b]	Financial Sector[a]
1970	11.4	9.6	1.8	5.8
1971	11.2	8.9	2.3	5.9
1972	9.6	11.1	−1.5	6.0
1973	9.1	9.6	−0.5	6.0
1974	9.1	5.7	3.4	5.7
1975	10.9	6.5	4.4	5.5
1976	12.7	11.0	1.7	5.3
1977	14.8	11.6	3.2	5.2
1978	16.0	13.8	2.2	9.5
1979	18.7	13.7	5.0	
1980	20.1	14.5	5.6	
1981	16.8	13.5	3.3	
1982	15.5	13.5	2.0	
1983[c]	10.5	10.0	0.5	

Source: CEPAL, on the basis of official data.

[a]Computed in national currency. Financial sector is value-added generated by financial institutions, insurance, real estate, and indirect services to firms.

[b]Computed using deficit in current account in 1970 dollars converted to current dollars using implicit deflator of U.S. GNP.

[c]Preliminary figures.

ing that experience in both Argentina and Chile (table 5.4).[2] Only Uruguay showed significant improvement in this regard. In short, whereas financial savings proved to be highly sensitive to interest rates, real national savings proved to be far less so.

Third, foreign savings (foreign debt) grew sharply during the neoconservative period, partly as a response to highly favorable interest rates but partly also to the generalized expansion of international liquidity (tables 8.7, 8.8,

Table 8.3.   Argentina: Share of Savings and Financial Sector in Gross National Product, 1970–1983 (*percentage*)

Year	Gross Domestic Savings[a]	Gross National Savings[a]	Foreign Savings[b]	Financial Sector[c]
1970	22.0	21.5	0.5	4.3
1971	25.5	24.3	1.2	4.3
1972	25.2	24.6	0.6	4.2
1973	22.7	24.6	−1.9	4.1
1974	22.4	22.7	−0.3	3.9
1975	22.1	19.4	2.7	4.3
1976	23.6	24.9	−1.3	3.9
1977	26.2	23.9	2.3	4.3
1978	24.3	27.5	−3.2	8.0
1979	25.7	24.9	0.8	8.0
1980	26.6	22.9	4.4	9.0
1981	22.5	18.0	4.5	9.1
1982	19.0	16.4	2.6	8.5
1983[d]	16.2	13.5	2.7	7.6

Source: CEPAL, on the basis of official data.

[a]Computed in national currency.

[b]Computed using deficit in current account in 1970 dollars converted to current dollars using implicit deflator of U.S. GNP.

[c]Computed in national currency 1970–77; in dollars, 1978–83. Financial sector is value-added generated by financial institutions, insurance, real estate, and indirect services to firms.

[d]Preliminary figures.

---

2. Inasmuch as interest payments abroad strongly increased during the neoconservative period, a better indicator of the national savings *effort* (or its restriction in consumption) would be national savings plus factor payments to the outside world, all expressed as a proportion of gross disposable income (this latter being GNP adjusted by the effect of variations in the terms of trade on national income). The national savings effort, so measured, as a proportion of gross disposable income fell 3 percentage points in Chile between the historic period and the neoconservative period, but rose in both Uruguay (3 percentage points) and Argentina (1 to 1.5 percentage points).

8.9). Foreign debt grew only moderately during the first phase (up to 1977–78); only the public sectors of Argentina and Uruguay increased their indebtedness significantly. However, in 1980–81, because of high domestic interest rates, a preannounced and increasingly overvalued exchange rate, and an increased financial opening to the outside, foreign savings increased markedly, close to 13 percent, 6 percent, and 5 percent of GNP in Chile, Uruguay, and Argentina, respectively (tables 8.1, 8.2, 8.3). It is notable that, although Chile had the least internationally open financial sector and, although its public sector was deliberately restrained from borrowing from abroad, it was Chile and not Uruguay that received the heaviest inflows of foreign capital throughout the neoconservative period, not only in relation to GNP and exports but in absolute terms (tables 8.7 through 8.10).[3]

Table 8.4.   Chile: Credit and Money Measures, 1970–1983

	Credit to Private Sector				
	Nominal (billions of current pesos)	Real (1975 pesos)	Ratio to Gross National Product (percentage)		
Year			Credit	$M1^a$	$M2^b$
1970	0.01	1.94	7.1	10.2	17.3
1971	0.01	2.80	7.9	12.8	17.0
1972	0.02	2.86	8.5	13.7	17.5
1973	0.09	2.37	7.0	10.6	12.9
1974	0.58	2.71	5.9	5.3	6.4
1975	3.07	3.07	8.3	4.5	7.1
1976	13.11	4.20	10.2	3.9	7.6
1977	49.65	8.29	17.3	4.5	10.5
1978	114.43	13.65	23.5	4.8	12.5
1979	200.90	17.96	26.0	4.9	14.6
1980	379.25	25.09	35.2	5.5	16.2
1981	546.29	30.20	44.5	5.0	19.6
1982	879.30	44.21	71.6	6.6	31.9
1983[c]	956.06	37.79	63.4	6.8	27.3

Source: CEPAL, on the basis of official data; International Monetary Fund, *International Financial Statistics; Statistical Yearbook;* Banco Central de Chile 1983.

[a]Bills and coins in circulation plus demand deposits.

[b]M1 plus time and savings depostis.

[c]Preliminary figures.

---

3. This may have been so either because of Chile's greater interest-rate spread for the foreign investor, at least in relation to Uruguay (which still fails to explain why the spread did not fall), or because of Chile's better growth prospects in relation to Argentina.

Fourth, notwithstanding the sharp increase in capital inflows and financial savings, investment as a proportion of GNP actually declined in the neoconservative period in Chile, increased only marginally in Argentina, and increased significantly only in Uruguay (table 5.3). In fact, the three countries showed signs of substitution of foreign savings for national savings in the years 1979–81, which helps explain why investment did not increase markedly during the neoconservative period. The most striking case of such substitution is that of Chile in 1981, when external savings rose from 6 to 13 percent of GNP whereas national savings fell from 18 to 11 percent (table 8.1).

Fifth, as expected, upon their liberalization interest rates rose from systematically negative during the years of financial repression to generally positive (table 8.11). Indeed, borrowing rates proved to be unexpectedly and dangerously high for most of the neoconservative period, averaging in real terms 41 percent per year in Chile, 17 percent per year in Argentina, and 15 percent per year in Uruguay for the period from financial liberalization to the

Table 8.5. Uruguay: Credit and Money Measures, 1970–1983

	Credit to Private Sector		Ratio of Gross National Product (percentage)		
Year	Nominal (millions of current pesos)	Real (1975 pesos)	Credit	$M1^a$	$M2^b$
1970	83	1,150	13.6	14.4	21.2
1971	123	1,353	16.7	18.3	26.8
1972	253	1,602	20.4	16.0	25.5
1973	414	1,331	16.3	14.1	21.3
1974	841	1,525	18.3	12.7	20.0
1975	1,596	1,596	19.1	11.5	21.1
1976	2,706	1,797	20.8	12.3	26.7
1977	4,919	2,064	24.7	11.1	31.1
1978	8,678	2,519	28.4	13.0	38.3
1979	19,109	3,325	34.7	12.3	39.3
1980	34,332	3,654	36.5	10.6	39.8
1981	48,267	3,833	38.2	8.4	43.6
1982	95,255	6,355	74.2	9.2	73.5
1983^c	111,380	4,980	59.6	7.0	47.5

Source: CEPAL, on the basis of official data; International Monetary Fund, International Financial Statistics; Statistical Yearbook.

[a]Bills and coins in circulation plus demand deposits.

[b]M1 plus time and savings deposits.

[c]Preliminary figures.

maxidevaluations.[4] While no one can specify exactly what the equilibrium interest rate is, to judge from other countries' experiences or even from LIBOR (which never exceeded 6 percent in real terms during the neoconservative period, and averaged much less), it is hard to believe that this could be much above, say, 10 percent per year real.

The spread between domestic borrowing and deposit rates averaged at least 13 percent per year in the three countries for the period (table 8.12). The

Table 8.6. Argentina: Credit and Money Measures, 1970–1983

| | Credit to Private Sector | | | | |
| | Nominal (billions of current pesos) | Real (1975 pesos) | Ratio to Gross National Product (percentage) | | |
Year			Credit	$M1^a$	$M2^b$
1970	20	24.1	22.7	17.0	30.7
1971	29	25.9	21.8	15.0	26.3
1972	45	25.3	20.5	15.0	24.5
1973	74	25.8	20.3	18.4	29.6
1974	118	33.3	24.5	23.7	36.7
1975	299	29.9	20.5	23.4	28.9
1976	1,211	22.3	15.1	16.9	24.1
1977	4,334	28.9	20.8	16.2	31.5
1978	12,180	29.5	23.7	15.3	33.9
1979	40,023	37.3	28.8	13.3	36.0
1980	83,449	38.7	29.6	12.8	34.0
1981	221,970	50.4	40.7	11.3	34.1
1982	689,280	59.2	43.2	10.2	28.8
1983[c]	2,905,220	56.2	33.2	8.6	26.3

Source: CEPAL, on the basis of official data; International Monetary Fund, International Financial Statistics; Statistical Yearbook.

[a]Bills and coins in circulation plus demand deposits.

[b]M1 plus time and savings deposits.

[c]Preliminary figures.

---

4. Borrowing rates are the nominal rates of interest deflated by the wholesale-price index, for this latter is in all likelihood the most appropriate deflator for the debtor. Should these be deflated by the consumer-price index, average real rates of interest would remain unchanged in Chile but fall from 17 to 5 percent per year in Argentina and from 15 to 14 percent in Uruguay. Interest paid to depositors also rose during the period, averaging 12 percent per year in Chile, 1 percent per year in Uruguay, and −7 percent per year in Argentina (negative, but far less so than in the past). Deposit rates naturally are deflated by the consumer-price index—the more pertinent deflator for depositors.

cost of reserve requirements explains a small part of this differential, especially in the early years of high inflation, in which it was important to control monetary growth and during which the central bank paid no interest on such reserves.[5] However, the remainder of this unusually high spread (well above the historic one, which ranged between 3 and 5 percent) seems to have constituted a quasi rent, which would be a sign of insufficient competition in this activity.[6]

Table 8.7.   Chile: Global External Debt, 1970–1983

| | Billions of Dollars of Debt | | | | Ratios of Global Debt | |
| | | | Global | | | |
Year	Private	Public	Total	Net[a]	Percentage of GNP[b]	Percentage of Exports
1970	0.6	2.2	2.8	2.4	30.9	224
1971	0.5	2.3	2.8	2.6	27.0	248
1972	0.4	2.6	3.0	2.9	28.2	305
1973	0.7	2.9	3.6	3.5	33.8	246
1974	0.8	3.6	4.4	4.3	37.7	189
1975	1.1	3.6	4.7	4.8	42.3	256
1976	1.0	3.5	4.5	4.4	37.2	186
1977	1.3	3.9	5.2	4.8	36.9	200
1978	2.0	4.7	6.7	5.4	40.9	228
1979	2.4	5.1	8.5	5.9	44.1	184
1980	6.0	5.1	11.1	6.5	49.0	186
1981	10.1	5.5	15.5	11.0	59.7	280
1982	12.0	5.2	17.2	14.5	72.0	370
1983[c]	10.5	7.0	17.5	15.5	71.0	379

Source: 1970–76, Banco Central de Chile 1982; 1977–81, ODEPLAN 1983; 1982–83, Informe del Ministro de Hacienda, 2 July 1984.

[a]Net international reserves.

[b]1970 GNP converted to current dollars using implicit deflator of U.S. GNP.

[c]Preliminary figures.

---

5. This is suggested by an analysis of the Chilean case (see table 8.12), in which the cost of maintaining such noninterest-bearing reserves is estimated and in which, nevertheless, the average spread for the period remained close to 15 percent. For a fuller treatment of this point see Arellano 1984 and Cortés and Sjaastad 1978.

6. See, in this regard, Spiller and Favaro 1982. Although in Uruguay there were twenty-one private banks, one state bank, and many nonbank intermediaries, the authors argue that the legal barriers to further entry of new banks encouraged oligopolistic behavior by the financial system. It is striking, however, that spreads were similarly high in Argentina and Chile and behaved in much the same way, despite the absence of such barriers in the latter. This suggests that *in practice* it took a good deal of time for the pressure of competition to

That this spread declined over the course of time—almost up to 1981–82, when the risk of a major financial crisis was quite high—certainly suggests that the increased number of financial intermediaries, and the ensuing competition, was responsible.

Moreover, domestic interest rates failed to converge to international ones, as had been expected and hoped for, not even during the period in which the exchange rate was being devalued in programmed and preannounced fashion. And this notwithstanding the heavy inflows of capital. On the contrary, domestic interest rates for both deposits and borrowing proved to be well above LIBOR plus the rate of devaluation. This spread varied from a minimum of 10 to 20 percentage points per year in Uruguay, to 20 to 30 in Chile, and a maximum of 30 to 40 percentage points in Argentina (table 8.12, indexes B and

Table 8.8.   Uruguay: Global External Debt, 1970–1983

	Billions of Dollars of Debt				Ratios of Global Debt	
			Global		Percentage of GNP[b]	Percentage of Exports
Year	Private	Public	Total	Net[a]		
1970	0.19	0.33	0.52	0.43	16.9	179
1971	0.22	0.39	0.61	0.52	19.4	244
1972	0.23	0.54	0.77	0.68	23.9	219
1973	0.18	0.54	0.72	0.64	20.5	176
1974	0.22	0.74	0.96	0.98	24.3	192
1975	0.17	0.86	1.03	1.10	22.8	187
1976	0.17	0.96	1.13	1.02	22.8	162
1977	0.29	1.03	1.32	0.98	24.7	163
1978	0.33	0.91	1.24	0.63	20.1	136
1979	0.67	1.01	1.68	0.99	22.9	141
1980	0.97	1.16	2.13	1.32	25.6	140
1981	1.66	1.47	3.13	2.29	34.7	183
1982	1.55	2.71	4.26	3.92	49.0	277
1983[c]	1.31	3.20	4.51	4.11	53.0	320

Source: Banco Central del Uruguay.

[a]Net international reserves.

[b]1970 GNP converted to current dollars using implicit deflator of U.S. GNP.

[c]Preliminary figures.

make itself felt. (High spreads may also have been due to the fact that most operations were for thirty days, which raised fixed costs. Yet this should have been largely compensated by the much greater number of operations than in the past—all the more so since the periodic renovation of most short-run credits was effected almost automatically requiring little additional evaluation.)

C). Except for exchange risk, this differential made it quite attractive for foreigners to bring capital into these countries and for nationals to borrow in foreign currency (table 8.11, especially last three columns). These spreads were large even in the period when the exchange rate was being devalued far more slowly than the difference between domestic and international inflation, when real domestic interest rates might therefore have been expected to be lower than international ones or even negative (at least so long as a max-idevaluation was not feared).[7]

Sixth, financial liberalization was accompanied by a more permissive regulatory environment, both in terms of practices formally permitted and, more importantly, practices informally condoned that circumvented the spirit of the regulation. Among the latter were (1) triangular lending operations, often-times through the creation of an investment firm whose principal equity was shares of its parent firm but which, as a "different" firm, could borrow and then relend to the parent firm, thereby circumventing lending limits to any single firm; (2) restrictions on ownership of banks that yet allowed effective control of a bank by a single economic conglomerate through the ownership of persons or firms related to or belonging to the same group.

Since bankruptcy was thought to be guaranteed against by the government, there was a built-in bias for banks to throw to the wind regulatory and common-sense limits on concentration of risk and to make unusually risky loans, especially to firms belonging to the same conglomerate as the bank, resulting in banks having unduly leveraged ratios of debt to equity (see Díaz-Alejandro 1983). This would be fine in upswings (when the gains were "privatized"), but would leave banks "holding the bag" in downswings (or the

---

7. In the absence of exchange risk and with no controls on capital flows, the nominal domestic interest rate should equal or converge toward the nominal international rate of interest plus the expected devaluation:

$$i_D = i_I + \dot{R}_e.$$

To the extent that the expected devaluation, $\dot{R}_e$, is equal to the announced and executed devaluation, $(\dot{R})$,

$$i_D = i_I + \dot{R}.$$

The exchange rate comes to lag inflation and be overvalued when $\dot{R} < \dot{P}_D - \dot{P}_I$. Therefore, when there is a lag in the exchange rate,

$$i_D < i_I + (\dot{P}_D - \dot{P}_I); \text{ or}$$

$$(i_D - \dot{P}_D) < (i_I - \dot{P}_I).$$

In other words, with an expected lag in the exchange rate, the real domestic interest rate should be less than the real international rate of interest. And if the expected lag in the exchange rate were greater than the real international rate of interest, real domestic interest should be negative (or close to it, for there are country risks and additional intermediation costs to be added in). Since LIBOR in this period (6 percent per year real) was less than the expected lag in the exchange rate, substantially *negative* real domestic interest rates should have been observed for some of the period in question.

Table 8.9.   Argentina: Global External Debt, 1970–1983

| | Billions of Dollars of Debt | | | | Ratios of Global Debt | |
Year	Private	Public	Global	Net[a]	Percentage of GNP[b]	Percentage of Exports
1970	1.8	2.1	3.9	3.1	13.1	185
1971	2.0	2.5	4.5	4.1	13.9	214
1972	2.7	3.1	5.8	5.2	16.8	252
1973	2.8	3.4	6.2	4.8	16.5	168
1974	3.4	4.6	8.0	6.6	18.4	174
1975	3.9	4.0	7.9	7.3	16.8	226
1976	3.1	5.2	8.3	6.5	16.8	180
1977	3.6	6.0	9.7	5.6	17.4	147
1978	4.1	8.4	12.5	6.5	21.6	167
1979	9.1	10.0	19.0	8.5	28.3	207
1980	12.7	14.5	27.2	19.5	36.5	275
1981	15.6	20.0	35.7	31.8	46.6	331
1982	15.0	28.6	43.6	40.5	58.0	484
1983[c]			45.5	42.1	56.0	485

Source: Banco Central de la República Argentina.
[a]Net international reserves.
[b]1970 GNP converted to current dollars using implicit deflator of U.S. GNP.
[c]Preliminary figures.

Table 8.10.   Southern Cone: Indicators of Capital Inflows, 1973–1983

Country and Year	Capital Account in Balance of Payments (millions of dollars)	Capital Account as Percentage of Exports	Long-Term Private Capital as Percentage of Exports	Short-Term Private Capital as Percentage of Exports
Chile				
1973	387.0	26.5	−0.1	12.8
1974	211.0	9.1	0.9	−4.0
1975	211.0	11.5	−4.1	7.7
1976	200.0	8.3	1.2	2.8
1977	737.0	28.3	7.7	21.4
1978	1,857.0	63.1	39.6	15.3
1979	2,261.0	48.9	30.5	10.2
1980	3,344.0	56.0	38.0	16.8
1981	5,008.0	90.9	69.7	20.1
1982	1,096.0	21.8	24.5	−11.8
1983[a]	693.0	15.1	0.0	−17.9

Table 8.10. *continued*

Country and Year	Capital Account in Balance of Payments (millions of dollars)	Capital Account as Percentage of Exports	Long-Term Private Capital as Percentage of Exports	Short-Term Private Capital as Percentage of Exports
Uruguay				
1973	9.0	2.2	−4.9	5.4
1974	96.0	19.2	1.2	21.0
1975	136.0	24.7	3.1	5.6
1976	156.0	22.4	5.7	11.8
1977	351.0	43.4	1.7	25.1
1978	262.0	28.7	−0.8	−5.9
1979	453.0	37.9	1.8	7.9
1980	811.0	53.1	0.9	20.4
1981	494.0	29.5	2.8	19.1
1982	−182.0	−25.9	4.5	33.3
1983[a]	111.0	8.0		
Argentina				
1973	147.0	4.0	−0.2	0.6
1974	−42.0	−0.9	−1.3	−1.4
1975	205.0	5.9	−1.2	10.7
1976	261.0	5.7	−1.7	−7.7
1977	556.0	8.4	8.1	1.7
1978	302.0	4.0	28.1	−16.6
1979	4,760.0	51.9	29.1	14.6
1980	2,176.0	22.0	31.1	−20.4
1981	1,520.0	14.0	63.9	−76.0
1982	1,809.0	20.1	5.8	−18.9
1983[a]	−13.0	0⁻	0⁺	−13.9

Source: CEPAL, on the basis of International Monetary Fund, *Balance of Payments*.
[a]Preliminary figures.

government would pay the cost if it guaranteed deposits, thus "socializing" the debt).

Seventh, asset prices (our data in this case are limited to Argentina and Chile) moved quite erratically (figures 8.1 and 8.2). The index of stock-market prices (expressed in real terms) in Argentina varied by a factor of one to four (and then back again) in the period between financial liberalization and the maxidevaluations (mid-1977 to the end of 1980); and the same index rose by more than one to ten in Chile, only to lose half of its value in the same reference period (mid-1975 to mid-1982). Urban real estate seems to have shown similar

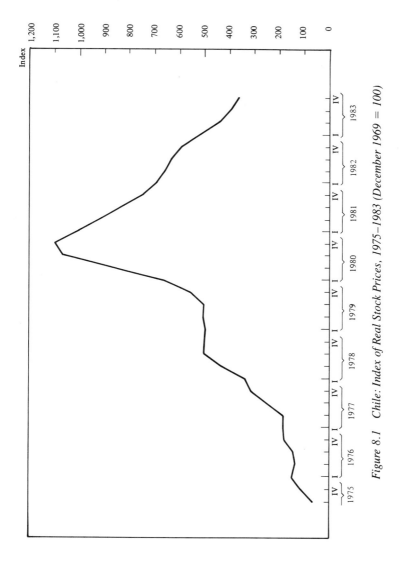

Figure 8.1 Chile: Index of Real Stock Prices, 1975–1983 (December 1969 = 100)

Table 8.11. Southern Cone: Interest Rates by Year (*percentage*)

Country and Year	Lending Rate			Deposit Rate		Domestic Debtor Rate		Foreign Creditor Rate (Index C)
	Nominal	Real[a]	Real[b]	Nominal	Real[a]	Index A	Index B	
Chile								
1975[c]	331.7	−40.8	−45.7	303.5	−44.9	−31.1	−35.0	132.2
1975[d]	498.3	127.1	84.0	234.5	25.2	11.4	−0.8	96.8
1976	250.7	17.7	39.4	197.9	0.0	−27.4	−14.0	45.4
1977	156.3	39.1	55.3	93.7	5.2	−7.6	3.1	20.7
1978	85.3	35.1	33.4	62.8	18.7	−4.0	−5.0	34.1
1979	62.0	16.6	2.3	45.0	4.4	−7.4	−18.7	26.2
1980	46.9	12.0	14.7	37.4	4.7	−12.8	−10.7	37.4
1981	51.9	38.7	58.1	40.8	28.6	6.4	21.2	40.8
1982	63.1	35.1	16.8	47.8	22.5	77.0	53.1	−21.5
1983[e]	42.7	15.9	14.0	27.9	3.9	6.3	4.5	7.3
Uruguay								
1977	65.7	5.3	14.4	38.3	−12.1	−8.8	−1.0	2.2
1978	73.9	19.1	9.0	47.2	0.8	−2.9	−11.2	12.9
1979	65.5	−9.6	−6.5	43.4	−21.7	−26.6	−24.1	19.5
1980	66.6	16.7	29.5	50.1	5.1	−5.2	5.3	26.8

154

1981	60.4	23.9	39.6	46.1	12.8	4.2	17.3	26.3
1982	61.5	34.0	21.0	53.3	27.2	174.1	147.4	−30.0
1983e	94.4	28.3	11.9	70.1	12.3	−7.2	−19.1	32.8
Argentina								
1977c	79.2	−23.3	−22.1	60.5	−31.3	135.9	139.6	−69.1
1977d	236.4	15.9	26.7	171.9	−6.3	−14.5	−6.5	16.1
1978	172.4	0.9	11.9	130.4	−14.6	−32.3	−25.0	37.2
1979	134.6	−2.2	2.6	117.1	−9.4	−24.7	−21.1	34.6
1980	98.3	5.7	25.9	79.4	−4.4	−25.0	−10.6	45.7
1981	175.9	19.3	−1.5	152.8	9.3	83.2	51.2	−30.5
1982	213.5	11.4	−13.5	148.8	−19.7	145.4	84.8	−62.9
1983e				272.6	−30.2	−1.4	2.9	−22.2

Source: Central banks of Argentina, Chile, and Uruguay; International Monetary Fund, *International Financial Statistics.*

Note: Year is from December to December. Index A is $[(1 + \text{LIBOR}) (1 + \text{nominal devaluation})/(1 + \text{consumer-price variation})] - 1$. Index B is $[(1 + \text{LIBOR}) (1 + \text{nominal devaluation})/(1 + \text{wholesale–price variation})] - 1$. Index C is $[(1 + \text{nominal deposit rate})/(1 + \text{nominal devaluation})] - 1$.

aDeflated by consumer-price index.
bDeflated by wholesale-price index.
cFirst semester (before liberalization of interest rates).
dSecond semester (after liberalization of interest rates).
ePreliminary figures.

Table 8.12.   Southern Cone: Interest-Rate Differentials by Year (*percentage*)

Country and Year	Index A	Index B	Index C
Chile			
1975[a]	7.0	117.0	132.2
1975[b]	78.9 (44)	83.9	228.9
1976	17.8 (16)	37.7	62.1
1977	32.3 (28)	13.9	50.6
1978	13.8 (13)	23.3	40.4
1979	11.7 (9)	12.7	25.9
1980	6.9 (6)	20.1	28.5
1981	7.9	20.8	30.4
1982	10.7	−30.8	−23.7
1983[c]	11.6	−18.0	9.0
Uruguay			
1977	19.8	−3.6	15.5
1978	18.1	3.8	22.7
1979	15.4	6.7	23.2
1980	11.0	10.9	23.0
1981	9.8	8.4	19.0
1982	5.1	−56.3	−54.0
1983[c]	14.3	−5.6	38.2
Argentina			
1977[a]	11.6	−70.9	−67.5
1977[b]	23.7	9.5	35.5
1978	18.2	26.2	49.2
1979	8.0	20.2	29.9
1980	10.5	27.4	40.8
1981	9.1	−40.3	−34.9
1982	26.0	−67.3	−58.8
1983[c]		−85.2	

Source: Table 8.1. Chile's index A rates in parentheses from Ffrench-Davis and Arellano 1981.

Note: Index A, difference between loan rate and deposit rate. Ffrench-Davis and Arellano figures includes cost of legal reserve requirements. Index B, difference between interest (U.S. dollars) received by the foreign creditor who lends in the internal market and the LIBOR rate: $\{[(1 + \text{deposit rate})/(1 + \text{nominal exchange-rate variation})]/(1 + \text{LIBOR})\} - 1$. Index C, difference between interest in internal market and in external market for domestic borrower: $\{(1 + \text{lending rate})/[(1 + \text{LIBOR})(1 + \text{nominal exchange-rate variation})]\} - 1$.

[a]First semester.

[b]Second semester.

[c]Preliminary figures.

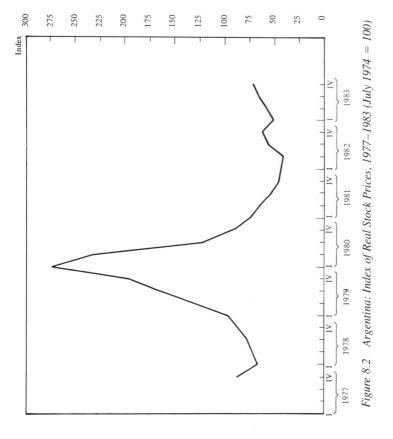

Index

300

275

250

225

200

175

150

125

100

75

50

25

0

I IV I IV I IV I IV I IV I IV I IV
1977 1978 1979 1980 1981 1982 1983

Figure 8.2   Argentina: Index of Real Stock Prices, 1977–1983 (July 1974 = 100)

157

swings, though far less extreme. Thus enormous capital gains (and losses) were made during this period. Somewhat paradoxically, to the extent that the prices of shares and of urban real estate are good indicators of asset values, financial liberalization (higher real interest rates) was accompanied by increases, not decreases, in asset values; the subsequent sharp declines were associated not so much with higher interest rates as with the growing gap between "paper" wealth and the even dimmer prospects of income growth—a prelude of the sharp recessions these countries were about to suffer and of the domestic financial crises that preceded these recessions.

THREE POLICY QUESTIONS

Many questions emerge on viewing the results of financial liberalization. I should like to address three, the answers to which, I think, can shed much light on the financial crisis that finally ensued. (1) Why were domestic interest rates so high, and for so long, and so far above international rates despite such high capital inflows? (2) Why didn't national savings and investment rise significantly (except for Uruguay), despite the unusually high interest rates and despite the very strong increase in time and savings deposits? (3) Why did asset prices rise so much, rather than falling when interest rates rose, as we would normally expect?

Why Were Interest Rates So High?

The perception of a high exchange risk explains part of the differential between domestic and international interest rates in 1980 in Argentina, in 1981 in Chile, and in 1982 in Uruguay. Nevertheless, the differential had been high in the preceding years, when the exchange risk was virtually nonexistent and capital inflows were quite heavy. The differential between LIBOR adjusted by devaluation and domestic lending rates (index C in table 8.12) was never less than 30 percentage points in Argentina in 1978–79, nor less than 23 percentage points in Uruguay in 1979–80; and what is particularly perplexing, it reached 29 percentage points in Chile in 1980, the year after the exchange rate was fixed—and in the middle of a boom. In other words, exchange risk is undoubtedly a factor contributing to this differential, but it is far from being the sole or most important one.

The degree in which the capital accounts were opened up is also likely to have influenced this interest-rate differential. This may well explain why Uruguay had the lowest differential. But even then, several problems remain that suggest that the relation is not all that simple. For one thing, despite the greater ease with which capital could flow into Uruguay, its capital flows were comparable to those received by Chile, which had more restrictions (tables 8.7 through 8.10). For another, the differential moved contrary to the direction of financial liberalization both in Uruguay, where it was extensive from its inception, and in Chile, where the process was more gradual. The ratio of credit and $M2$ in GNP rose sharply in both countries as expected, but the differential between domestic and international rates (indexes B and C of table 8.12), instead of declining, rose in Uruguay between 1977 and 1980 and in Chile between 1979 and 1981. And while this differential did fall in Argentina, it never fell below 10 percentage points.

Thus, apart from exchange risk and the degree of financial liberalization, other factors seem to explain high domestic interest rates and their lack of convergence toward international rates. Undoubtedly, the restrictive monetary policy common to the price-stabilization policies initially pursued in all three countries was one such factor, which would help explain high interest rates in the early years of these experiences. Yet, since these interest rates continued to remain high in real terms, even in periods of very heavy capital inflows and when stabilization policy moved from controlling the money supply to controlling the exchange rate, it is reasonable to look for additional explanations on the side of the demand for credit.

Among the principal factors increasing this demand above normal levels in different moments during the neoconservative experience were:

1. The unexpected appearance of opportunities for exceptional capital gains naturally raises the real demand for credit. This is what happened in Argentina in 1977, when, as part of one more attempt at price stabilization, a four-month price freeze was announced. This encouraged firms to demand credit to buy inputs and to stockpile output in order to sell it later at the higher prices expected once the price freeze was lifted. The most notable case was that of Chile in 1975, when, in the midst of a severe depression, the government announced its program to auction off a large number of banks and enterprises that had come into its hands during the Allende government.

2. The rise in the real value of assets, under normal conditions, is closely related to the rate of economic growth soon expected. Nevertheless, during various years after financial liberalization, the sharp upward revaluation of stocks and real estate far exceeded what could be justified by any reasonable expectation of likely economic growth, indicative of a speculative euphoria (a point to which I shall soon return). In any case, whatever the reason, the real market value of assets did grow substantially for several years, at least in Argentina and Chile. To the extent this happens, the demand for credit can rise because of a wealth effect.

3. Public-enterprise deficits, which in the past had been largely "financed" via the direct creation of money by the central bank, were now financed by borrowing in the domestic capital market. Chile used this mechanism quite extensively, especially at the beginning, whereas Argentina and Uruguay borrowed heavily from external sources to cover public-sector needs throughout the entire process.

4. The opening up of trade and the elimination of administrative controls on

the allocation of credit immensely expanded demand for consumer credit—especially for consumer durables, for the relative price of these had fallen considerably within the three countries because of lower tariffs.

5. The belief that high real rates of interest would soon fall to reasonable (equilibrium) levels—say, 5 to 10 percent per year. This was all the more important because much short-term credit was being utilized to finance operations of a longer-term nature, thereby supposing its automatic renovation.

6. The above factors explain a demand for credit originating in expectations (correct or not) of higher future income. One would suppose that the demand for credit would fall should expectations be reversed. Nevertheless, demand for credit can also go up in the short run not only for possible gains in income but to avoid or postpone possible losses in wealth brought on by unexpected reversals in key economic indicators—for example, to avoid either being forced to liquidate excess inventories accumulated because of an unexpected decline in sales or being forced to sell assets during periods of recession and, consequently, at depressed values. It was thus quite tempting to postpone such capital losses in a recession thought to be transitory (Argentina between the end of 1977 and the end of 1978 and Chile in 1974–75). The temptation was naturally irresistible in a generalized situation affecting many firms (after the maxidevaluations of 1981–82), since the sale of assets would have been at such low prices that it implied the firm's bankruptcy. The path to bankruptcy is seldom smooth and gradual, and just when bankruptcy might happen is not always evident. When possible bankruptcy is sudden and widespread (as in 1981–82), it is likely to induce the acquiescence of bank creditors, for their own solvency is at stake (a point to which I shall return; also see Ho and Saunders 1980; Bullow and Shoven 1978; and Perez and Moreno 1984).

These six factors introduced an important asymmetry and upward bias in the demand for credit. To the extent that potential capital losers demand more credit, and not less, in order to avoid or postpone losses, the increased demand for credit of would-be capital gainers is not compensated by a decrease in the demand for credit of prospective capital losers. Indeed, rather than canceling each other out, these effects combine and reinforce each other, and the overall effect is all the stronger the greater the fluctuations in the perceived value of capital assets. Precisely one of the central features that characterized the neo-conservative experiences was the sharp changes in the relative price structure—of prices with respect to wages; of agricultural prices with respect to prices of manufactures; of the price of tradables with respect to that of nontradables—all of which necessarily gave rise to important capital gains and losses. Thus to the extent that capital losses in particular were perceived as transitory (an excusable perception, for to perceive them as permanent might have implied recognizing insolvency, all the more so since key macroeconomic variables fluctuated substantially and never approximated equilibrium), an important asymmetry was introduced in the demand for credit. Wealth transfers led both potential capital gainers and losers to demand more credit, consequently moving real interest rates well above equilibrium levels.[8]

In much the same vein, the failure of domestic interest rates to converge to international ones was due to the fact that the demand for credit grew far more than what the international market was willing to finance. This latter market is rationed by quantity as well as by price: while certainly an interest-rate differential can attract capital inflows, it will do so in practice only as long as the exchange risk is low.[9] So long as the demand for foreign credit increased in step with the capacity to service such debt (as with rising exports and reserves), exchange risk was likely to be perceived as low. However, once the increased demand for credit, as during the close of phase II, was due to a deterioration in the capacity to service such debt (because of the lag in the exchange rate, the international recession, and growing interest payments), the supply of foreign credits was sharply cut back. As might be expected, capital inflows then became rather insensitive to interest-rate differentials but quite sensitive to exchange risk. Domestic interest rates were thus pulled upward, worsening the recession, and ultimately precipitating an acute financial crisis, all of which forced the maxidevaluations.

For this reason, domestic and international interest rates failed to converge and certainly failed to equalize. To be sure, had it been possible to maintain this exchange policy indefinitely, interest-rate convergence would eventually have taken place. But the point is that the longer the preannounced exchange rate policy was maintained, the more it became overvalued, and the less credible was its continuance. For it was hard to believe that the government would be willing to persevere in its exchange policy however sharp an economic contraction it required. No guarantee on such policy would have been believable, short of closing the central bank and counting on an indefinite supply of foreign exchange—and thus "dollarizing" the economy, as in Panama.

Why Were Financial Savings So High, National Savings and Investment So Low?

Financial liberalization was expected to raise interest rates and induce greater savings and investment. Interest rates rose indeed, as did time and savings deposits. Yet except for Uruguay, ex post national savings (that is, income less consumption) did not increase, nor did investment. Why didn't the increased

---

8. I owe this insight concerning the association of asymmetry in the demand for credit and the degree of relative price (and so, wealth) changes to Carlos Massad.

9. Capital inflows are not simply and solely dependent on the differential in real interest rates between the domestic and international capital markets. In this period, significant amounts of capital came in because the expected rate of return in dollars of direct investment was also high (at least, so long as the exchange policy was expected to continue). Much of the capital brought in from overseas by nationals was not for investment in the domestic capital market but for direct investments in the economy.

financial savings translate itself into increased effective national savings and investment?[10]

The counterpart of controlled interest rates during the former period of financial repression in the Southern Cone was the administrative allocation of credit. Credit during this period strongly favored investment in fixed capital and public-works infrastructure at the expense of consumer credit, private-sector infrastructure (that is, commercial construction), and housing. Whether such an allocation maximized welfare or not—implying that the social discount rate of interest was less than the free-market rate—is an open question. The fact remains that financial liberalization both freed interest rates and eliminated controls on credit use. Thus the repressed demand for credit—especially for consumer durables but also for private commercial infrastructure—manifested itself upon financial liberalization, and so the increase in financial savings did not necessarily yield an increase in effective, ex post savings and investment, but rather helped finance consumer credit.

In addition, Chile, unlike Argentina and Uruguay, purposely reduced public-sector infrastructure investment so as not to crowd out private investment, a reduction which, it turned out, was only partially offset by the increase in private investment. For these reasons, overall savings and investment in Chile were actually much lower during the neoconservative period than in the previous period, and in Argentina they were virtually similar to those of the previous period, notwithstanding the sharp increase in financial savings. Effective (ex post) national savings thus proved rather insensitive to the rate of interest in this period, at least in Argentina and Chile.

On the other hand, national savings seem to have responded (1) positively to growth in national income and especially to the ups and downs in disposable gross income (that is, after output is adjusted by variations in the terms of trade); (2) inversely to the increase in the availability of domestic credit for consumer durables as well as to the relatively low cost of dollar-denominated credit for imports (at least up to 1981); (3) inversely to the decline in the relative price of durable goods, especially imported ones (due to the overvalued exchange rate of phase II stabilization and the reduction in tariffs); and (4) inversely to the apparently greater market value of most fixed assets, which led economic agents to believe (mistakenly) that their permanent income was higher and that they could well afford to spend more on consumption.

---

10. Not only is it a fascinating question *how* financial savings could go up without effective national savings and investment also doing so, but also *where* these financial savings came from. On both these issues, see Arellano 1984. As to the latter question, he suggests, first, that 35 percent of the increase in domestic financial assets was the counterpart of foreign debt that was not spent on imports but that augmented reserves until 1981. A second major source is simply capitalized interest rates on deposits, which between 1977 and 1981, alone, were the equivalent of close to half of existing nonmonetary financial assets; third, much of the savings represented a shift of government direct investment from public-sector firms to the financial sector.

Thus, whatever the long-term effects of higher interest rates on national savings, the evidence of the Southern Cone is certainly mixed. In Uruguay, real savings and investment rose. In Argentina and Chile, consumption rose (possibly because it had been heretofore so repressed). In any case, it should be clear that, as important as the impact of financial liberalization on interest rates was, so too was the dismantling of credit controls it entailed. To the extent that these were formerly biased in favor of investment, the impact of liberalization was to increase financial savings yet reduce real savings (and investment).

For much the same reason, the increase in foreign savings (debt) associated with increased financial opening up to the outside world need not have resulted in like increases in investment. Some debt indeed was used to increase foreign exchange reserves (at least up to the period preceding the maxidevaluations). Some substituted national savings with foreign savings, as earlier noted, especially in the years 1979–81, giving rise to massive increases in consumer imports. Much went to satisfy the armed forces' pent-up demand for the import of military hardware (less valued by previous civilian administrations, which were concerned with fostering productive investment). Finally, much augmented private savings and investment overseas, since foreign debt was socialized, whereas foreign exchange was privatized. The end result is that, notwithstanding unprecedented increases in the share of foreign savings in gross national product in the neoconservative period (1 percent in Uruguay, 2 percent in Argentina, and 3 percent in Chile), overall investment rose by only 1.5 percent in Argentina and actually fell in Chile.[11] Only Uruguay showed a marked increase in investment during the period.

Why Were Asset Prices So High?

I have already commented on the extraordinary volatility of asset prices during the period of financial liberalization; that they varied far more than any other variable is not unusual, but rather that they varied by as much as they did: four to one in Argentina and over ten to one in Chile. The puzzle is all the more enigmatic given the noted tendency of interest rates to rise sharply and remain high during the period of financial liberalization. In short, how account for such extraordinary increases in the prices of stocks (in real terms) precisely in a period characterized by unusually high interest rates?

Most economic theories prepare us for the reverse result: that stock prices vary inversely with real interest rates. Since higher interest rates discount future income streams at ever greater percentages, their present value is thereby lowered. Traditional hypotheses regarding the relation between interest rates, money supply, and stock prices predict that increased money supply in time t

11. Share of foreign savings in GNP was estimated by comparing the average net increase in the annual flow of debt before and during the neoconservative periods as a percent of GNP.

will lead to higher stock prices in $t + 1$, because, first, increased money supply lowers interest rates and so raises the present value of future earnings; second, when there is idle capacity, increased money supply may increase aggregate demand and so real earnings; and third, in the short term, increased money supply may be transferred into stocks more rapidly than into goods or bonds. These reasons point to a positive relation between increased money supply in previous time periods and increased stock prices in the same and following time periods, and so to an inverse relation between interest-rate behavior and stock prices in the same or following time periods (see Sprinkel 1964, Homa and Jaffe 1971, and Hamburger and Kochin 1972).

This traditional approach has been successfully challenged by the most modern formulation of stock-market behavior, the efficient-capital-market hypothesis, which argues that the price of a stock already incorporates all past and current information concerning the best estimate of future values of its determinants (including the interest rate; see Fama 1970, Pesando 1974, and Contador 1974). Hence, it cannot vary systematically *today* as a response to *past* variations in money supply or interest rates.

Nevertheless, even the efficient-capital-market hypothesis suggests that, since financial liberalization can be expected to raise interest rates, stock-market prices should fall when liberalization is announced or is expected. This conclusion could be avoided if one believed, as did those who argued on behalf of financial liberalization, that freeing interest rates would not only raise real interest rates in the formal market (lowering them in informal markets), but raise the quantity and quality of investment—leading to far greater growth. Such growth did not take place, but that may only show that buyers of stocks erred in expecting it, an expectation that raised the demand (and so the price) for stocks, notwithstanding the expectation that interest rates would also rise. Once expectations of strong growth were dashed, stock prices tumbled down.

This explanation fits the general swing in stock prices, though it hardly explains their magnitude. For example, in Chile, lending rates rose from 39 percent per year (real) in 1976 to 55 percent per year in 1977. Such a rise in interest rates implied discounting earnings of future years so heavily that earnings as of the third year and beyond would have a present value of less than 9 percent! Obviously, then, for stock prices to rise in 1977, enormous growth would have to have been expected for the years 1977, 1978, and 1979. Chile's growth did accelerate quite strongly in these three years, from just under 2 percent per capita to about 7 percent per capita, but when one discounts such growth by 55 percent in the first year, 80 percent in the second, and 90 percent in the third, it is obvious that no reasonable expectation of accelerated growth could compensate the increased interest rates. And yet Chilean stock prices rose 76 percent in real terms between the fourth quarter of 1976 and the fourth quarter of 1977 (after close to doubling, as well, in the previous four quarters).

This great growth in stock prices reflected both very favorable expectations of economic growth and the belief that interest rates would soon settle down at much lower rates.[12] Only in some such way could one rationalize the quadrupling of real stock prices between the first quarter of 1978 and the first quarter of 1980 in Argentina or the sixteenfold increase in Chile between the third quarter of 1975 and the fourth quarter of 1980. Such optimistic assessments as to future increases in economic growth and decreases in interest rates so as to lead to such enormous increases in real stock values can only be characterized as generalized euphoria; in short, the upswing of a speculative bubble.

The econometric test for a bubble and crash have been ably demonstrated by Meller and Solimano (1984) for Chile. I will use their formal definition of a speculative bubble: a situation in which the price of shares between two periods (adjusted by dividends) grows faster than the interest rate and continues to so grow for several succeeding periods, only to be followed by repeated periods of slower growth than the interest rate. In an efficient market, the growth in the price of shares (adjusted by dividends) should equal the interest rate. Thus any growth persistently and *systematically* beyond that explicable by real economic forces (that is, the interest rate) is symptomatic of the formation of a speculative bubble; the existence of the bubble is corroborated if it is followed by a crash (stock prices growing far less than the interest rate).

Using this concept, a bubble clearly developed in Chile between the third quarter of 1979 and the end of 1980 (figure 8.1), when the return to stock purchases far exceeded the interest rate for five successive quarters—stock prices more than doubling in real terms in that brief spell (the boom), after which they declined to a third of their peak value over the next twelve successive quarters (the crash). Similarly, in Argentina (figure 8.2), stock prices quadrupled in real terms in the eight quarters from the beginning of 1978 through the beginning of 1980, to be followed by a decline to a sixth of their peak value over the next nine quarters before they began a recovery.

Another way to present the above phenomenon is to note that in neither of the two countries was the level of stock prices (in real terms) correlated with the interest rate during the period of financial liberalization. Indeed, what correlation there was (especially in Chile) seems to have been with $M1$ (in real terms) and $M2$ (in real terms); positively with the former, as if the excess supply of money was spent far more on stocks than on goods, thus raising stock prices in real terms; and negatively with the latter, as if short-term time deposits were good substitutes for stocks.[13] But in neither country was the level of interest

---

12. Of course, such factors as the formation of economic conglomerates and mutual funds also fed price speculation.

13. For Chile, a multiple regression (corrected for second order autocorrelation) between a real index of stock prices, *RISP*, and, for the same period, real $M1$, ($M1P$), real $M2$ ($M2P$), and the real interest rate, iR, yields

$$RISP = -436 + 19M1P - 2M2P + 11\ iR,$$
$$t \quad (-6.9) \quad (9.4) \quad (-3.2) \quad (0.9)$$

rates negatively correlated with the level of stock prices, as might have been expected. Nor was there any significant correlation, even in the short run, between quarterly percentage changes in stock prices and variations in the interest rate; and the sign was positive (contrary to the inverse relation that might have been expected).

For Chile, however, there are two interesting results related to interest-rate variations. Interest-rate increases in period $t - 1$ are followed by a rise in stock prices in period t; moreover, stock prices in period t rise when interest rates fall in period $t + 1$.[14] This suggests that interest rates did not affect stock prices in the long run, but economic agents behaved in the short run as if they thought they did. They raised stock prices in time t as if they expected interest rates to fall in time t or time $t + 1$. And such an occurrence was expected if, among other things, interest rates had risen in time $t - 1$. Thus stock-market behavior, while bearing no correlation to interest rates in the long run, was correlated in the short run, at least in Chile, with what economic agents thought short-run interest behavior would be.

In any case, a bubble did form in stock prices in both Argentina and Chile. Since stock prices reflect the market value of fixed capital, a nontradable, the value of assets seemed to rise far more than the value of foreign debt (at the fixed exchange rate). Firms and other asset holders thus thought themselves far wealthier in real terms than they were (and especially in terms of tradables, given the lag in the exchange rate), and so capable of paying high domestic interest rates while spending more on consumption. Thus the bubble in asset values led to further divergences from equilibrium in the credit and exchange markets.

CONSEQUENCES

For all the above reasons, the demand for credit remained strong and domestic interest rates remained high during the neoconservative experiences (at least up to the maxidevaluations). But how can an economy function properly if its

---

with an adjusted R^2 of 88 percent. The same regressions for Argentina had far weaker explanatory power (less than 5 percent), and the interest rate was likewise not significant. The best result in Argentina was achieved with

$$RISP_t = f(M1P)_{t + 1},$$

but again iR was not correlated and had the wrong sign. The data are six-month moving averages for each quarter. Incidentally, since the stock-price index and $M1P$ and $M2P$ are correlated in the same time period, these results could be fit into the efficient-capital-market model as framed by Cooper 1974, where stock-market prices lead money (since money supply for the same time period would, in effect, be an expected value).

14. The quarterly percentage variation in $RISP$ ($VRISP$) regressed on the quarterly percentage variation in real $M1$ ($VM1P$), real $M2$ ($VM2P$), and in the absolute change in iR (ViR), and when corrected for autocorrelation, showed no significant correlation with interest-

productive sectors are paying real interest rates on the order of 20 percent per year or more? For it is really quite difficult to imagine that a large number of investment opportunities existed that allowed paying such interest rates for a prolonged length of time when average growth rates were as modest as they were.[15]

Part of the explanation no doubt lies in the fact that not all borrowing was in pesos at domestic rates; much was in dollars at international rates. Thus, at least so long as the lag in the exchange rate persisted, firms that borrowed abroad paid negative real rates of interest on those loans (table 8.11), thus allowing them to pay high interest rates on domestic loans. The fact that the bulk of long-term credit was in foreign currency, whereas the bulk of domestic credit was short term, largely explains why it was virtually impossible for any but a small part of dollar-denominated debt to be transferred into peso-denominated debt toward the end of phase II, when the risk of a major devaluation loomed large.

Access to foreign credit was neither uniform nor generalized (see Petrei and Tybout 1985; Galvez and Tybout 1985). Rather, it was a wholesaler's market, largely limited to big firms or to firms belonging to the same owners as the banks. Thus economic conglomerates found it much more attractive to buy up assets from those with less access to foreign or domestic credit than to invest, a fact that tended to raise the value of assets all the more. Moreover, the fact that such conglomerates devised mechanisms to invest without significantly drawing on their own limited financial resources (but on that of the community as a whole, through the banking system) gave them great leverage (high debt to equity ratios), which accelerates booms (bubbles) but which also accentuates declines (once the bubble bursts).

Indeed, because of the implicit guarantee against bankruptcy that at least the major banks were thought to have (that is, that the government would bail them out rather than allow a run on the financial system) and because many of these banks were controlled by parent firms desirous of credit, the banking system itself acquiesced in allowing highly leveraged, pyramidal and triangular lending operations. If all went well (as during upswings), huge profits would accrue to the most leveraged firms. If not, firms' and banks' losses would be limited to their relatively low equity, the bulk of the loss being incurred by depositors; or if—as expected, and as it largely turned out—deposits were

---

rate variations in time t. But in Chile, $V(iR)_{t+1}$ was negatively correlated with $V(iR)_{t+1}$ (with 90 percent confidence) and positively correlated with $V(iR)_{t-1}$ (with 99 percent confidence). In Argentina $(VRISP)_t$ was correlated with $VM2P$ (with 89 percent confidence), lending some additional weight to the hypothesis of Cooper 1974 that stock-market price variations may actually lead money supply changes.

15. For a detailed treatment of the financial crisis in the Southern Cone and alternative ways of dealing with it, see Arellano 1984, Barandiarán 1983, Díaz-Alejandro 1983, and Fernández 1982. A somewhat more upbeat interpretation of the prelude to the crisis in Chile can be found in Mathieson 1983.

guaranteed by governments to avoid a financial run, most of the loss would be absorbed by the public at large.

Thus interest rates and asset values grew hand in hand, establishing an ever-increasing distance between the fast-growing and overblown value (on paper) of assets and the much more modest growth of output and income. Yet such a financial bubble could continue to maintain itself only if fed with an ever-increasing supply of foreign credit, attracted to a large extent by the highly favorable interest-rate differential, which itself was the result of the lagging exchange-rate policy such flows made possible. *Thus the financial bubble rested on a growing influx of foreign capital and the corresponding lag in the exchange rate that it made possible, neither of which were sustainable in the long run.* The lagged exchange rate could not be maintained indefinitely, because the Southern Cone's production of tradables was becoming increasingly less competitive. Nor could capital be expected to continue to come in at such high rates, for capital inflows ultimately depend on effective increases in a country's capacity to service such a debt (that is to say, on increased reserves, more imports, improved terms of trade, and so on). And this capacity was simply not growing proportionately.

Once the growth in the value of assets slowed and the inflows of capital decelerated, high interest rates did the rest. Toward the end of phase II, the bubble burst, and the process reversed itself: asset prices plummeted, and capital inflows came to a virtual halt. The demand for credit became clearly destabilizing: the higher the interest rates rose, the greater the financial costs became—and, therefore, the greater the demand for credit. The only alternative to demanding more credit was liquidating assets; but under the then-prevailing conditions, liquidation was tantamount to bankruptcy, for the capital losses would be enormous even if buyers could be found. The obvious reluctance of firms to incur such capital losses led them to demand credit in the hope that somehow something would turn up. At this stage, they really had nothing to lose and much to gain by postponing liquidation. Thus, asset-market disequilibrium (an unwillingness to sell at a significant loss) was thrust on the financial market for its resolution, increasing the demand for credit and driving up interest rates even further. The burden of adjustment thus fell on credit markets and the interest rate.

Given such short time horizons, it was small wonder that firms were now willing to "pay" inordinately high domestic interest rates (these averaged 26 percent in Argentina, 40 percent in Uruguay, and 58 percent in Chile in real terms in the year preceding their maxidevaluations). For their part, the banks (firms' creditors) were forced to renew credit, for their only alternative was to try to make good on guarantees now worth but a fraction of the overblown values at which they had been assessed when credit was first provided. (In yet other cases, banks provided credit on call to debtor firms that in fact belonged to the same economic conglomerate as the banks.) As a result, the solvency of the banks and of the financial system as a whole came to be completely jeopardized, for they were overwhelmingly dependent on the financial state of very precarious firms.

Toward the end of phase II (1981–82), the domestic financial crisis exploded. The contractionary effects of the international recession and the overvalued exchange rates were apparent, and capital inflows fell sharply: 30 percent in Argentina in 1980, 78 percent in Chile in 1982, and over 100 percent in Uruguay in 1982 (when net capital inflows were negative). Capital inflows were thus reduced precisely when they were most necessary (the end of phase II and the beginning of phase III), whereas they were exaggerated (most of phase II) when they were far from indispensable. Thus capital inflows proved to be highly procyclical.

This financial run by foreign banks severely aggravated the contractionary effects in the Southern Cone of the overvalued exchange rate, of the international recession (on export volumes, terms of trade, and interest rates), and of the domestic financial crisis. Together, all these factors eroded confidence in the maintenance of the exchange policy, so that not only was bank lending cut back sharply but capital flight between 1980 and 1983 grew to massive proportions (except in Chile), thus precipitating the cataclysm all feared.[16] Once reserves were finally depleted, there was no practical alternative but to devalue massively.

Given the magnitude of the disequilibria and the brief time in which external accounts had to be brought into line, adjustment could only be of the worst type—contractive (output reducing) rather than expansive (output switching). Consequently, in the two or three years that followed, GNP fell some 10 percent in each of the three countries (as opposed to an average of 4 percent in the rest of Latin America, and unemployment sharply increased. Moreover, the central banks of the three countries were obliged to intervene in the domestic banking system, renegotiating or writing off much of firms' domestic debts and renegotiating foreign debt.

CONCLUSIONS AND THEORETICAL IMPLICATIONS

There is no doubt that at the beginning of the neoconservative experiences the domestic capital market was quite repressed and underdeveloped. Nevertheless, the profound changes that financial liberalization brought about did not translate themselves, despite intentions, into systematically higher savings

---

16. Analysis of debt and balance-of-payments data suggests that capital flight between 1980 and 1982 may have amounted to as much as 40 percent in Argentina and 60 percent in Uruguay of the increment in external debt over that same period. Capital flight amounted to far less in Chile. Whether this was because of its tighter controls on capital flows (requiring a two-year minimum stay) or because of possibly greater confidence—misplaced or not—in the soundness of its macroeconomic policy is worth exploring.

nor clearly improved resource allocation. Indeed, the three experiences came to a close with their financial systems in a shambles.

The principal failing seems to have been in the persistently high real rate of interest throughout almost all of the neoconservative period, a rate of interest that far exceeded the rate of growth of output or any reasonable rate of return on productive assets. Real interest rates of 2 to 3 percent per month cannot be paid systematically without jeopardizing the solvency of firms and, ultimately, of the financial system itself. The bursting of the financial bubble was thus inevitable.

Unlike normal, well-behaved markets, in which divergences from equilibrium automatically set in motion forces to restore equilibrium, deviations from equilibrium in financial markets may lead to even further divergences, if certain minimum thresholds of confidence in the ability to service such debt are not met. Once such confidence is lost, incentives are set in motion that lead debtors to demand more credit (to postpone insolvency) and banks to acquiesce in that demand for fear of having to take losses that may exceed their own reserves. In such conditions, divergences from equilibrium (unduly high interest rates) may lead to behavior that further accentuates such divergences (raises interest rates further). The system comes to rest, then, only when the bubble bursts and a major financial crisis erupts, as was the case in the Southern Cone.

The real significance of high interest rates, even in the early stages, was incorrectly interpreted by the authorities. Rather than see it as a sign that something serious was amiss in the workings of the economy—a sign of a possibly major disequilibrium—they considered that, inasmuch as it was the rate that equalized the supply and demand for credit, it was by definition the equilibrium rate. This, of course, was a major theoretical error: a confusion of the market-clearing rate of interest with the equilibrium rate of interest. For the equilibrium rate of interest is that which equalizes supply and demand when all other markets (asset, foreign exchange, labor, and goods markets) are also in equilibrium. If these other markets are not in equilibrium, the rate of interest that clears the credit market is the rate required to absorb the disequilibrium of other markets. During the bulk of the neoconservative period, the high rate of interest was a reflection of disequilibria in other markets: foreign exchange (due to the overvaluation of the exchange rate and the expectations of devaluation), goods (inflated prices), and assets (the bubble). Hence, disequilibria in these markets were thrust on the credit market for resolution, inasmuch as the credit market adjusts to prices relatively quickly.[17]

---

17. Of course, how best to overcome such disequilibria is another question. Intervene in the money market, the goods market, or the asset market? Expand the quantity of money and validate the prevailing level of prices to avoid a recession? Control interest rates directly? Prohibit the renewal of credits without adequate guarantees? Put an end to loans to firms in the same conglomerate as the bank and thereby speed the liquidation of assets? These questions, although important, go beyond the purposes of this study.

This analysis thus confirms the views of those who insisted all along that such unusually high real interest rates were indicative of a basic disequilibrium in the economy and rejects the views of those who argued in somewhat panglossian fashion that, if the market so dictates, they are necessarily the correct rates. It was thus a grave policy error to liberalize financial markets so rapidly and so extensively precisely at a time when, because of the stabilization policy, important disequilibria still remained in other critical sectors of the economy.

Domestic and international interest rates failed to converge, much less equalize, because credit markets have important peculiarities. Credit cannot be efficiently rationed solely by price (rate of interest), because credit is a future commitment. Hence, the higher its price, the lesser is the credibility in the debtor's capacity to meet this commitment. Thus credit must be rationed both by *quantity* and by *price,* which means that capital inflows will be sensitive not only to interest rate differentials but to the amount demanded. Inasmuch as other markets were transferring their disequilibria to the credit market for resolution, the demand for credit (and so the demand for capital inflows required to equalize domestic and international interest rates) was enormous—far in excess of what it would have been were other markets in equilibrium. It is not strange, then, that international banks were not willing to lend the amount demanded, thus preventing the law of one price from fully operating in the financial market. Indeed, it is now quite clear that more foreign capital came in than was in fact prudent from a long-run perspective.

The fact that credit, especially foreign credit, was rationed by quantity and not just by price gave an additional advantage to firms belonging to economic conglomerates, or that were themselves large, or that were dedicated to exports, for they had much better access to this rationed but cheaper foreign credit. These firms had the privilege of bringing in capital to the country at negative real rates of interest (in terms of domestic currency) for a long period of time and then of relending it in domestic currency for short periods of time and at high real rates of interest; or of using it to buy assets at good prices (to the extent that other asset holders had access only to credit at high interest rates), and obtaining in this way substantial profits.[18]

Such privileged access for some was not due to legal discrimination but was a reflection of reality. Capital markets were (and still are) segmented. International capital markets are largely wholesale markets, with access naturally restricted in practice to the principal firms and banks of a country (or to firms linked to such banks or to the export sector). Thus, most small and medium-sized firms, or those in the production of nontradables, or those whose production is geared primarily to the domestic market, found themselves restricted largely to the domestic credit market, paying high interest or intermediation charges.

---

18. This was especially the case in Chile, where financial liberalization was more limited. As noted earlier, Zahler (1980) estimates that such segmentation implied a transfer of a billion dollars to those firms that enjoyed privileged access to foreign credits.

In short, much as liberalization stimulated financial intermediation, the capital market remained largely segmented and underdeveloped, especially long-term credit. For this reason, too, it proved difficult to raise savings and improve resource allocation. It could have been foreseen that foreign credit would be differentially available and that direct intervention in this market was justified to control the rationing of credit and to redress this type of segmentation.

To be sure, to borrow in dollars was to run the risk of devaluation, a risk that was to prove all too real in phase III, when each country was forced to realize a maxidevaluation. Nevertheless, this risk was remote in the beginning of phase II, so that the incentive to borrow abroad was almost irresistible. By the time the accumulated overvaluation had become unsustainable and the exchange risk was high, the accumulated stock of foreign debt was quite large. Hence, the impact of the much-needed maxidevaluations on debtors in foreign currency was devastating, wiping out much of the gains of previous years.

The new capital market was almost exclusively limited to short-run instruments. It would have been wiser in retrospect to have inverted the order, first generating long-run instruments (indexed) for various years' duration and with good interest rates, and paying low interest rates to depositors for short-run money. For, given the disequilibria and uncertainty, it could have been foreseen that the market, if left to itself, would naturally favor the creation of short-run instruments at high interest rates, and once these instruments were established, that it would be very difficult for long-run instruments to emerge. Bonds, especially, require stability and predictability—in other words, that other markets be at or close to equilibrium, which, of course, they were not.

There were important differences among the three countries in the legal controls and limits on the entry and exit of capital as well as in the timing and sequence of financial liberalization relative to trade liberalization. Yet such differences do not suffice to explain differences in the rate of capital inflows (strongest in Chile, despite its greater controls) nor the failure of interest rates to converge (in all three countries). More important in explaining these phenomena are the various disequilibria experienced and the resulting excess demand for credit.

Also overlooked by most policymakers was the fact that financial repression not only kept interest rates artificially low but, by rationing credit, necessarily repressed the demand for certain types of credit (generally that for consumption). It was thus a serious oversimplification of neoconservative theorists to focus on the favorable effects of financial liberalization on effective savings and investment (via higher interest rates) and to neglect the unfavorable effects on these once the pent-up demand for consumption was released.[19]

---

19. Although a case can be made that consumer durables are a form of savings—and certainly they do improve welfare—the point is that the hoped-for increase in *productive* investment may thereby have been squelched.

None of this is to deny that financial repression had its costs and that a move toward financial liberalization was in order. In retrospect, however, it seems clear that financial liberalization should not have taken place until after price stabilization had been achieved or was well under way. The simultaneous pursuit of both jeopardized the success of each, all the more so given the financial sector's sensitivity to disequilibria in other sectors, its segmentation, its tendency to concentration, its bias toward the short run, and its proclivity to bubbles.

9

In Closing

It would not be very fruitful at this stage simply to repeat conclusions spelled out in detail in preceding chapters. Nor would it serve much purpose to try to formulate some global evaluation of these experiences, since such a judgment would necessarily depend on the relative weight assigned to variables as different as inflation, economic growth, income distribution, and external equilibrium, as well as on the importance attached to the difficult initial conditions that each country confronted. And how can one adequately make a global evaluation of experiences so different as the Uruguayan one, somewhat successful in several dimensions, and the Argentinian one, a failure on almost all counts? Moreover, it should be clear by now, given the treatment I have accorded the central issues in preceding chapters, that my overall assessment is rather negative, so that little would be gained by attempting one final justification of this position.

Hence, I think that it would be more useful in this last chapter to refer to the general approach that characterized the three neoconservative experiences and, in particular, their view of the appropriate roles of the market, of regulation, and of private-sector and public-sector economic activity. For in my estimation it was this view that determined, in the final analysis, the successes and failures of the experiences.

THE NEOCONSERVATIVE APPROACH

While there is no doubt that the neoconservative critique of past development strategy in the Southern Cone often bordered on easy caricature—that is, that government intervention is bad and inefficient, per se—it must be recognized that much of its criticism was valid. It is likely that the very same heterodoxical economic intervention that helped the Southern Cone pull out of the Great Depression also helps explain its subsequent slow growth and high inflation.

174

For policies designed for overcoming transitory demand-deficient recessions are grossly inappropriate as long-run development strategies. It is one thing to stimulate demand in the face of overwhelmingly underutilized capacity; it is quite another to expand productive capacity.

Neoconservatism reacted against government interventions in the market, whose appeal lay in that their benefits were clear and direct, but whose costs were diffuse and indirect and therefore underestimated. These interventions included (1) tariffs in accordance with private need, which saved foreign exchange but which failed to take into account social costs; (2) overvalued exchange rates, which cheapened imported intermediate inputs but which made activities with comparative advantage more costly; (3) price controls, which benefited consumers but which discouraged the production of basic necessities; and (4) subsidized credits, which encouraged industrialization, but at such an artificially low cost that an overly mechanized and excessively large capacity was built.

Moreover, as interventions became widespread, it became increasingly difficult to determine whether a specific intervention further distorted the market or simply offset an existing distortion; hence it was also unclear whether eliminating it would lessen or accentuate existing distortions. All that was certain was that activities favored by economic policy would expand and those that were discouraged would stagnate. Unfortunately, it was not always clear whether in net terms policy favored or discouraged a specific activity. It is for reasons of this sort that neoconservatives argued for the restoration of free prices as the central mechanism for the efficient allocation of resources.

One does not have to be a neoconservative *à outrance* to recognize that there is much truth in their criticism. Certainly one need not share neoconservatism's almost diabolical view of government intervention and public-sector activity or its belief that prices are the sole and best allocator of resources. And certainly neoconservative policies are themselves open to criticism. Nevertheless, it is difficult to deny that many neoconservative policies were moves in the right direction; it was necessary to redefine the roles of the market and regulation, of private-sector and public-sector activities, allowing each to specialize in those roles in which it had comparative advantage. This required, given the conditions prevailing in the Southern Cone in the early seventies, improving the price system.

MICROECONOMIC EFFICIENCY
AND MACROECONOMIC INEFFICIENCY

It is ironic, notwithstanding the importance neoconservatives accorded to "getting prices right," that the key prices of the economy (interest rates, wages, exchange rate) and the principal markets for those goods (credit, labor, and foreign exchange) should have remained so far from equilibrium, for so long, in each of the three neoconservative experiences.

At least four critical markets were in serious disequilibrium throughout important phases of the neoconservative experiences:

1. The goods market was well out of equilibrium, especially during phase I. Inflationary expectations kept prices well above those implicit in the stabilization policy, thus making it impossible for consumers to buy all that firms could produce. The resulting redistribution of income toward producers eased the pressure on them to lower prices—and thus to decelerate inflation faster. Recession and stagnation followed in Chile and Argentina.

2. The labor market was in serious disequilibrium throughout most of the three experiences. Wage costs well below historic, normal, or long-run equilibrium levels nevertheless did not reduce unemployment and, indeed, may have worsened it. For unemployment was due more to problems of insufficient aggregate demand (a reflection of the aforementioned goods-market disequilibrium), than to rigidities in the labor market. Restoration of labor-market equilibrium (fuller employment and restored wage levels) had to await the resolution of the goods-market disequilibrium (lower relative prices and higher sales).

3. The financial market was far out of equilibrium throughout. High real interest rates—at well above any reasonably expected long-term value—reflected (1) high demand for credit arising from disequilibria in the goods market and the foreign exchange market; (2) asymmetrical demand for credit arising from capital gains and losses induced by major changes in relative prices; and (3) collective, speculative euphoria. What these extraordinary interest rates certainly did not reflect was the likely growth of productivity, perhaps the key determinant of normal interest rates.

4. The market for foreign exchange was clearly in disequilibrium during most of phase II. The exchange rate's value reflected the transitory surge in capital inflows made possible by international liquidity, rather than long-run, sustainable capital inflows or coming comparative advantage. Thus goods lost much-needed competitiveness, a point that became all too evident once capital inflows abruptly decelerated at the end of phase II.

In the face of such major disequilibria, private agents reacted in timely and rational microeconomic fashion, thus leading to overindebtedness, excessive imports, a severe financial crisis, a regressive redistribution of income, and, especially in Chile and Argentina, underutilized capacity and unemployment. Diverse indicators show that within-firm productivity improved; but given the inconsistent and disequilibrated macroeconomic setting within which firms operated, this improved microeconomic efficiency led to social inefficiency. In other words, while the role of prices in the economy was restored, neoconservatives failed to assure that these reflected true social-opportunity costs.

Errors in Policy Design and Implementation

The causes of such severe price and market failures can be traced to errors both in policy design and in policy implementation. Price liberalization, for example, could not simultaneously achieve both price stabilization and faster growth. To achieve the former, it would have been desirable to guide prices toward equilibrium, not to free them all at once. A major error in financial liberalization was to initiate it while the economy was in disequilibrium from premature price liberalization and a poorly conceived stabilization policy. Given its sensitivity and rapid adjustment to other markets, the financial market thus absorbed the brunt of these disequilibria, giving rise to unduly high interest rates—with ultimately disastrous results for the economy. Also problematic was the policy of preannounced devaluations, for these were programmed at a rate well below that compatible with inflation and inflationary expectations.

Errors in Conception of the Way the Economy Works

Underlying such policy errors were a set of assumptions as to the working of the economy that can only be characterized as excessively naive idealizations. First, the belief that relations that hold in the long run are also true in the short run gave rise to a systematic neglect of the short run and of the dynamics or transition from one long-run state to another. To be sure, these issues are on the frontier, and even beyond the frontier, of the current state of economic knowledge. But certainly one does not resolve the problem simply by assuming it away. The short run is not the long run, and the dynamics of the move from one to the other is not necessarily continuous and smoothly convergent.

For example, few today seriously doubt that in the long run the rate of inflation is very closely associated with the growth of money supply, so that if one wishes to bring down inflation, one must eventually slow monetary growth correspondingly. What is at issue, however, and was all too sadly evident in these experiences, is that monetary restriction alone will not bring down inflation except with unnecessary costs. If monetary restriction is not accompanied by measures aimed at reducing inflationary expectations—and so decelerating the values of other key variables simultaneously—a sharp recession is all too likely to ensue. Similarly, few doubt that if exchange rates are fixed, domestic inflation eventually will equal international inflation.

Yet this long-run relation admits of wide deviations in the short run. Indeed, short-run deviations can prove so great that a maxidevaluation may be less costly than the maintenance of exchange parity and the corrective deflation it necessarily entails (and the likely recession that will ensue if the deflation is large and the time frame to achieve it is brief).

In short, only if the movement to equilibrium were rapid or at least systematically convergent, would short-run and long-run objectives not conflict. But if price movements were slow or were they to deviate transitorily from equilibrium, prices could provide misleading signals to markets, inducing behavior on the part of private agents that would *increase* divergences from equilibrium for some time.

Second, as a variant of the above, neoconservatives disregarded the theory of the second best—to them any move toward an optimum was the best policy, even though the remaining conditions for the optimum were not given. For example, they thought it preferable to free prices and interest rates, even at the risk of temporary disequilibrium, rather than to control them transitorily and keep them close to equilibrium, since in the optimum state, prices should be free.

Third, neoconservatives tended to confuse microeconomic and macroeconomic relations—or what amounts to much the same thing, to privilege partial-equilibrium analysis to the neglect of general-equilibrium analysis. Possibly the clearest example of this is their failure to recognize that a full understanding of unemployment needs take into account not only the labor market but the goods market, as well. Thus they systematically explained high unemployment by what they considered unduly high wage costs, though this ran smack in the face of the fact that, from the beginning, real wages fell by a third in all three countries while unemployment shot up. Equally trying was their surprise to see that employment rose during most of phase II (especially in Chile) as real wages recovered. This, of course, ran completely counter to what their microeconomic analysis of the labor market led them to expect. This microeconomic perspective blinded them to the fact that unemployment was largely due to overblown prices in the goods market, with the concomitant reduction in sales and output, and that fuller employment and labor-market equilibrium required resolution of the goods-market disequilibrium (by lowering prices and raising sales) and not further reductions in wages.

Fourth, neoconservatives had a very strong faith in the natural forces of competition but disregarded forces working against competition. Their belief in the law of one price in both the goods and financial markets was premised on the rapid and strong competitive pressure that arbitragers were expected to bring to bear on these markets. The painfully and fatally slow convergence of prices and interest rates both in Chile, which pursued a strong policy of trade liberalization, and in Uruguay, which opened to outside financing from the start, shows just how much the neoconservatives underestimated the forces blocking effective competition.

Few producers failed to pursue the quasi rents gained from their semimonopolistic positions in product markets during the transition to the full opening up of trade, resulting in the upward rather than downward convergence of the prices of domestic goods and imports. Firms with access to international capital markets made large capital gains by relending domestically at much higher interest rates or by gobbling up domestic firms. In time, capital markets might have become sufficiently integrated and homogeneous to assure interest-rate convergence and the allocation of credit to its socially most productive uses—but the fact is that the three experiences failed before they moved beyond this transition stage. Thus the neoconservatives' exaggerated faith in competition led them to design a permissive regulatory structure, which paved the way for the bubble and the subsequent crash that left the financial system in a shambles.

Two Blinders

At the root of such oversimplifications were two assumptions, blinding them to these facts. One is theoretical, one ideological. The central neoconservative theoretical premise was that market-clearing prices are the same as equilibrium prices, so that any deviation between the two will be readily resolved within that same market, with no significant repercussions on other markets. As I have been at pains to insist throughout, prices that equalize supply and demand in one market are not necessarily equilibrium prices. Rather, equilibrium prices are a subset of market-clearing prices: equilibrium prices in any one market are those prices that clear that market *when all other markets are also in equilibrium*. However, if other markets are in disequilibrium (say the goods market or the market for foreign exchange), the price that clears the remaining markets (say the financial market or the labor market) is not that market's equilibrium price, for it has been forced to absorb part of the disequilibrium existing in other markets.

At the heart of this distinction, of course, is the neoconservatives' belief (in the tradition of rational expectations) that only prices adjust, not quantities. At the heart of my criticism is the affirmation that, unfortunately, oftentimes quantities do adjust. Once quantity adjustments take place in one market, disequilibrium sets in, and price movements become quantity constrained, moving market-clearing prices *away* from equilibrium.

Obviously if one believes that market-clearing prices must be equilibrium prices, as the neoconservatives did, one will fail to perceive, or will misinterpret, evidence to the contrary: exceptionally high real rates of interest together with the sudden upward revaluation of assets, exaggerated rates of foreign indebtedness, considerable lags in the exchange rate, record-breaking unemployment rates, and unusually high levels of plant underutilization. Hence, it is not surprising that neoconservative policymakers in the Southern Cone first tended to doubt or ignore the evidence of the economic and social deterioration that their policies brought on; then they minimized the evidence or rationalized it away; and only belatedly did they act. Their faith in an idealized market (if prices are free, then whatever prices prevail are those that ought to prevail) limited their capacity to respond.

The neoconservative ideological premise was that, whereas public-sector spending could result in inefficiencies and disequilibria, the private sector would never behave in a destabilizing or inefficient fashion. To be sure, en-

trepreneurs do risk their own capital, not someone else's, and this potential
dynamism was not heretofore adequately tapped in the Southern Cone. Once
price and interest-rate controls were removed, once wider access was provided
to foreign capital, and once firms were permitted to invest according to their
own criteria and not the government's, this energy and initiative were released.
Undoubtedly, this entrepreneurial response to neoconservative incentives helps
explain the boom in nontraditional exports, as well as the industrial sector's
subsequent survival despite the severe recession, lags in the exchange rate, and
lower tariffs.

Nevertheless, the private sector was not exempt from major social inefficiencies and destabilizing behavior. For example, producers' inflationary expectations introduced into the price system a rigidity that gave rise to the
recession; the collective euphoria of private agents caused the financial market
bubble; and the linkages between banks and firms of the same conglomerate
were a destabilizing force. And what are we to say of the excessive foreign
indebtedness incurred by the private sector and concurred in by private foreign
banks?

Private agents do not possess a view of the whole economy. They are
unaware of each other's plans and are utterly dependent on market signals for
acting in a socially efficient manner. Yet when these key signals—interest rates,
prices, wages, the exchange rate—are well out of line, what is profitable for the
individual may be far less so for society. For example, for long stretches of time
it was systematically more profitable to invest in commercial and financial
activities than in production, especially in Chile and Argentina.

Neoconservatives did not understand that, if the economy was in significant disequilibrium, private-sector initiative could be channeled into such socially unproductive activities to the extent that competition was neither strong
nor widespread. Therefore, they intervened too little and too late—insuffi-
ciently and reluctantly—because of their almost limitless faith that the market,
the private sector, and the free play of prices would rapidly and automatically
resolve all economic disequilibria. The counterpart to this belief was their
conviction that the state was hopelessly and inescapably inefficient both in
intervening in and regulating the market and in directly engaging in productive
activity. Such an extreme position—possibly a pendular reaction to the contrary prejudices in the Southern Cone before the onset of the neoconservative
experiences—was at the root of one of its principal failures: *private and microeconomic efficiency in a context of social and macroeconomic inefficiency.*
Where macroeconomic distortions were most severe (Argentina), social efficiency was most compromised; where such distortions were least (Uruguay),
social efficiency was least jeopardized.

It is obvious, then, that the attractiveness of these premises stemmed not
from the evidence in their favor but from their accordance with a prior ideological position; namely, that these premises justified minimum government intervention in the economy.

DISTRIBUTIVE BIASES

In addition to leading to macroeconomic inefficiency, the neoconservative experiences ended with a more regressive distribution of income. This was not their intention, at least if one takes at face value the bulk of official declarations, which often criticized past policies precisely on this basis. Thus neoconservatives argued for general, distributionally neutral rules and opposed the discretionary policies of the past, which favored, so they argued, the strongest pressure groups. There is certainly much truth in this observation, although one might still prefer discretionary policies with a progressive bent.

What then failed in this highly critical area? As is shown in previous chapters, the bulk of the regressive redistribution of income can be attributed to the specific policy instruments adopted to achieve price stabilization and financial liberalization. The distributional bias of stabilization policies arose from the combination of wage controls and price liberalization; that of financial liberalization arose from (1) the provision of privileged access to cheap credit to those banks and domestic firms with international contacts, even in the face of the financial crisis; and (2) the special treatment accorded to debtors: those indebted in dollars (via special exchange rates) and those indebted in local currency (via subsidized interest rates, the central bank's purchase of bad loans, retroactive government guarantees on the private sector's foreign debt, and so on). To be sure, these measures had apparent justifications, yet these rested on three further dubious assumptions.

First, neoconservatives believed that institutional arrangements abetted or permitted by government were the main source of the rigidities and imperfections in the price system. Since the bulk of these were considered to be in the labor market, wages had to be controlled. Unfortunately, this assumption overlooked far more serious rigidities stemming from (1) economic collusion in banking, industry, and importing (rigidities that appeared with intensity during these experiences) and (2) the inertia of inflationary expectations (which meant that the asymmetrical treatment of wages and prices resulted in a regressive redistribution of income).

Second, neoconservatives assumed that capital markets were highly efficient, assigning credit in accordance with the expected rate of return of projects and not as a function of wealth (which served as a guarantee). This assumption proved not to be the case, so that the opening up of the economy to the international capital market provided privileged access to cheap credit to large firms and to firms linked to banks, while smaller firms had to resort to the far more expensive credit available in the domestic market. This is an example of the theory of the second best, in which the elimination of one of the distortions in the price system—restricted access to external capital—possibly had a net negative impact, inasmuch as the remaining conditions necessary to achieve optimality were not given (to wit, a perfect and nonsegmented international and domestic capital market with low costs of information).

Third, neoconservatives considered government intervention to be justified in a financial crisis because of the negative externalities associated with it,
yet they neglected the disproportion in the benefits of such government intervention: debtors' net wealth was salvaged, whereas workers' jobs were saved
only for the duration of the crisis. Moreover, they failed to consider alternatives. While continuing to hold society as a whole responsible for private
debt, they could have redistributed the fruits of future recovery far more widely
(for example, issuing stocks or bonds to workers, to their social security funds,
or to other social organizations in order to balance the socialization of the debt).

The fact that the errors of both commission and omission fell systematically on certain social groups (wage earners and small businessmen without
access to foreign capital) suggests not only technical errors of implementation
or analysis but also the low priority given to distributive questions by neoconservative policymakers. It was far more important for them to bring inflation
down than to maintain or recover employment levels; and the severe reduction
of real wages seemed far less serious than the risk of an inflationary rebound.

WERE THE FAILURES DUE TO THE MODEL?

We are finally in a position to directly address the question, To what extent were
the failures of the neoconservative experiences in the Southern Cone caused by
deficiencies in the model and to what extent by errors in implementation? To be
sure, every experience in the real world generates errors. However, when such
errors are systematically biased in one direction, it is likely that the errors are
due neither to the way policy was implemented nor to the underlying theory but
rather to the values and biases held by policymakers. The ideological presup-
positions of Southern Cone neoconservatives shaped their interpretation of
reality, favorably predisposing them to extremely idealized constructs of the
economy, while blinding them to anomalies in these constructs. Thus the model
they built was itself faulty, not so much the theory behind it nor its technical
implementation (both of which left much to be desired), not certainly the
principles of a market economy, nor the outward-oriented strategy, nor even
financial liberalization (costly as it was). At the root of the faulty model lay the
antiinterventionist biases of neoconservative policymakers in the Southern
Cone and the low priority they attached to distributive issues.

Whether these biases and priorities are intrinsic to neoconservative thinking as such is an academic question. For our purposes, it suffices to understand
that they were part and parcel of the Creole version of the neoconservative
model put into effect in the Southern Cone. It need not be stressed, I trust, that
such a narrow set of biases and values could have come to be the dominant ones
only under authoritarian regimes, where countervailing social forces had been
either severely restricted or forcibly demobilized.

CONCLUSION

This critical assessment of the neoconservative experiences of the Southern Cone in no way implies that we should return to the past, with all of its biases and failures. The validity of much of the neoconservative critique of the excessive interventionism of the past must be recognized: (1) the use of prices (controls) to redistribute income or to repress inflationary pressure, disregarding the eventually negative effects of such policies on resource allocation and growth; (2) an excessively short-run outlook; (3) insufficient fiscal discipline, manifest in the tendency to raise expenditures without corresponding increases in taxes or other fiscal revenues; (4) exaggerated optimism in the possibilities provided for industrialization by generally narrow domestic markets, and the corresponding neglect of achieving economies of scale and greater specialization by producing for export markets; (5) extraordinarily high tariffs, differentiated according to private, not social, needs; (6) the general assumption of supply inelasticity, and the ensuing underestimation of the effect (positive as well as negative) of price variations on output; and (7) an excessive faith in the virtues of government management and in mechanisms of direct and visible control, with a tendency to overlook indirect and long-run effects.

Southern Cone neoconservative experiences thus provide us with important lessons for the future—what ought to be done and what ought to be avoided. Significantly better advantage ought to be taken of private initiative and of the market than had been done before the neoconservative experiences. On the other hand, the government should play a qualitatively more active role in the economy than it did during the neoconservative experiences. Such intervention should aim, at least, at maintaining key prices (such as the real interest rate, the real exchange rate, and the real wage rate) reasonably close to their long-run equilibrium values, so as to minimize recession and regressive redistributive effects.

The need to define and establish an appropriate balance between the roles of the government and the market, on the basis of a realistic and not simply ideological assessment of the merits and drawbacks of each, is the great economic lesson provided by the experiences of the Southern Cone countries over the last fifty years. *Better* planning and *better* markets would seem to be a more fruitful approach than either *more* planning or *more* markets. In any case, to improve both while achieving an appropriate balance between the two is the principal challenge facing any future strategy of economic development in the Southern Cone.

Bibliography

Anichini, J., Caumont, J., and Sjaastad, L. 1977. *La política commercial y la protección en el Uruguay*. Montevideo: Banco Central del Uruguay.

Ardito Barletta, N., Blejer, M., and Landau, L., eds. 1984. *Economic Liberalization and Stabilization in Argentina, Chile, Uruguay: The Monetary Approach to the Balance of Payments*. Washington, D.C.: World Bank.

Arellano, J. 1981. "Elementos para el análisis de la Reforma Previsional." In *Colección Estudios CIEPLAN*, December.

————. 1983. "De la Liberalización a la Intervención: El Mercado de Capitales en Chile 1974–83." *Colección Estudios CIEPLAN*, December.

————. 1984. "La difícil salida al problema del Endeudamiento Interno." In *Colección Estudios CIEPLAN*, June.

Arellano, J., and Cortazar, R. 1982. "Del Milagro a la Crisis: Algunas Reflexiones sobre el Momento Económico." In *Colección Estudios CIEPLAN*, July.

Baer, W., and Kerstenetzky, I., eds. 1964. *Inflation and Growth in Latin America*. New Haven: Yale University Press.

Balassa, B. 1974. "Exchange Rates and Inflation in Chile." Confidential memo.

————. 1980. "Policy Response to External Shocks in Selected Latin American Countries." Washington, D.C.: World Bank. Mimeo.

————. 1984. "Experimentos de Política Económica en Chile—Diez años del Experimento Chileno con Políticas de Mercado Libre, 1973–1983." In *Estudios Públicos*, 14.

Banco Central de Chile. 1982. *Deuda Externa 1981*.

————. 1983. *Indicadores Económicos y Sociales, 1960–1982*.

Banco Central de la República Argentina. Various years. *Memoria Anual*.

————. 1977. *Ensayos Económicos*, no. 4, pt. 2.

Banco Central del Uruguay. Various years. *Indicadores de la Actividad Económica y Financiera*.

Banco Nacional de Comercio Exterior (Mexico). 1981. *Comercio Exterior*, January–February.

Barandiarán, E. 1983. "Nuestra crisis financiera." Mimeo.

Barro, R., and Grossman, H. 1971. "A General Disequilibrium Model of Income and Employment." In *American Economic Review*, March.

Bension, A., and Caumont, J. 1979. "Política Económica y Distribución del Ingreso en el Uruguay." Mimeo.

Blejer, M. 1984. "Recent Economic Policies of the Southern Cone Countries and the Monetary Approach to the Balance of Payments." In Ardito Barletta, Blejer, and Landau, eds., 1984.

Boeninger, E. 1983. "Bases Ideológieas del Neoliberalismo." In ILADES, 1983.

Brunner, K., and Meltzer, A., eds. 1982. *Economic Policy in a World of Change*. Vol. 17. Carnegie Rochester Series on Public Policy. Amsterdam: North Holland.

Bullow, J., and Shoven, J. 1978. "The Bankruptcy Decision." In *Bell Journal of Economics*, Autumn.

Cáceres, C. 1982. "La vía chilena hacia una economía de mercado." In *Estudios Públicos*, no. 6.

Campos, R. 1961. "Two Views on Inflation." In Hirschman, ed., 1961.

Canitrot, A. 1982. "Teoría y práctica del liberalismo: política anti-inflacionaria y apertura económica en la Argentina, 1976–1981." In *Desarrollo Económico*, no. 82.

Cavallo, D. 1977. "Los efectos recesivos e inflacionarios iniciales de las políticas monetarias de estabilización." In Banco Central de la República Argentina, 1977.

CEPAL. 1962. Inflación y Crecimiento. 6 vols. N.d. Mimeo. Summary in *Economic Bulletin for Latin America*, February, under title "Inflation and Growth."

———. 1978. *Series Históricas del Crecimiento de América Latina*. Santiago: CEPAL.

———. 1983. "Indices del tipo de cambio real efectivo de las exportaciones y de las importaciones." In *Estudio Económico de América Latina 1981*. Santiago: CEPAL.

Cline, W., and Weintraub, S. ed. 1981. *Economic Stabilization in Developing Countries*. Washington, D.C.: Brookings.

Collier, D., ed. 1979. *The New Authoritarianism in Latin America*. Princeton, N.J.: Princeton University Press.

Contador, C. 1974. "Politica Monetaria, Inflacao e Mercado de Acoes no Brasil—uma Sintese de Conclusóes." In *Revista Brasileira de Economia*, March.

Cooper, R. 1974. "Efficient Capital Markets and the Quantity Theory of Money." In *Journal of Finance*, June.

Corbó, V., Edwards, S., Lüders, R., and Koenig, L. 1984. "Commentary on Recent Experiences in the Southern Cone: Chile," and the discussions thereafter. In Ardito Barletta, Blejer, and Landau, eds., 1984.

Corbo, V., De Melo, J., and Tybout, J. 1985. "What Went Wrong with the Recent Reforms in the Southern Cone?" Washington, D.C.: World Bank. Mimeo.

Corbo, V., and Meller, P. 1977. "Sustitución de Importaciones, Promoción de Exportaciones y Empleo: el caso Chileno." In PREALC, 1977.

Corbo, V., and Pollack, M. 1982. "Fuentes del Cambio en la Estructura Económica Chilena: 1960–1979." In *Estudios de Economía*, primer semestre.

Cortázar, R. 1983a. "Políticas de Reajustes y Salarios en Chile: 1974–1982." In *Colección Estudios CIEPLAN*, June.

———. 1983b. "Resultados distributivos: Chile 1973–1982." In CIEPLAN, *Notas Técnicas*, June.

Cortázar, R., Foxley, A., and Tokman, V. 1984. *Legados del Monetarismo, Argentina y Chile*. Buenos Aires: Ediciones Solar.

Cortázar, R. and Marshall, J. 1980. "Indice de precios al consumidor en Chile: 1970–1978." In *Colección Estudios CIEPLAN*, November.

Cortés, H. 1981. "Trade Reform and the Economy: The Chilean Experience." Documento de trabajo no. 3. In *Centro de Estudios Públicos,* November.

Cortés, H., and Sjaastad, L. 1978. "El Enfoque Monetario de la Balanza de Pagos y las Tasas de Interes real en Chile." In *Estudios de Economía,* primer semestre.

Dagnino Pastore, J. M. 1984. "Assessment of an Anti-inflationary Experiment: Argentina in 1976–1981," In Ardito Barletta, Blejer, and Landau, eds., 1984.

Dahse, F. 1979. *Mapa de Extrema Riqueza.* Santiago: Editorial Aconcagua.

De Melo, J., Pascale, R., and Tybout, J. 1985. "Uruguay 1975–1981: Interrelación entre Shocks Financieros y Reoles." In *Cuadernos de Economía,* April.

Díaz-Alejandro, C. 1970. *Essays on the Economic History of the Argentine Republic.* New Haven: Yale University Press.

———. 1980. "A América Latina em Depressao, 1929–1939." In IPEA, *Pesquisa e Planejamento Económico,* August.

———. 1981. "Southern Cone Stabilization Plans." In Cline and Weintraub, eds., 1981.

———. 1983. "Goodby Financial Repression, Hello Financial Crisis." Mimeo.

Di Tella, G., and Zymelman, M. 1970. *Las Etapas del Desarrollo Económico Argentino.* Buenos Aires: Editorial Universitaria de Buenos Aires.

Dornbusch, R. 1982. "Stabilization Policies in Developing Countries: What Have We Learned?" In *World Development,* vol. 10.

———. 1984. "Commentary on Evaluation and Experience." In Ardito Barletta, Blejer, and Landau, eds., 1984.

Economía y Sociedad. 1978. September–October.

Edwards, S. 1985. "Stabilization with Liberalization: An Evaluation of Ten Years of Chile's Experience with Free Market Policies, 1973–1983." In *Economic Development and Cultural Change,* January.

Esser, K., Almer, G., Greischel, P., Kürzinger, E., and Weber, S. 1983. *Monetarismo en Uruguay: Efectos sobre el Sector Industrial.* Berlin: Instituto Alemán de Desarrollo.

Fama, E. 1970. "Efficient Capital Markets: A Review of Theory and Empirical Work." In *Journal of Finance,* May.

Felix, D. 1961. "An Alternative View of the 'Monetarist-Structuralist' Controversy." In Hirschman, ed., 1961.

Fernández, R. 1982. *La Crisis Financiera Argentina: 1980–1982.* Buenos Aires: CEMA.

Ferrer, A. 1977. *Crisis y Alternativas de la Política Económica Argentina.* Mexico City: Fondo de Cultura Económica.

———. 1979. "El Retorno del Liberalismo, Reflexiones sobre la Política Económica vigente en la Argentina." In *Desarrollo Económico,* no. 72.

———. 1981. "El Monetarismo en Argentina y Chile." In Banco Nacional de Comercio Exterior, 1981.

Ffrench-Davis, R. 1980. "Liberalización de Importaciones: La Experiencia Chilena en 1973–1979." In *Colección Estudios CIEPLAN,* November.

Ffrench-Davis, R., and Arellano, J. P. 1981. "Apertura Financiera Externa: La Experiencia Chilena en 1973–1980." In *Colección Estudios CIEPLAN,* July.

Ffrench-Davis, R., Fontaine, J., García, A., and Wisecarver, D. 1983. "Que pasó con la Economía Chilena." In *Estudios Públicos,* no. 11.

FIDE. 1982. *Coyuntura y Desarrollo,* December. Buenos Aires: FIDE.

Foxley, A. 1980. "Stabilization Policies and Stagflation: The Cases of Brasil and Chile." In *World Development,* vol. 11.

———. 1983. *Latin American Experiments in Neoconservative Economics.* Berkeley and Los Angeles: University of California Press.

Frenkel, J. 1982. "The Order of Economic Liberalization: Lessons from Chile and Argentina." In Brunner and Meltzer, eds., 1982.

Frenkel, R. 1979. "Decisiones de Precios en Alta Inflación." In *Estudios CEDES,* vol. 2, no. 3.

———. 1980. "El Desarrollo reciente del Mercado de Capitales en la Argentina." In *Desarrollo Económico,* no. 78.

Friedman, M. 1953. "The Methodology of Positive Economics." In Friedman, *Essays in Positive Economics.* Chicago: University of Chicago Press.

———. 1962. *Capitalism and Freedom.* Chicago: University of Chicago Press.

———. 1970. "A Theoretical Framework for Monetary Analysis." In *Journal of Political Economy,* March–April.

———. 1982. Interview. In *Revista Cosas,* June 17. (Santiago).

Galbis, V. 1977. "Financial Intermediation and Economic Growth in Less Developed Countries: A Theoretical Approach." In *Journal of Development Studies,* January.

Galvez, J., and Tybout, J. 1985. "Chile 1977–1981: Impacto Sobre Empresas Chilenas de Algunas Reformas Económicas e Intentos de Estabilización." In *Cuadernos de Economía,* April.

Grunwald, J. 1961. "The 'Structuralist' School on Price Stability and Development." In Hirschman, ed. 1961.

Hamburger, M., and Kochin, L. 1972. "Money and Stock Prices: The Channels of Influence." In *Journal of Finance,* May.

Haq, K., and Massad, C., eds. 1984. *Adjustment with Growth: A Search for an Equitable Solution.* Islamabad: North-South Roundtable.

Harberger, A. 1982a. "The Chilean Economy in the 1970's: Crisis, Stabilization, Liberalization, Reform." In Brunner and Meltzer, eds., 1982.

———. 1982b. "La Ciencia Económica es una Sola, depende de la capacidad del Economista adaptarla correctamente a cada realidad." In Riffka, 1983.

———. 1984. "Commentary on Evaluation and Experience." In Ardito Barletta, Blejer, and Landau, eds., 1984.

Hayek, F. 1960. *The Constitution of Liberty.* Chicago: University of Chicago Press.

Hirschman, A., ed. 1961. *Latin American Issues.* Washington, D.C.: Twentieth Century Fund.

———. 1968. "The Political Economy of Import-Substituting Industrialization in Latin America." In *Quarterly Journal of Economics,* February.

———. 1979. "The Turn to Authoritarianism in Latin America and the Search for Its Economic Determinants." In Collier, ed., 1979.

Ho, T., and Saunders, A. 1980. "A Catastrophe Model of Bank Failure." In *Journal of Finance,* December.

Homa, K., and Jaffee, D. 1971. "The Supply of Money and Common Stock Prices." In *Journal of Finance,* December.

ICHEH. 1978. *Chile 1940–1975: Treinta y Cinco años de Discontinuidad Económica.* Santiago: Instituto Chileno de Estudios Humanísticos.

ILADES. 1983. *Del Liberalismo al Capitalismo Autoritario.* Santiago: Instituto Latinoamericano de Doctrina y Estudios Sociales.

Instituto de Economía, Universidad de la República. 1969. *El proceso económico del Uruguay—Contribución al Estudio de su Evolución y Perspectiva.* Montevideo: Instituto de Economía.

Instituto Nacional de Estadísticas de Chile. 1979. "Encuesta de Presupuesto Familiar 1969," and "Encuesta de Presupuesto Familiar 1978." In *Compendio Estadístico.* Santiago: Instituto Nacional de Estadísticas.

International Monetary Fund. Various issues. *Balance of Payments.* Washington, D.C.: IMF.

————. Various issues. *International Financial Statistics.* Washington, D.C.: IMF.

————. Various issues. *International Financial Statistics Supplement on Trade Statistics.* Washington, D.C.: IMF.

————. Various years. *Statistical Yearbook.* Washington, D.C.: IMF.

Jarvis, L. 1985. *Chilean Agriculture under Military Rule.* Berkeley and Los Angeles: University of California Press.

Lavín, J. 1980. *El enriquecimiento de las personas en Chile.* Concepción: Universidad de Concepción.

Leijonhufvud, A. 1968. *On Keynesian Economics and the Economics of Keynes.* London: Oxford University Press.

Lepage, H. 1979. *Mañana el Capitalismo.* Madrid: Alianza Editorial.

Lerdau, E. 1984. "Commentary on Evaluation and Experience." In Ardito Barletta, Blejer, and Landau, eds., 1984.

Lewis, W. A. 1954. *Economic Development with Unlimited Supplies of Labor.* Manchester: Manchester School of Economics.

Linz, J., and Stepan, A., eds. 1978. *The Breakdown of Democratic Regimes: Latin America.* Baltimore: Johns Hopkins University Press.

Lüders, R. 1985. "La Razón de ser de la Intervención del 13 de Enero." In *Revista Economía y Sociedad,* March.

Macadar, L. 1982. *Uruguay 1974–1980: un nuevo ensayo de reajuste económico.* Montevideo: CINVE.

McKinnon, R. 1973. *Money and Capital in Economic Development.* Washington, D.C.: Brookings.

————. 1979. "Represión Financiera y el Problema de la Liberalización dentro de los Países menos Desarrollados." In *Cuadernos de Economía,* April.

Mallon, R., and Sourrouille, J. 1975. *La Política Económica en una Sociedad Conflictiva: el Caso Argentino.* Buenos Aires: Amorrortu.

Mamalakis, M. 1976. *The Growth and Structure of the Chilean Economy from Independence to Allende.* New Haven: Yale University Press.

Mathieson, D. 1983. "Estimating Models of Financial Market Behavior during Periods of Extensive Structural Reform: The Experience of Chile." In *IMF Staff Papers,* June.

Meller, P. 1984. "Análisis del Problema de la Elevada Tasa de Desocupación Chilena." In *Colección Estudios CIEPLAN,* September.

Meller, P., Cortázar, R., and Marshall, J. 1979. "La Evolución del Empleo en Chile, 1974–1978." In *Colección Estudios CIEPLAN,* December.

Meller, P., Livacich, E., and Arrau, P. 1984. "Una Revisión del Milagro Económico Chileno (1976–1981)." In *Colección Estudios CIEPLAN,* December.

Meller, P., and Solimano, A. 1984. "El Mercado de Capitales Chileno: Laissez Faire, Inestabilidad Financiera y Burbujas Especulativas." Mimeo.

Mesa Lago, C. 1985. *El Desarrollo de la Seguridad Social en América Latina.* Santiago: CEPAL.

Mezzera, J. 1981. "El Proceso de Apertura Uruguayo en la Esfera Real." CEPAL. Mimeo.

Nogués, J. 1981. "Distorsiones en Mercados de Factores, Empleo y Ventajas Comparativas en el Sector Manufacturero Argentino." In *Ensayos Económico*, no. 20.

———. 1982. "Sustitución de Importaciones versus Promoción de Exportaciones: Impactos Diferenciales sobre el Empleo en el sector Manufacturero Argentino." In *Desarrollo Económico*, no. 86.

Notaro, J., and Wonsewer, I. 1980. "La Liberalización de los Precios y los Mercados y la Reducción de la Acción Económica del Estado." CEPAL. Mimeo.

ODEPLAN. 1983. *Informe Económico 1982.* Santiago: ODEPLAN.

Patinkin, D. 1956. *Money, Interest and Prices.* 2d. ed. New York: Harper and Row, 1965.

Perez, F., and Moreno, A. 1984. "Teoría Financiera, Contratos y Políticas Económicas." In *Estudios Públicos*, Fall.

Pesando, J. 1974. "The Supply of Money and Common Stock Prices: Further Observations on the Econometric Evidence." In *Journal of Finance*, June.

Petrei, A., and Tybout, J. 1985. "Argentina 1976–1981: La Importancia de Variar los Niveles de Subsidios Financieros." In *Cuadernos de Economía*, April.

Pinto, A. 1973. *Chile, un caso de Desarrollo Frustrado.* 3d. ed. Santiago: Editorial Universitaria.

PREALC. 1977. *Investigaciones sobre empleo*, no. 4. Santiago: PREALC.

———. 1984. "Reactivación con Transformación: el Efecto Empleo." In *Documento de Trabajo*, April.

Prebisch, R. 1950. *Economic Development of Latin America and Its Main Problems.* New York: UN ECLA.

Ramos, J. 1973. "El Comportamiento de los Precios y Salarios desde el 11 de Septiembre de 1973." Universidad de Chile. Mimeo.

———. 1975. "El Costo Social: Hechos e Interpretaciones." In *Estudios de Economía*, segundo semestre.

———. 1977. "Inflación Persistente, Inflación Reprimida e Hiperestanflación." In *Cuadernos de Economía*, December.

———. 1980. "The Economics of Hyperstagflation." In *Journal of Development Economics*, December.

———. 1982. "El Liberalismo Económico de Hayek." In *Estudios Sociales*, no. 33.

Riffka, S. 1983. *Los Modelos de la Crisis: Políticas Económicas y Perspectivas Democráticas an América Latina.* Quito: Editorial El Conejo, ILDIS.

Rodríguez, C. 1983. "Políticas de Estabilización en la Economía Argentina 1978–1982." In *Cuadernos de Economía*, April.

Sargent, T. 1981. "The End of Four Big Inflations." In *NBER Conference Paper*, no. 90. Washington, D.C.: National Bureau of Economic Research.

Sjaastad, L. 1982. "The Failure of Economic Liberalism in the Southern Cone." 1982 Bateman Memorial Lecture, University of Western Australia. Mimeo.

Sociedad de Fomento Fabril (Chile). Various issues 1975–82. *Informes Mensuales.*

Sourrouille, J., and Lucángeli, J. 1983. *Política Económica y Procesos de Desarrollo: la Experiencia Reciente de Argentina.* Santiago: CEPAL.

Spiller, P., and Favaro, E. 1982. "An Econometric Test of Interaction among Oligopolistic Firms: The Uruguayan Banking Sector." Central Bank of Uruguay. Mimeo.

Sprinkel, B. 1964. *Money and Stock Prices.* Homewood, Ill.: Richard Irwin.

Tironi, E. 1981. "Políticas Económicas y Procesos de Desarrollo: la Experiencia de Chile desde 1973." Mimeo.

Valenzuela, A. 1978. *The Breakdown of Democratic Regimes: Chile.* Baltimore: Johns Hopkins University Press.

Vergara, P. 1980. "Apertura Externa y Desarrollo Industrial en Chile 1974–1978." In *Colección Estudios CIEPLAN,* November.

Williamson, J. 1984. "Commentary on Evaluation and Experience." In Ardito Barletta, Blejer, and Landau, eds., 1984.

Willmore, L. 1982. "Economic Recession and Trade Liberalization: Chilean Manufacturing, 1975–1981." CEPAL. Mimeo.

Wonsewer, I., and Saráchaga, D. 1980. "La Apertura Financiera en Uruguay." Mimeo.

World Bank. 1977. *Argentina: Reconstruction and Development.* Washington, D.C.: World Bank.

———. 1979. *Chile: An Economy in Transition.* Washington, D.C.: World Bank.

———. 1982. *Economic Memorandum on Uruguay.* Washington, D.C.: World Bank.

Zahler, R. 1980. "Repercusiones Monetarias y Reales de la Apertura Financiera al Exterior: el Caso Chileno 1975–1978." In *Revista de la CEPAL,* April.

———. 1982. "El Neoliberalismo en una version Autoritaria." In CPU, *Estudios Sociales,* no. 31.

———. 1983. "Recent Southern Cone Liberalization Reforms and Stabilization Policies: The Chilean Case (1974–1982)." In *Journal of Interamerican Studies and World Affairs,* vol. 25.

Index